of this
in

degree
stine,
rich
a
d ... psycho-analysis. His wide scholarly interests and deep reading led him to develop revolutionary theories regarding the origins of the Earth, natural phenomena in pre-history, the craters on the Moon and the surface and atmosphere of Mars. These ideas first reached the public in his bestselling book, *Worlds in Collision*, which was first published in 1950 and caused an upheaval in academic circles whose reverberations – as *The Velikovsky Affair* shows – are still being felt today. In works written since then, including *Ages in Chaos* and *Earth in Upheaval*, he has pursued his theories and extended them to create a radical revision of ancient history. His latest book, *Peoples of the Sea*, was completed recently and appears in Abacus in 1979.

Alfred de Grazia, compiler of and contributor to this volume, is Professor of Social Theory at New York University.

By Immanuel Velikovsky in Abacus.

WORLDS IN COLLISION
EARTH IN UPHEAVAL
AGES IN CHAOS
PEOPLES OF THE SEA (to be published in Spring 1979)

Also about Immanuel Velikovsky in Abacus:

VELIKOVSKY RECONSIDERED by the editors of *Pensée*

The Velikovsky Affair

Scientism *versus* Science

ALFRED DE GRAZIA
RALPH E. JUERGENS
and
LIVIO C. STECCHINI

SPHERE BOOKS LIMITED
30/32 Gray's Inn Road, London WC1X 8JL

First published in Great Britain by Sidgwick and Jackson Ltd 1966

Revised edition published in 1978 in Abacus by Sphere Books Ltd
30/32 Gray's Inn Road, London WC1X 8JL

TRADE
MARK

Set in Monotype Times Roman

Printed in Great Britain by
Hazell Watson & Viney Ltd
Aylesbury, Bucks

CONTENTS

THE VELIKOVSKY AFFAIR

INTRODUCTION TO THE SECOND EDITION

We dedicate this book to people who are concerned about the ways in which scientists behave and how science develops. It deals especially with the freedoms that scientists grant or withhold from one another. The book is also for people who are interested in new theories of cosmogony – the causes of the skies, the earth, and humankind as we see them. It is, finally, a book for people who are fascinated by human conflict, in this case a struggle among some of the most educated, elevated, and civilized characters of our times.

These lines are being written a few weeks after the launching of a carefully prepared book attacking the growing position of Immanuel Velikovsky in intellectual circles.[1] The attack was followed promptly by a withering counter-attack in a special issue of the journal, *Kronos*.[2] The events reflect a general scene which, since the first appearance of this volume, has been perhaps more congenial to the temperament of war correspondents than of cloistered scholars.

The philosophical psychologist, William James, who once proposed sport as a substitute for warfare, might as well have proposed science and scholarship for the same function. Scientific battles also have their armies, rules, tactics, unexpected turns, passions bridled and unbridled, defeats, retreats, and casualty lists. All of the motives that go into warfare are exercised. In the present controversy, the minds of the combatants must also carry into the fray images of a distant past when the world was ruined by immense disasters, whether or not they deny the images.

Unlike sport, the outcomes of scientific battles are as important, if not more so, than the results of outright warfare. At stake in the controversy over Velikovsky's ideas is not only the system used by science to change itself – which is largely the subject of this book – but also the substantive model of change to be employed by future science – whether it shall be comprehended mainly as revolutionary and catastrophic or as evolutionary and uniform.

The controversy has had many striking facets. One has been the large participation of the public. It continues to increase. Velikovsky has managed to talk to people about mythology, archaeology, astronomy, and geology, *without doing injustice to those disciplines*, in an amazing and unprecedented manner. Socrates, Aristotle, Galileo, Freud, and Einstein – to name a few thinkers who were implicated in 'crowd phenomena' – were not public figures in the sense here taken. His public – a well-behaved, educated, well-intentioned and diversified aggregate – has supported Velikovsky on every possible occasion. That he was a foreigner with a Russian accent, a psychiatrist, unequivocably a Jew, denounced by some of the most respected scientists of America and Britain, unbending in his person and in his allegiance to science and in refusing every opening for support from demagogic or religious quarters: these facts hardly disturbed the favourable reception granted him by a large public.

That he is a charismatic figure is obvious: fourteen hundred people attended his talk and awarded him a standing ovation at a critical scientific symposium in San Francisco in 1974. But 'charisma' is a bit of jargon; the question remains 'why'. Although I must reserve the answer until another occasion, I would here suggest that his ideas have represented all the legitimate anxieties about present-day 'knowledge' that educated people possess, whether it be their own knowledge or that of their scientific tutors.

I have lived with 'the Velikovsky Affair' for fifteen years. Often I have been asked how I came to be involved. Sometimes the question comes from my colleagues, who, like myself, have wondered how a million, perhaps two million, serious readers can find that a book like *Worlds in Collision* makes sense, while a great many scientists and scholars cannot even come to grips with the book, turn away from it angrily, and irritably consign the whole lot of favourable readers to the ranks of religious revivalists who have received The Word.

But there was little heroic, charismatic, revelatory, or even extraordinary about my initiation. The year 1950, which saw the publication of *Worlds in Collision*, was a busy one in my younger life; I had several infants, a new professorship, and a more than passing engagement with psychological operations in the Korean War, then raging. So the scandal over the book's suppression and success left only a faint scratch upon my mind.

However, in 1962, when I was publishing and editing the *American Behavioral Scientist* magazine in Princeton, Dr Livio Stecchini, a historian of science also resident there, spoke to me more than once about a man named Dr Velikovsky who also lived in Princeton and had been victimized by the scientific establishment. I listened without enthusiasm to Stecchini, for the annals of science and publishing, like politics, are crowded with cases that are falsely or ineptly brought up, of hopeless theories trying to engage public attention, of feelings of persecution.

Then, one evening, as I was saying my goodbyes at the home of my brother, I espied a book entitled *Oedipus and Akhnaton*, by one Immanuel Velikovsky. The residual stimuli precipitated a gestalt of curiosity. I borrowed it. I read it from cover to cover, brooking no minor interruption. I thought that it was a masterpiece of true detective literature (a judgement that I think is now confirmed), and telephoned Dr Stecchini to arrange a meeting.

As I talked with Dr Velikovsky – an impressive experience in a person's life – I was introduced to his archive of materials on the case. It was astonishingly rich and ordered. I concluded after several long meetings and much reading among his materials that the history of science had few, if any, cases that were so well documented. I decided to devote a special issue of the *American Behavioral Scientist* to 'the Velikovsky Affair'.

It was this issue, finally appearing in September 1963 after prolonged, gruelling, and enlightening sessions with Dr Velikovsky and my co-authors, Ralph Juergens and Livio Stecchini, and after long hours spent amidst the archive of Velikovsky itself, that formed the basis for the present book. I would not go as far as some commentators in saying that the book brought the great controversy to life when the cause seemed lost; my concept of history is more Tolstoian. Still, the response to the issue was immediate. Eric Larrabee, a publicist, who had had a long-standing contract with the Doubleday Company publishers to write a book on the subject, was spurred to publish an article in *Harper's* magazine about the Velikovsky case. The *American Behavioral Scientist* issue was expanded, with new contributions by Juergens and Stecchini, and published by University Books two years later. (In the present edition, Dr Stecchini has revised and added much new material to his contributions.)

With notable exceptions, to be described in the pages to come, the book was well received. It was resented by many in the underground of science, which includes the mysterious realms of foundations and government agencies. There, any association whatsoever with Dr Velikovsky is likely to provoke discrimination and reprisals. But the distinction of the panel of readers who endorsed my decision to publish its materials no doubt acted as a formidable obstacle to public assaults upon it. It is difficult for someone, in the face of the evidence offered, to contradict the book's two main ideas: that Dr Velikovsky was unjustly treated, and that he maintains a set of propositions that must be seriously considered by the sciences and humanities. A reading of the book apparently positions one reasonably to annoy many scientists encountered in classrooms, professional meetings and cocktail parties.

When my attention was first drawn to the sociological

and legalistic aspects of the Velikovsky Affair in 1962, my interest in the substantive problems of catastrophism and uniformitarianism, or revolutionism and evolutionism, was that of a charmed spectator. However it was not long before a question began persistently to intrude upon my mind: 'Was there only misguidance and foolishness in the jungle-buried history of catastrophist thought or was there lurking in it an alternative model of cosmogony?' I have pursued now for over a decade the substance of what, for lack of a better term, I sometimes call 'holocene cosmogony' and at other times 'revolutionary primevalogy', and am much more committed intellectually to Dr Velikovsky's approach than I was when this material was first published.

With the encouragement afforded by others who were travelling the same route, I have achieved a measure of confidence in a two-part reciprocal answer: there is no 'fact' in the great and varied growth of today's science that is 'true' enough to block a complete cosmogonic model that is antithetical to uniformitarianism; there is enough of 'fact' to supply the construction of a revolutionist model.

Dozens of pertinent incidents have marked my association with the realm of Velikovskian politics and science over the years. One of the neatest, and of course indirect and noncommittal, testimonials to the validity of the present book occurred lately. The new edition of the *Encyclopedia Britannica* has recently appeared. In its vast uniformitarian and evolutionist terrain there is set a biographical article upon Velikovsky, which I discovered to be on the whole acceptable in the general frame of the Encyclopedia. Nevertheless, two years or so later, Lawrence K. Lustig, the Managing Editor of the Encyclopedia's *Book of the Year*, was possessed to write an article there containing an orthodox, negative pronunciamento upon Velikovsky in the course of a general attack upon pseudoscience. I wrote to Dr Lustig, decrying his position; he replied without retracting his position by as much as a centimetre.

Yet, on the same day as the proposal to publish the present book arrived from Sphere Books, Ltd, in England, there arrived also a letter from Dr Lustig, now Editor-in-Chief of a large, new encyclopedia-in-the-making at Princeton, New Jersey. He asks me to write for the encyclopedia the articles on 'Freedom', 'Freedom of Religion', and 'Freedom of Speech'. If this story may be taken as a compliment to the integrity of the present work, it may also be heartening to those scholars, young and old, who fear that their advocacy of the philosophical principles of the book would deny them certain fruits of their long and arduous studies and careers.

Professor William Mullen and I have separately published articles 'indexing in advance' the fallout of Velikovsky's ideas upon the many academic disciplines.[3] In the politics of exploiting this fall-out, the scholar-aspirant or scholar-turncoat can be shown two paths. For the cautious soul, who would evade controversy and is shy of ridicule, it will be relatively easy, now that many barriers are down, to introduce revolutionary hypotheses into scientific areas where the ruling order is evolutionary, provided that one avoids citing the works of Velikovsky and his school. One can, for example, speak of a revolutionary turn of mind on the part of *homo sapiens* without mentioning Velikovsky, and be applauded, as was Jaynes this past year.[4] One can discuss the catastrophically deposited ash layers on the ocean bottoms, as has Worzel, with only a tiny escape hatch for 'the fiery end of bodies of cosmic origin'.[5] One need not cite Isaacson,[6] either, in disposing of the century-old concept of the Greek 'Dark Ages', especially since Isaacson does not exist, it being the *nom de plume* of a young scholar in fear for his career; one might criticize the concept without mentioning Velikovsky, given the new climate of thought.

A scholar can play safe in elaborating the evidence for hundreds of hypotheses in the Velikovskian literature that are already clearly stated and buttressed by evidence, and do so without mentioning him and with the indulgence of authorities who are ordinarily fanatic about the citation of sources. Scholars may now indulge in the heady alcohol of revolutionary theory, so to speak, provided that they label their brew as medicinal, because, after all, the police are in cahoots, if indeed they have not already taken to drink themselves. There comes to mind the chemical geologist and Nobel prize winner, Harold Urey, who has on occasion reprimanded Velikovsky's supporters even though he has himself speculated that errant celestial bodies might be the great age-breakers in geological morphology and paleontology[7] (just as the ancients said that the ages were made and broken by the birth and death of the planetary gods).

Alternatively credit may be given where credit is due. A scholar may virtuously confess his research sources, hoping that the court for criminals such as he will soon be too crowded for him to have to worry about being brought to trial for a long time, trusting that before that time occurs the rapidly changing climate of belief will have transformed his crime into a propriety.

When will this Great Day befall? By 1973, a decade after *The Velikovsky Affairs* was first published, his group was cheered by the news that the American Association for the Advancement of Science (AAAS) would stage a symposium upon his work. On February 25, 1975, the symposium took place before the greatest audience that this convention of the largest American scientific organization produced. A full volume about the activities preceding the symposium, of its proceedings, and of its aftermath would be a worthy objective of a sociologist of science; it is yet to be written. However, the two works alluded to at the beginning of this essay have already appeared, the one sharply anti-Velikovsky and the other just as strongly pro-Velikovsky. Both works related mostly to the substantive theories about the Venus and Mars scenarios that had been presented in *Worlds in Collision.*[8]

Without presenting a mass of evidence, it would be improper for me to pass judgement here on the complicated hassle. I shall, however, go so far as to say that the reader of this book will experience few surprises should he happen finally to hear the full story. All the actors who were involved, both *pro* and *con*, including the group actors – the AAAS and the press – performed true to type.

The scientific establishment, I should add, was now more subtle in preserving proper forms and a correct public posture – as if they had read the present book and were trying to conduct themselves accordingly. There was even some familiarity with Velikovsky's *Worlds in Collision* evident among the five panel-members (I inclue the Moderator) who opposed Velikovsky, he standing alone. As it developed, the establishment advocates were in a state of 'partial assimilation'; so Professor Harold Lasswell has termed the process by which a political revolution like the French or Russian is in part absorbed by its conservative opponents as a defensive measure.

Indeed here was an interesting development. Little cordiality was exhibited among the panelists. And no happiness was displayed at exploring new realms of scientific inquiry. But apparently, without admitting so much, the critics of Velikovsky were being forced to move into combat upon his terrain. Science as a whole cannot help but benefit from this. For, as Adam Smith long ago pointed out, private competition may result in public gain. Velikovsky has enlarged the scientific marketplace, J. S. Mill's marketplace of ideas, by designing a new product. So we encounter the first halting steps of the so-called 'hard sciences' to deal with the 'soft' materials of legends, myth, psychology, archaeology, and history.

Scientists cannot any longer remain specialists and hope to deal for more than a moment in this marketplace with its changed conditions. I recall the weeks of intensive study that Velikovsky put in, not long ago, to master several points of chemistry for an article in reply to chemistry Professor Albert Burgstahler. Hence, we should add that the same is true of the 'soft' scientists – the Graves, the Schliemanns, the Freuds, the Jungs, the Campbells and the Eliades: these must treat of oceanography, geophysics, and celestial dynamics.

Also, and merely as one of 'the halt leading the blind', I would suggest that scientists and scholars repair to the philosophical foundations of science and humanism, upon which the disciplinary structures rest; upon reading and reviewing Plato, Hegel, Dewey, Bridgman and the like, and understanding the critical decisions of Galileo, Newton, Marx-Engels, Nietzsche, Darwin, Freud, Einstein and the like, they may prepare new footings and erect new structures. The history of science and natural history are composed of psycho-social-empirical problems, inextricably intertwined, approachable by a science that is neither 'hard' nor 'soft', but malleable. If few persons can master learning of such scope and depth, does not such learning then constitute a principal goal for that vaunted 'collective enterprise', science?

It is not that the broader view will only help understand and give support to Velikovsky's work; the broader view is also needed to criticize it adversely. I do not refer to his manner and style as worthwhile targets. His writings are vigorously assertive. He does not indulge in the polite and evasive mannerisms of most social scientists and humanists. Nor can he rightly employ mathematics where the variables cannot be fixed or the date measurably assembled. He has granted that he is dealing in hypotheses – and what empirical scientist is not?

I mean that should one reasonably and incredulously ask: 'Is there nowhere an anti-Velikovsky treatise of serious consequence?' the answer, regrettably, is still 'no'. Not in general nor even in a special discipline such as astrophysics or archaeology. Thousands of scientists and scholars have impugned his work. A few have stepped up to bat against him or one of his team: they put on airs; they dance about; they come up unprepared; they take blundering swipes at the ball; they strike out. When all is done, they say that it was not a real professional ballgame.

In two cases major intellectual projects have been directed against Velikovsky. The aforesaid Cornell Press book was promptly shredded by the aforesaid special issue of *Kronos*. The second attack, indirectly launched to contradict Velikovsky and not even mentioning him, came earlier; it was *Hamlet's Mill* by G. de Santillana and H. von Dechand;[9] it concentrated upon mythology and the earliest scientific knowledge; its structure is mysterious; it is useful largely because it indeed goes to show that proto-historic mankind could be disciplined and scientific, and that mythology everywhere derives from the behaviour of the planets. Both books received ample support. Both are being cannibalized by the revolutionists, who are resource-starved and have become quite adapted to feeding upon the evidence and criticism offered by their opponents.

Writing at the end of 1977, an historian of science, A. M. Paterson, declared:[10]

> Actually, the battle is over. Dr Velikovsky has emerged the victor because his scientific hypothesis that there have been physical planetary catastrophes in historical times has been proven to have enormous predictive power. For example, a few from very, very many may be listed: Radio noise from Jupiter, strong charge on Jupiter (1953); Earth's extensive magnetosphere (1956); An extensive magnetic field in the solar system extending to Pluto (1946); The Sun is charged (1950); Venus is very hot, has a heavy atmosphere, and was disturbed in its rotation and may have an anomalous rotation (1950); Mars' atmosphere contains quantities of argon and neon (1945); Mars is moon-like, battered and geologically active (1950); There have been many reversals of Earth's magnetic poles (1950); Some of Earth's petroleum was deposited only a few thousand years ago (1950).
>
> And successful deduction about the Moon: Hydrocarbons, carbides, and carbonates will be found (July 2 and July 21, 1969); Strong remanent magnetism in rocks (May 19, 1969); Pockets of radioactivity (March 14, 1967); Excessive argon and neon in the regolith (leading to incorrect age estimates) (July 23, 1969); Steep thermal gradient under the surface (July 2, 1969).

Perhaps Professor Paterson would be quick to agree that her first sentence was the hyperbole of an enthusiast. As she points out elsewhere in her article, 300 years of science may be used up in conflict over a great paradigm.

Furthermore, we have to contend with the possibility of real explosive warfare, occasioned by the inane and insane politics of the age, which would foreclose the warfare of science. Dr Velikovsky has been acutely aware of the threat of nuclear missiles. On the occasion of receiving an honorary doctrate of philosophy at the University of Lethbridge, Alberta, Canada, in 1974, he speculated that the threat to humanity as a whole could be traced to the suppression of the memory of early catastrophes and the unconscious, typically neurotic urge of persons in power to recapitulate the terrible ancient scenes.[11]

Here, however, we must assume that such a catastrophe will not occur. Then, if only because the present world, unlike the past, rushes into the resolution of issues, a vindication of Velikovsky's theories and hence a major shift in the ruling paradigm or model of science may take place in a fairly short period of time. The challenge of the revolutionary to the evolutionary view is sharp and clear, no matter what synthesis evolves in the end. There are now available, yet unassimilated to either model of the world, hundreds of studies of catastrophic import performed by uniformitarians who shrink from drawing appropriate conclusions. Hence, when the philosophical and ideological barriers are dropped, and an archway of revolutionary theory is erected over the cleared roadway, empirical studies will enter in veritable troops. The changeover-time from one to another model of holocene and early human history might not be long.

Alfred de Grazia, 3 January 1978

REFERENCES

1. Isaac Asimov *et al.*, *Scientists Confront Velikovsky*, (Ithaca, N.Y.: Cornell University Press, 1977).

2. *Velikovsky and Establishment Science*, Vol. III, no. 2 (1977). *Kronos* (Glassboro State College, Glassboro, N.J., USA) and

The Society for Interdisciplinary Studies, which publishes the *SIS Review* (c/o T. B. Moore, Central Library, Hartlepool, Cleveland, Eng.) carry continuously information on the controversies surrounding Immanuel Velikovsky, as well as publishing articles by him and associated scholars on substantive concerns of revolutionary primevalogy.

3. Mullen, 'The Center Holds', in *Velikovsky Reconsidered*, by the editors of *Pensée* (Abacus, 1978), p. 239–49; A. de Grazia, 'The Coming Cosmic Debate in the Sciences and Humanities', in Nahum Ravel, ed., *From Past to Prophesy: Velikovsky's Challenge to Conventional Beliefs*, Proceedings of the Symposium held at the Saidye Bronfman Centre, Montreal, Quebec, Canada, January 10–12, 1975.

4. Julian-Jaynes, *The Origin of Consciousness in the Breakdown of the Bicameral Mind*, (Boston: Houghton Mifflin, 1977).

5. J. L. Worzel, 'Extensive Deep Sea Sub-Bottom Reflections Identified as White Ash', *Proc. Nat. Acad. Sci.*, 43:349–55, March 15, 1959, 355; B. Heezen, Ewing, and Ericson, 'Significance of the Worzel Deep Sea Ash', *ibid*, 355–61.

6. Israel Isaacson, 'Applying the Revised Chronology', *Pensée*, IV: 5–20 (1974).

7. 'Cometary Collisions and Geological Periods', *Nature* 242:32 (March 2, 1973).

8. With what seems a comic touch, the science fiction author and popular science writer, Isaac Asimov, was brought in, very much after the fact, to introduce the book of the 'serious' scientists and the 'non-commercial' Cornell University Press. Also added was a paper of Professor Donald Morrison, that had been tempered by earlier heated encounters with Velikovsky's associates. *Cf.* R. E. Juergens, 'On Morrison', in *Kronos, loc. cit.*, 113.

9. Boston: Gambit, 1969.

10. 'Velikovsky versus Academic Lag', in *Velikovsky and Establishment Science, op. cit.*, pp. 121–31, p. 126.

11. 'Cultural Amnesia', in Earl Milton, ed., *Recollections of a Fallen Sky* (Lethbridge, Can.: Lethbridge U. Press, 1978).

INTRODUCTION TO THE FIRST EDITION

In 1950, a book called *Worlds in Collision*, by Dr Immanuel Velikovsky, gave rise to a controversy in scientific and intellectual circles about scientific theories and the sociology of science. Dr Velikovsky's historical and cosmological concepts, bolstered by his acknowledged scholarship, constituted a formidable assault on certain established theories of astronomy, geology and historical biology, and on the heroes of those sciences. Newton, himself, and Darwin were being challenged, and indeed the general orthodoxy of an ordered universe. The substance of Velikovsky's ideas is briefly presented in the first chapter of this book.

What must be called the scientific establishment rose in arms, not only against the new Velikovsky theories but against the man himself. Efforts were made to block dissemination of Dr Velikovsky's ideas, and even to punish supporters of his investigations. Universities, scientific societies, publishing houses, the popular press were approached and threatened; social pressures and professional sanctions were invoked to control public opinion. There can be little doubt that in a totalitarian society, not only would Dr Velikovsky's reputation have been at stake, but also his right to pursue his inquiry, and perhaps his personal safety.

As it was, the 'establishment' succeeded in building a wall of unfavourable sentiment around him: to thousands of scholars the name of Velikovsky bears the taint of fantasy, science-fiction and publicity.

He could not be suppressed entirely. In the next years he published three more books. He carried on a large correspondence. And he was helped by a very few friends, and by a large general public composed of persons outside of the establishments of science. The probings of spacecraft tended to confirm – never to disprove – his arguments. Eventually the venomous aspects of the controversy, the efforts at suppression, the campaign of vilification loomed almost as large, in their consequences to science, as the original issue. Social scientists, who had been generally unaware of Dr Velikovsky's work, and its importance, and who had been almost totally disengaged, now found themselves in the thick of the conflict.

The involvement of the social and behavioural sciences in the scientific theories of Velikovsky was higher than had been earlier appreciated. The social sciences are the basis of Velikovsky's work: despite his proficiency in the natural sciences, it is by the use of the methodology of social science that Velikovsky launched his challenge to accepted cosmological theories. No one pretends that this method is adequate. New forms of interdisciplinary research are needed to wed, for example, the study of myth with the study of meteorites. Nor does one have to agree that Velikovsky is the greatest technician of mythology, even while granting his great conceptual and synthesizing powers.

Whatever the scientific substance, the controversy itself could not be avoided or dismissed by behavioural science. The politics of science is one of the agitating problems of the twentieth century. The issues are clear: Who determines scientific truth? Who are its high priests, and what is their warrant? How do they establish their canons? What effects do they have on the freedom of inquiry, and on public interest? In the end, some judgement must be passed upon the behaviour of the scientific world and, if adverse, some remedies must be proposed.

It was in this light that, in a special issue, the *American Behavioral Scientist* published three papers dealing with the Velikovsky controversy. The first, by Ralph Juergens, recounts the story of Dr Velikovsky from its beginnings to the present; tells something of the man and his works. The second, by Livio Stecchini, analyzes the roots of the controversy in the scientific past. A third, by the editor, searches for means by which new discoveries may be brought into the corpus of science, and offers suggestions for reform of present procedure.

The *American Behavioral Scientist* did not enter the Velikovsky controversy heedlessly. The papers were read by a number of respected scientists and scholars, who did not necessarily share, of course, all of the views expressed by the authors, nor necessarily subscribe to Dr Velikovsky's views. They agreed, however, to the usefulness of their publication; their general help and encouragement in the original studies is now again gratefully acknowledged as the studies go to press in book format. Our thanks are owing to:

HADLEY CANTRIL, Chairman of the Board, Institute for International Social Research; past president, Society for the Psychological Study of Social Issues.

SALVADOR DE MADARIAGA, Honorary Fellow, Exeter College, Oxford University.

LUTHER H. EVANS, Director of International and Legal Collections, Columbia University, former Director General, UNESCO.

MOSES HADAS, Jay Professor of Greek, Columbia University.

R. H. HILLENKOETTER, Vice Admiral, U.S.N. (Retired); former director, Central Intelligence Agency.

HORACE M. KALLEN, Research Professor of Social Philosophy, New School for Social Research; past president, Society for the Scientific Study of Religion.

HAROLD D. LASSWELL, Professor of Law and Political Science, Yale University Law School; past president, American Political Science Association.

HAROLD S. LATHAM, former Editor-in-Chief and Vice-president, Macmillan Co.

PHILIP WITTENBERG, Partner, Wittenberg, Carrington and Weinberger.

Publication of the papers brought immediate response. Numerous scholars, both in the natural and social sciences, have written to the *American Behavioral Scientist*, commenting favourably, on the whole, upon the presentation of the matter to the scientific public. All documentation is being preserved, in the hope that the archives will be of use to future discussion.

The new material in the present book is considerable. Ralph Juergens has brought the story of the Velikovsky case up to date in a new paper. There is also a new paper by Dr Livio Stecchini, carrying on from his first paper, this time on the uses of historical data for astronomical theory. We publish here, too, Dr Velikovsky's own paper from the special issue of the *American Behavioral Scientist*.

The Velikovsky case is in no sense closed. There is no reason why it should be. Undeterred by the attacks upon him, and the obstacles placed in his way, Dr Velikovsky is pursuing his studies, and now has several books nearing completion: three on the substance of his theories, others of a general autobiographical character. He remains a faithful and indefatigable correspondent, and his letters point to new challenges.

It is our hope that the publication of these papers in the present volume will make it less easy for his new work to be suppressed, or lightly dismissed. We hope, too, that they will help scientists and interested laymen everywhere to rehearse the problems and to reform the errors of the vast enterprise of science.

Alfred de Grazia, 1966

MINDS IN CHAOS

by Ralph E. Juergens

Seventeen years ago the appearance of Immanuel Velikovsky's *Worlds in Collision* precipitated an academic storm. Prominent American scientists, roused to indignation even before the book was published, greeted it with a remarkable demonstration of ill will that included a partially successful attempt to suppress the work by imposing a boycott on its first publisher's textbooks. The reading public witnessed the unique spectacle of a scientific debate staged not in the semi-privacy of scientific meetings and journals, but in the popular press, with scientists – in rare accord – on one side and lay champions of free speech on the other. With the might of authority all on one side of the issue, the debate was resolved in a predictable manner; Velikovsky and his book were discredited in the public eye.

From the start there was more to the controversy than the simple question of a dissenting scholar's right to be published and read; the atmosphere generated by scientific consternation was charged with a peculiar emotion that *Newsweek* termed 'a highly unacademic fury'. Even if Velikovsky's book were, as one astronomer put it, the 'most amazing example of a shattering of accepted concepts on record', the violence of the reaction against it seemed all out of proportion to the book's importance if, as most critics insisted, the work was spurious and entirely devoid of merit. Many nonscientist observers concluded that Velikovsky's work was not run-of-the-mill heresy, but a thesis that presented a genuine threat to the very ego of science. It seemed that *Worlds in Collision* was being attacked with a fervor 'reserved only for books that lay bare new fundamentals'. Caught up in this fervor, more than one scientist-reviewer of Velikovsky's book adopted tactics even more surprising than the overt and covert deeds of the would-be suppressors.

Before attempting to trace the course of the Velikovsky affair, we might first recall the unsettling message of the book that initiated that strange chain of events. In Britain, where *Worlds in Collision* was also rejected by almost all scientists, but with a lesser show of emotion, Sir Harold Spencer Jones, the later Royal Astronomer, summarized its thesis this way:

> The central theme of *Worlds in Collision* is that, according to Dr Velikovsky, between the fifteenth and eighth centuries B.C. the earth experienced a series of violent catastrophes of global extent. Parts of its surface were heated to such a degree that they became molten and great streams of lava welled out; the sea boiled and evaporated; . . . mountain ranges collapsed, while others were thrown up; continents were raised causing great floods; showers of hot stones fell; electrical disturbances of great violence caused much havoc; hurricanes swept the earth; a pall of darkness shrouded it, to be followed by a deluge of fire. This picture of a period of intense turmoil within the period of recorded history is supported by a wealth of quotations from the Old Testament, from the Hindu Vedas, from Roman and Greek mythology, and from the myths, traditions and folklore of many races and peoples . . .
>
> These catastrophic events in the earth's history are attributed by Dr Velikovsky to a series of awe-inspiring cosmic cataclysms. In the solar system we see the several planets moving round the sun in the same direction in orbits which are approximately circular and which lie nearly in the same plane. Dr Velikovsky asserts that this was not always so, but that in past times their orbits intersected; collisions between major planets occurred, which brought about the birth of comets. He states that in the time of Moses, about the fifteenth century B.C., one of these comets nearly collided with the earth, which twice passed through its tail. [The earth experienced] the disrupting effect of the comet's gravitational pull, . . . intense heating and enormous tides . . . incessant electric discharges . . . and the pollution of the atmosphere by the gases in the tail . . . Dr Velikovsky attributes . . . oil deposits in the earth to the precipitation, in the form of a sticky liquid (naphtha), of some of the carbon and hydrogen gases in the tail of the comet, while the manna upon which the Israelites fed is similarly accounted for as carbohydrates from the same source.
>
> This comet is supposed to have collided with Mars . . . and,

as the result of the collision, to have lost its tail and to have become transformed into the planet Venus . . .

Further catastrophes . . . ensued . . . Mars was shifted nearer to the earth so that in the year 687 B.C. . . . Mars nearly collided with the earth.

These various encounters are supposed to have been responsible for repeated changes in the earth's orbit, in the inclination of its axis, and in the lengths of the day, the seasons and the year. The earth on one occasion is supposed to have turned completely over, so that the sun rose in the west and set in the east. Dr Velikovsky argues that between the fifteenth and eighth centuries B.C. the length of the year was 360 days and that it suddenly increased to 365¼ days in 687 B.C. The orbit of the moon and the length of the month were also changed . . .[1]

In short, Velikovsky's research among the ancient records of man – records ranging from unequivocal statements in written documents, through remembrances expressed in myth and legend, to mute archaeological evidence in the form of obsolete calendars and sundials – and his examination of geological and paleontological reports from all parts of the globe led him to conclude that modern man's snug little world, set in a framework of celestial harmony and imperceptible evolution, is but an illusion. Velikovsky's reappraisal of world history ravages established doctrine in disciplines from astronomy to psychology: universal gravitation of masses is not the only force governing celestial motions – electromagnetic forces must also play important roles; enigmatic breaks in the geological record denote, not interminable ages of languorous erosion and deposition gently terminated by cyclic submergence and emergence of land masses, but sudden, violent derangements of the earth's surface; the remarkably rapid annihilation of whole species and genera of animals and the equally remarkable, almost simultaneous proliferation of species in other generic groups bespeak overwhelming catastrophe and wholesale mutation among survivors; the mechanism of evolution is not competition between typical and chance-mutant offspring of common parents, but divergent mutation of whole populations simultaneously exposed to unaccustomed radiation, chemical pollution of the atmosphere, and global electromagnetic disturbances; ancient cities and fortresses were not brought low individually by local warfare and earthquakes, but were destroyed simultaneously and repeatedly in worldwide catastrophes; calamities described in clear-cut terms in surviving records of the past – records almost universally interpreted allegorically by late-classical as well as modern scholars – were common traumatic experiences for all races of mankind, and as such have been purged from conscious memory.

The author of this strange new concept of universal history was born in Vitebsk, Russia, in 1895. His formal schooling began in Moscow at Medvednikov Gymnasium, from which he graduated with full honours. Following a brief period of study at Montpellier, France, and travels in Palestine, he began pre-medical studies in natural science at Edinburgh, Scotland, in 1914. When his schooling abroad was interrupted by the outbreak of World War I, Velikovsky enrolled in the Free University in Moscow and for a few years studied law and ancient history. Meanwhile, in 1915 he resumed work towards a medical degree at the University of Moscow, and in 1921 he received his medical diploma.

The next few years Velikovsky spent in Berlin, where he and Prof. Heinrich Loewe founded and published *Scripta Universitatis* with funds supplied by Velikovsky's father. In this series of volumes, conceived as a cornerstone for what would become the University of Jerusalem, contributions from outstanding Jewish scholars in all countries were published in their native languages and in Hebrew translation. The late Albert Einstein edited the mathematical-physical volume of the *Scripta*.

In Berlin Velikovsky met and married violinist Elisheva Kramer of Hamburg. Later the same year the young couple moved to Palestine, and the doctor began his practice of medicine. For fifteen years this practice – first as a general practitioner in Jerusalem, and later, after psychiatric training in Europe, as a psychoanalyst in Haifa and Tel Aviv – occupied most of Velikovsky's time. Nevertheless, he published a number of papers on psychology, some in Freud's *Imago*. In one paper, to which Prof. Eugen Bleuler wrote a preface,[2] Velikovsky was the first to suggest that pathological encephalograms would be found characteristic of epilepsy; distorted and accentuated brain waves of epileptics were later found to be important clinical diagnostic symptoms. He also conceived a plan for an academy of science in Jerusalem and started a new series, *Scripta Academica*, to which Prof. Chaim Weizmann, president of the World Zionist Organization and a noted scientist, contributed the first monograph in biochemistry. This series was dedicated to the memory of Velikovsky's father, who had died in Palestine in December 1937.

Velikovsky also had an idea for a book, and to complete the necessary research he decided to interrupt his practice for an extended visit to America. The Velikovskys and their two school-age daughters arrived in New York in the summer of 1939, and the doctor plunged into his library research. The intended book had been conceived as an analytic study of Freud's own dreams, as recorded in his writings, and a comparative study of the lives of three personages – Oedipus, Akhnaton, and Moses – who had figured prominently in Freud's thoughts and works.

The research was nearly completed by the spring of 1940, and Velikovsky began to make preparations for the return home. Then, at the last moment before an already-postponed sailing, he chanced upon an idea that was to completely alter his life plans and keep him in America for decades.

Reflecting upon events in the life of Moses, Velikovsky began to speculate: Was there a natural catastrophe at the time of the Exodus of the Israelites from Egypt? Could the plagues of Egypt, the hurricane, the parting of the waters, and the smoke, fire, and rumblings of Mt Sinai described in the Bible have been real and sequential aspects of a single titanic cataclysm of natural forces?

If the Exodus took place during – or because of – an upheaval, perhaps some record of the same events has survived among the many documents of ancient Egypt; if so, might not such a record be a clue to the proper place of the Exodus in Egyptian history?

After weeks of search Velikovsky came upon the story he sought. A papyrus bearing a lamentation by one Ipuwer had been preserved in the library of the University of Leiden, Holland, since 1828. Translation of the document by A. H. Gardiner in 1909 had disclosed an account of plague and destruction closely paralleling the Biblical narrative, but the similarities escaped Gardiner's attention. Ipuwer bewailed the collapse of the state and social order during what seemed to be a calamity of natural forces. Mention of Asiatic invaders (Hyksos) made it appear that the sage Ipuwer had witnessed the downfall of the Middle Kingdom (Middle Bronze Age) in Egypt.

For nearly 2000 years scholars have conjectured and debated about the proper place of the Exodus in Egyptian history. But the end of Middle Kingdom which is conventionally assigned to the eighteenth century B.C., had never been considered; it seemed much too early according to Hebrew chronology. All efforts have been directed towards finding a likely niche in New Kingdom history. Velikovsky, however, felt confident that his method of correlation was valid; he resolved to establish the coevality of the Exodus and the Hyksos invasion as a working hypothesis and pursue the inquiry through subsequent centuries. He discovered so much apparent substantiation for the novel synchronization that he was soon compelled to face up to its inherent dilemma: either Hebrew history is too short by more than five centuries – an inconceivable premise – or Egyptian chronology, a proud joint achievement of modern historians, archaeologists, and astronomers, and the standard scale against which all Near Eastern histories are calibrated, is too long by an equal number of centuries. The latter alternative seemed just as inconceivable; all the excess centuries would have to be found and eliminated from post-Middle Kingdom history, that portion of Egyptian history considered by all scholars to be unalterably reconstructed and fixed in time. But soon Velikovsky found the apparent explanation for the discrepancy: certain Egyptian dynasties appear twice in conventionally accepted schemes – first, their stories appear as they have been pieced together from the monuments and other relics of Egypt; then in history gleaned from Greek historians, the same characters and events are given secondary and independent places in the time table. 'Many figures . . . are "ghosts" or "halves" and "doubles". Events are often duplicates; many battles are shadows; many speeches are echoes; many treaties are copies.'

In the fall of 1940 Velikovsky traced events similar to those described in the Pentateuch and the Book of Joshua in the literature of ancient Mexico. This confirmed his growing suspicion that the great natural catastrophes that visited the Near East had been global in scale. Immediately he expanded his research to embrace records of all races. The next five or six years he spent developing parallel themes – reconstructions of ancient political history and recent cosmic history – and as month followed month the intimate details of a new concept of the world emerged. Two manuscripts were the product of his labours: *Ages in Chaos* traced Near Eastern history from —1500 to —300; *Worlds in Collision* documented the evidence and sequence of catastrophes on earth and in the solar system.

The late Robert H. Pfeiffer, then Chairman of the Department of Semitic Languages and Curator of the Semitic Museum at Harvard University, read an early draft of *Ages in Chaos* in 1942 and conceded that the revolutionary version of history might well be correct. He felt the work should receive a fair trial and objective investigation. He also read subsequent drafts of the manuscript and made efforts to help find a publisher for it. To one prospective publisher he wrote: 'I regard this work – provocative as it is – of fundamental importance, whether its conclusions are accepted by competent scholars or whether it forces them to a far-reaching and searching reconstruction of the accepted chronology'. Notwithstanding Pfeiffer's endorsement, eight publishers returned the manuscript.

Before seeking a publisher for *Worlds in Collision*, Velikovsky tried to enlist the help of scientists in arranging for certain experiments that would constitute crucial tests for his thesis, which was essentially three-fold: (1) There were global catastrophes in historical times; (2) these catastrophes were caused by extraterrestrial agents; and (3) these agents, in the most recent of the catastrophes, can be identified as the planets Venus and Mars, Venus playing the dominant role. All three postulates would be largely substantiated if it could be shown that, contrary to all conventional expectations, Venus (1) is still hot – evidence of recent birth, (2) is enveloped in hydrocarbon clouds – remnants of a hydrocarbonaceous comet tail, and (3) has anomalous rotational motion – evidence suggesting that it suffered unusual perturbations before settling in its orbit as a planet. The first two of these points were selected by Velikovsky in 1946 as the most crucial tests for his entire work.

THE EVIDENCE FROM MARINER II

He was confident of ultimate vindication for his conclusion that Venus is hot despite the fact that the outer regions of its envelope were known to have a temperature of −25°C. Even as recently as 1959 astronomers believed that because of the great reflecting power of its clouds the ground temperature on Venus could differ little from that on earth. Venus orbits closer to the sun, but more solar radiation is reflected away from Venus than from the earth. Nevertheless, Velikovsky argued that the seeming contradiction in evidence long available – apparent slow rotation, yet nearly identical temperatures on shadowed and sunlit surfaces of the envelope of

Venus – is illusory because the planet is young; it is hot and radiates heat from day and night hemispheres alike. [Fifteen years later, in 1961, radio astronomers announced that radiation from Venus indicated that its surface must have a temperature of 600°F. And in February 1963, after analyzing data from Mariner II, scientists raised this temperature estimate by another 200 degrees.[3] No convincing explanation has yet been advanced to square this evidence with orthodox cosmologies.]

Velikovsky thought his second deduction about Venus – hydrocarbon dust and gases must be present in its atmosphere and envelope – might be investigated spectroscopically. To this end in April 1946 he approached Prof. Harlow Shapley, then director of Harvard College Observatory. Without going into detail, Velikovsky explained that he had developed a hypothesis about recent changes in the order of the solar system and that his conclusions might be checked in part by spectral studies of Venus. Shapley pointed out that sudden changes in the planetary order would be inconsistent with gravitational theory; nevertheless, he agreed to consider performing such experiments if another scholar of known reputation would first read and then recommend Velikovsky's work. At Velikovsky's behest, Prof. Horace M. Kallen, co-founder of the New School of Social Research and at that time dean of its graduate faculty – a scholar already familiar with the work – wrote Shapley to urge that he conduct the search for hydrocarbons on Venus if at all possible. But to Kallen's plea, Shapley, who had refused to read the manuscript, replied that he wasn't interested in Velikovsky's 'sensational claims' because they violate the laws of mechanics; '*if Dr Velikovsky is right, the rest of us are crazy*'. Nevertheless, Shapley recommended that Velikovsky contact either Walter S. Adams, director of Mt. Wilson Observatory, or Rupert Wildt at McCormick Observatory.

In the summer of 1946 Velikovsky directed identical inquiries to both Wildt and Adams, stating that he had a cosmological theory implying that 'Venus is rich with petroleum gases and hydrocarbon dust'. So strong were these implications that he believed the presence or absence of these materials in the atmosphere and envelope of Venus would constitute crucial support or refutation for his thesis, and therefore he wished to know if the spectrum of Venus might be interpreted in this sense. Wildt replied that the absorption spectrum of Venus shows no evidence of hydrocarbons. Adams pointed out that the absorption bands of most petroleum molecules are in the far infra-red, below the range of photographic detection, and that hydrocarbons known to absorb in the detectable range are not apparent in the spectrum of Venus.

All this notwithstanding, Velikovsky elected to defer once more to his historical evidence; he left in his manuscript and later in the published book the statement that a positive demonstration that petroleum-like hydrocarbons are or are not present in the envelope of Venus would be a decisive check on his work. [On the basis of an apparent ability to condense and polymerize into heavy molecules at a temperature near 200°F in the atmosphere, the clouds of Venus must consist of heavy hydrocarbons and more complex organic compounds; thus concluded Mariner II experimenter Lewis D. Kaplan in February 1963.][4]

At the end of July 1946 the late John J. O'Neill, science editor of the New York *Herald Tribune*, agreed to read Velikovsky's manuscript. O'Neill was immediately impressed, and he devoted his column for August 14 to the work. In his opinion, 'Dr Velikovsky's work presents a stupendous panorama of terrestrial and human histories which will stand as a challenge to scientists to frame a realistic picture of the cosmos.'

Between June and October 1946 Velikovsky submitted his manuscript to one publisher after another, but the consensus was that the heavily annotated text was too scholarly for the book trade. Eventually, however, the trail led to Macmillan Company, where trade-books editor James Putnam saw possibilities in the book. In May of 1947 an optional contract was signed, and then, after another year in which various outside readers – among them, O'Neill and Gordon Atwater, then Curator of Hayden Planetarium and Chairman of the Department of Astronomy of the American Museum of Natural History – examined the manuscript and recommended publication, a final contract was drawn and signed.

By March 1949 word of the book Macmillan was preparing for publication had spread among people in the trade. Frederick L. Allen, editor-in-chief of *Harper's Magazine*, sought authorization to present a two-article synopsis of *Worlds in Collision* and had Eric Larrabee, then an editor on the *Harper's* staff, prepare a tentative condensation from galley proofs. Allen wished to submit this for approval, but Velikovsky did not respond to the proposal for more than six months. In the fall, however, after more urging, he agreed to see Larrabee to discuss a one-article presentation of his theme; Larrabee then rewrote his piece completely.

Larrabee's article, 'The Day the Sun Stood Still', appeared in *Harper's* for January 1950. The issue sold out within a few days, and so great was the demand from readers that a number of dailies both here and abroad reprinted Larrabee's text in full.

In February 1950 *Reader's Digest* featured a popularization of Velikovsky's findings prepared by the late Fulton Oursler, who emphasized their corroboration for Old Testament history.

Collier's Magazine, in February and March 1950, published two instalments of an announced three-part series. Velikovsky, who had agreed only to serialization – not adaptation or condensation, was so dismayed by the cavalier treatment being accorded his work in the highly sensationalized manuscripts submitted for his approval that he threatened to make a public disavowal of the *Collier's* articles unless each was severely revised. After long, stormy sessions, the first two manuscripts were approved; *Collier's* abandoned the third.

Early in February 1950, when *Worlds in Collision* was about to go to press, Putnam called on Velikovsky to show him two letters Macmillan had received from Harlow Shapley. In the first, dated January 18, Shapley expressed gratification over a rumour that Velikovsky's book was not going to appear, and astonishment that Macmillan had even considered a venture into the 'Black Arts'. In his second letter, written on January 25 after Putnam had answered the first, discounting the alleged rumour and assuring him that the book would appear on schedule, Shapley, who had still not seen the manuscript, remarked: 'It will be interesting a year from now to hear from you as to whether or not the reputation of the Macmillan Co. is damaged by the publication of "Worlds in Collision".' At the very least, release of the book would 'cut off' all relations between Shapley and Macmillan. He also announced that, at his request, one of his colleagues who was also a classicist was preparing a 'commentary' on Larrabee's article. He concluded with an expression of his hope that Macmillan had thoroughly investigated Velikovsky's background; however, 'it is quite possible that only this "Worlds in Collision" episode is intellectually fraudulent.'

This second letter apparently struck close to home for Macmillan president George Brett, for he personally answered Shapley to thank him for 'waving the red flag'. Brett promised to submit the book to three impartial censors and to abide by the majority verdict of the three.

Apparently the majority again voted thumbs up; the book was published on schedule. The identities of the last-minute censors were never officially revealed, but one of them, Prof. C. W. van der Merwe, Chairman of the Department of Physics at New York University, later disclosed to John O'Neill that he had been enlisted by Macmillan and had been one of the two who voted in favour of publication.

Meanwhile, the February 25, 1950, issue of *Science News Letter*, a publication then headed by Harlow Shapley, printed denunciation of Velikovsky's ideas by five authorities in as many fields: Nelson Glueck, archaeologist; Carl Kraeling, orientalist; Henry Field, anthropologist; David Delo, geologist; and Shapley himself, speaking for astronomers. This medley of protest came forth just as *Worlds in Collision* went to press – none of the critics had seen the work.

On March 14, the commentary on Larrabee's article by Shapley's colleague, astronomer Cecilia Payne-Gaposchkin, appeared in *The Reporter*. (An earlier draft of the article had been mimeographed and circulated widely by direct mail to scientists, science editors, and publishers.) Stringing phrases from three sentences appearing on as many pages of Larrabee's article into a sentence of her own, Gaposchkin set it in quotation marks and introduced it as 'Dr Velikovsky's astronomical assertions'. The gist of her thoroughly abusive article was that electromagnetic phenomena are of no importance in space, and in a purely mechanical solar system the events of *Worlds in Collision* are impossible. The March 25 issue of *Science News Letter*, in a 'Retort to Velikovsky', who had as yet not been heard from, cited Gaposchkin's critique as recommended reading for all scientists – 'a detailed scientific answer to Dr Velikovsky.'

On April 11 *The Reporter* reproduced letters to the editor from Larrabee and Gaposchkin. Larrabee challenged the propriety of her attack on a book she had not yet seen, and Gaposchkin acknowledged that her review had been based on popularized preview articles only; she remarked that she had since read the book (published April 3, 1950) and found it to be 'better written . . . but just as wrong'.

The last few weeks before *Worlds in Collision* made its appearance were spent in strategic manoeuvring by the leaders of the resistance forces. The late Otto Struve, then director of Yerkes Observatory at the University of

Chicago and an ex-president of the American Astronomical Society, penned letters to both John O'Neill and Gordon Atwater, requesting them to abandon their earlier positions with respect to *Worlds in Collision*. Atwater, unaware that he was facing an inquisition, replied that he believed Velikovsky's work had great merit, and although he did not accept all its conclusions in detail, he was preparing a favourable review of the book for *This Week* magazine. He was planning – indeed had already publicly announced – a planetarium programme to depict the events of *Worlds in Collision*. O'Neill composed a heated reply, but then destroyed it. He let it be known that his earlier appraisal of the book had not since been altered in any way.

Atwater's planetarium programme was scuttled immediately. During the last week of March he was summarily fired from both his positions with the museum – as Curator of Hayden Planetarium and Chairman of the Department of Astronomy – and requested to vacate his office immediately. Thus, when his review in *This Week* appeared on April 2, an article in which he pleaded for open-mindedness in dealing with the new theory, the credentials printed alongside Atwater's name were already invalid. Last-minute attempts to influence *This Week* not to publish this cover story failed when the editor sought and followed O'Neill's advice.

THE OPPOSITION TAKES ACTION

O'Neill's prepared review for the *Herald Tribune* had been scheduled to appear on April 2. But instead of O'Neill's article readers of that Sunday's issue found a review written by Struve. No concrete arguments were presented by Struve to justify his rejection of the book; 'It is not a book of science and it cannot be dealt with in scientific terms.' He went on: 'It was necessary for readers to wait until a recent issue of the "Reporter" to learn, through Mrs Cecilia Payne-Gaposchkin . . . that the observations of Venus extend back five hundred years before the Exodus, thus refuting the absurd theory of a comet that turned into a planet.' Velikovsky, however, had specified no date for the eruption of Venus from Jupiter, except that it had occurred some time before the Exodus. And, as Velikovsky pointed out in his book, the Babylonian tablets (Venus Tablets of Ammizaduga) cited by Gaposchkin to support her claim ascribe such erratic motions to Venus that translators and commentators have been baffled by them ever since they were discovered in the ruins of Nineveh in the last century; he also pointed out that even if the apparitions and periods of Venus recorded on the tablets date from early in the second millennium, which is disputed among scholars, they prove only that Venus already then moved erratically and quite unlike a planet.

Reviewing *Worlds in Collision* in the *New York Times Book Review*, also on April 2, the late chief science editor of the *Times*, Waldemar Kaempffert, followed Gaposchkin into the same territory and falsely accused Velikovsky of suppressing the Venus Tablets of Ammizaduga. Kaempffert seemingly had not read the book very carefully before condemning it, for not only did Velikovsky describe the tablets and quote the complete texts of observations from five successive years out of twenty-one, but he discussed opinions written by various orientalists and astronomers who had studied the tablets (Rawlinson, Smith, Langdon, Fotheringham, Schiaparelli, Kugler, Hommel).

In the next few months, 'a surprising number of the country's reputable astronomers descended from their telescopes to denounce *Worlds in Collision*', to quote the *Harvard Crimson* of September 25, 1950. Newspapers around the country were barraged with abusive reviews contributed by big-name scientists; some of these writings were syndicated to ensure better coverage.

Ignoring Velikovsky's alternate explanation that, perhaps in the grip of an alien magnetic field, a 'tilting of the [earth's] axis could produce the visual effect of a retrogressing or arrested sun', Frank K. Edmondson, director of Goethe Link Observatory, University of Indiana, wrote:[5] 'Velikovsky is not bothered by the elementary fact that if the earth were stopped, inertia would cause Joshua and his companions to fly off into space with a speed of nine hundred miles an hour.' This argument, first formulated by Gaposchkin, is at best disingenuous, for the all-important time factor – the rate of deceleration – is completely ignored.

Paul Herget, Director of the Observatory, University of Cincinnati, derided the ideas expressed in *Worlds in Collision*,[6] but advanced no specific counterarguments on scientific grounds. Nevertheless, he concluded that all the book's basic contentions were 'dynamically impossible'. Frank S. Hogg, director of David Dunlop Observatory, University of Toronto, and Oregon astronomer J. Hugh Pruett both reiterated the erroneous Gaposchkin–Struve notion that observations of Venus made before the time of the Exodus refute Velikovsky's theme.[7, 8] California physicist H. P. Robertson chose the easy path of invective: 'This incredible book . . . this jejune essay . . . [is] too ludicrous to merit serious rebuttal.'[9]

Atomic scientist Harrison Brown disdained to list the 'errors in fact and conclusion' that he estimated would fill a letter 'thirty pages in length'. Instead, in his review of *Worlds in Collision* in the *Saturday Review of Literature*,[10] Brown assured his readers that 'the combination of modern astronomy, geophysics, geochemistry, paleontology, geology, and physics can state the following:

> 'The earth did *not* stop rotating 3,500 years ago. [Brown, too, disregarded Velikovsky's alternative explanation for the visual effect of an arrested sun.]
>
> 'Venus was formed much earlier than 3,500 years ago. Indeed, it is probably about a million times older than Dr Velikovsky suggests.
>
> 'Venus was not formed from a comet emanating from Jupiter (or, for that matter, a comet emanating from anything else).'

The balance of Brown's review was devoted to 'book- and magazine-publishing irresponsibility'.

Despite the vigour of the protracted campaign to discredit its author, *Worlds in Collision* was heralded enthusiastically by many science writers and reviewers, and the book topped the best-seller lists of the New York *Times* and the New York *Herald Tribune* for twenty successive weeks in 1950. [By a strange oversight, however, the *Encyclopedia Britannica Book of the Year* covering 1950 failed to note the existence of Velikovsky's book in its recapitulation of the year's best sellers.]

On May 25, 1950, when sales of his book were at their peak, Velikovsky was summoned to Brett's office and told that professors in certain large universities were refusing to see Macmillan salesmen, and letters demanding cessation of publication were arriving from a number of scientists. Brett beseeched Velikovsky to save him from disaster by approving an arrangement that had been tentatively worked out with Doubleday & Company, which had no textbook department. Doubleday, with Velikovsky's consent, would take over all rights to *Worlds in Collision*. As evidence of the pressure being brought to bear, Brett showed Velikovsky a letter from Michigan astronomer Dean B. McLaughlin, who insisted Velikovsky's book was nothing but lies. On the same page McLaughlin averred he had not read and never would read the book.

While Velikovsky pondered his next move – whether to approve the transfer of rights to Doubleday, or to make an independent search for a new publisher – his scientist-critics apparently began to see their problem in a more serious perspective. Inability to dismiss the events of *Worlds in Collision*, gleaned from a multitude of sources, suggested that a substantial assault upon his method and sources was in order.

The June 1950 issue of *Popular Astronomy* carried another attack on Velikovsky by Cecilia Payne-Gaposchkin. Her words were prefaced by a few lines from the magazine editor, who explained, 'We are giving greater prominence to this analysis of "Worlds in Collision" than is usually accorded to book reviews . . . for two reasons. 1. This book has been brought to the attention of a large reading public by having been mentioned favourably in several popular magazines. 2. The analysis here given is by a recognized authority in the field of astronomy, the science with which the book comes into closest contact, or sharpest conflict.' Gaposchkin's 'analysis' was divided into two parts, first place being devoted to 'the Literary Sources'. By the simple ruse of ignoring both contextual material and corroborative references, she purported to show that Velikovsky had misrepresented his sources. Her 'Scientific Arguments' included restatements of undemonstrable dogmatisms and a highly sarcastic synopsis of Velikovsky's thesis.

Prof. Otto Neugebauer of Brown University, a specialist in Babylonian and Greek astronomy, in an article for *Isis*[11] that was mailed far and wide in reprint form, accused Velikovsky of wilfully tailoring quoted source material. To support this charge, Neugebauer specified that Velikovsky had substituted the figure 33°14′ for the correct value, 3°14′, in a quotation from the work of another scholar. When Velikovsky protested in a letter to the late George Sarton, then editor of *Isis*, that the figure given in his book was correct and the 33°14′ was in fact Neugebauer's own insertion, not his, Neugebauer dismissed the incident as a 'simple misprint of no concern' that did not invalidate his appraisal of Velikovsky's methods. And the reprint was circulated by an interested group long after its errors had been pointed out.

The fundamental position of Neugebauer is that the voluminous Babylonian astronomical texts from before the seventh century B.C., all of which are inconsistent with celestial motions as we know them, were composed in full disregard of actual observations; Velikovsky regards these records as representing true observations of the heavens before the last catastrophe.

Four Yale University professors collaborated in preparing a rebuttal to Velikovsky for the *American Journal of Science*,[12] which was edited by geologist Chester R. Longwell. Sinologist K. S. Latourette acknowledged that Velikovsky 'has combed an amazing range of historical records for evidence to corroborate his thesis', but apparently Latourette could find no specific arguments to refute that thesis. George Kubler, mexicologist, derided the suggestion set forth in *Worlds in Collision* that the Mesoamerican civilization must be much older than scholars then conceded; 'The Mesoamerican cosmology to which Velikovsky repeatedly appeals for proof did not originate until about the beginning of our era.' [In December 1956 the National Geographic Society announced: 'Atomic science has proved the ancient civilizations of Mexico to be some 1,000 years older than had been believed.'] Rupert Wildt took Velikovsky to task for doubting the validity of celestial mechanics based upon gravitation and inertia only, to the exclusion of electromagnetic forces. Longwell scorned the notion that petroleum might have a cosmic origin. [Prof. W. F. Libby, chemist of the University of California, has since suggested that petroleum may be found on the moon. Prof. A. T. Wilson of Victoria University, Wellington, New Zealand, in 1960 produced high molecular weight hydrocarbons by electric discharges in a methane–ammonia (Jupiter-like) atmosphere; in 1962 he, too, suggested that the earth's petroleum may be of cosmic origin and that oil may be found on the moon.]

The article authorized by the four Yale professors and signed by Longwell was given a preview run in the New Haven *Register* on June 25, 1950. A seven-column banner in blue ink above the text proclaimed: '4 Yale Scholars "Expose" Non-Fiction Best-Seller.'

After receiving assurances from Doubleday that it was immune to pressure from textbook writers and buyers, Velikovsky approved the transfer of rights on June 8, 1950. On June 11, columnist Leonard Lyons spread the news, and on June 18 the New York *Times* noted: 'The greatest bombshell dropped on Publishers' Row in many a year exploded the other day . . . Dr Velikovsky himself would not comment on the changeover. But a publishing official admitted, privately, that a flood of protests from educators and others had hit the company hard in its vulnerable underbelly – the textbook division. Following some stormy sessions by the board of directors, Macmillan reluctantly succumbed, surrendered its rights to the biggest money-maker on its list.'

Leonard Lyons reported that the suppression was engineered by Harlow Shapley. When queried, however, Shapley told *Newsweek*, 'I didn't make any threats and I don't know anyone who did.' The late George Sokolsky also discussed the case in his column, and shortly afterwards received a letter from Paul Herget, who was apparently disappointed that all the credit was going to Shapley. Herget wrote, and Sokolsky quoted: 'I am one of those who participated in this campaign against Macmillan. . . . I do not believe that [Shapley] was in any sense the leader . . . I was a very vigorous participant myself . . .' Dean McLaughlin wrote to Fulton Oursler: '*Worlds in Collision* has just changed hands . . . I am frank to state that this change was the result of pressure that scientists and scholars brought to bear on the Macmillan Company . . .'

On June 30, Fred Whipple, Shapley's successor as Director of Harvard College Observatory, informed the Blakiston Company, then owned by Doubleday, that, rather than continue to be a fellow author in the same house with Velikovsky, he would turn over to charity future royalties from his Blakiston-published *Earth, Moon and Planets* and would make no further updating revisions in the text so long as Doubleday controlled Blakiston.

Dumping its offensive best seller, however, was but the first step in the re-establishment of Macmillan's reputation. There remained matters of purgatorial sacrifice and public recantation.

James Putnam, a 25-year veteran with Macmillan, had been entrusted with making the arrangements to contract for and publish Velikovsky's manuscript. His judgement in urging that Macmillan accept *Worlds in Collision* had been confirmed in spectacular fashion when the book became a best seller. Nevertheless, the negotiations to transfer publishing rights to Doubleday were carried on without his knowledge, and as soon as the transfer had been consummated, Putnam's good friend, editor-in-chief H. S. Latham, was delegated to inform him that his services were being terminated immediately. [In January 1963 Latham expressed in a letter to Velikovsky the great regret he still feels for Macmillan's capitulation.]

At the annual meeting of the American Association for the Advancement of Science held in Cleveland in December 1950, a Mr Charles Skelley, representing the Macmillan Company, addressed the members of a committee specially appointed to study means for evaluating new theories before publication. He pointed out that, as a contribution to the advancement of science, his firm had 'voluntarily transferred' its rights to a 'book that the panel regarded as unsound . . .' His remarks were duly recorded and reported by panel chairman Warren Guthrie.[13] Harvard geologist Kirtley Mather was the main spokesman before the panel, discussing possible methods of censorship.

The British edition of *Worlds in Collision* was rushed into print within two months of a contract between Doubleday and Victor Gollancz, and in September British scientists began to publish reviews. Spencer Jones, quoted in part at the beginning of this account, concluded: 'It is a pity that so much erudition should have been wasted in following so false a trail.' However, he was mistaken in arguing that, if there had been catastrophes such as Velikovsky described, 'we should find that, at a certain epoch in past time, the positions of Mars and Venus were identical'. Velikovsky, in a letter published in *The Spectator* on October 27, 1950, called attention to the Royal Astronomer's error; the last catastrophe took place not between Mars and Venus, but between Mars and earth. He also pointed to the present close approaches of the earth and Mars every 15 years, the similar axial inclinations of these two planets, and the similar lengths of their days as vestiges of near contact and magnetic interference in the past.

Evolutionist J. B. S. Haldane, author of *Science and Ethics*, reviewed the book in the *New Statesman and Nation* for November 11, 1950. Haldane misquoted Velikovsky, then ridiculed the misquotation; he mismatched dates and the events Velikovsky had associated with them; he concluded that the book was 'equally a degradation of science and religion'.

THE ARTICLES IN *Harper's*

In the fall of 1950 Frederick Allen sought a scientist to participate in a debate with Velikovsky in the pages of *Harper's Magazine*. Shapley and Neugebauer, among others, declined the opportunity, but Princeton astrophysicist John Q. Stewart accepted. The debate appeared in *Harper's* for June 1951, introduced by several background paragraphs prepared by the editors, who noted that 'there has been a remarkable lack of explicit criticism of the book based on careful reading'.

Given the floor first, Velikovsky presented an 'Answer to my Critics'. One by one he described and analyzed fallacies in the principal physical or historical arguments that had been advanced against his book. Among these points were the matters of ancient eclipses, early observations of Venus, the substance of comets, electromagnetic forces and effects in the solar system, and the consequences of stopping the earth's spin or tilting its axis in space.

Stewart's article was titled 'Disciplines in Collision'. He relied heavily on Gaposchkin's earlier writings, quoting in full her synopsis of Velikovsky's theme – a passage filled with parenthetical sneers. Stewart charged that records of ancient solar eclipses contradict Velikovsky's thesis of changes in terrestrial and lunar movements in the second and first millennia B.C. But Velikovsky, in his rejoinder, printed in the same issue of *Harper's*, showed that the alleged eclipses, in the original sources, are accompanied neither by dates nor by locality specifications. Moreover, of the three mentioned records, the text of one (Chinese) referred to a disturbance of celestial motions which had prevented the occurrence of a predicted eclipse, and commentary about a second (Babylonian) by Kugler, the greatest authority on Babylonian astronomy, called attention to the fact that an eclipse would not be possible at all on the indicated day of a lunar month; Kugler conjectured that the phenomenon reported might have been a darkening of the sky due to passage of the earth through 'an immense train' of dust and meteorites. [In 1959 Prof. André Danjon, director of Paris Observatory, established that there are abrupt changes in the earth's rotational speed following solar flares; this he ascribes to electromagnetic influences. One implication of this discovery is that eclipses cannot be dated by retrospective calculation.]

Stewart also claimed that the geographic position of the terrestrial axis could never change; but since the debate of 1951 the idea of wandering of the axis with respect to the crust of the earth has gained the acceptance of science.

According to Stewart, 'Tombs dated from the fourth millennium B.C. were not destroyed by ocean floods in Ur (of the Chaldees)'. But Velikovsky, in his rejoinder, quoted Sir Leonard Wooley, the excavator of Ur: 'Eight feet of sediment imply a very great depth of water and the flood which deposited it must have been of a magnitude unparalleled in local history . . . a whole civilization which existed before it is lacking above it and seems to have been submerged by the water.'

The August 1951 issue of *Harper's* carried a letter to the editor from Julius S. Miller, professor of physics and mathematics at Dillard University. Miller cited what he called a 'glaring paucity and barren weakness of explicit criticism' on the part of Velikovsky's critics. He concluded: '(1) The Velikovsky notions are not altogether untenable'; and '(2) . . . not yet refuted.'

Laurence Lafleur, then associate professor of philosophy at Florida State University, brought a new argument to bear against Velikovsky in the November 1951 issue of *Scientific Monthly*: '. . . the odds favour the assumption that anyone proposing a revolutionary doctrine is a crank rather than a scientist.' Lafleur itemized seven criteria for spotting a crank. Examples:

> *Test 6.* Velikovsky's theory is in no single instance capable of mathematical accuracy. Its predictions, if capable of any, would certainly be so vague as to be scientifically unverifiable.
> *Test 7.* Velikovsky does show a disposition to accept minority opinions, to quote the opinions of individuals opposed to current views, and even to quote such opinions when they have been discredited to the point that they are no longer held even as minority views. For example, we may cite the notion that the earth's axis has changed considerably.

So Lafleur concluded that Velikovsky qualified as a crank 'perhaps by every one' of these tests. But having established this 'we must still deal with the feeling, first, that scientists should have attempted to refute Velikovsky's position, as a service both to him and to the public . . .' Thus the professor acknowledged that much of earlier criticism – thousands of words printed in the span of more than a year and a half – was denunciation rather than refutation. But in his own attempt to perform the recommended 'service', Lafleur, even with the aid of astrophysical theorems contrived for the occasion, fared no better than the scientists. On the assumption that an electroscope would detect it, he denied that the earth carries an electric charge. (No scientist corrected, in print, this mistaken notion or any other wrong statement by any critic during the entire *Worlds in Collision* controversy.) Lafleur also claimed that an approach between two celestial bodies close enough to bring their magnetic fields into conflict must inevitably bring about collision, evaporation, and amalgamation of the bodies.

The American Philosophical Society met in Philadelphia in April 1952, and as part of a symposium on 'Some Unorthodoxies of Modern Science' a paper,

'Worlds in Collision', by Cecilia Payne-Gaposchkin was read. Once again Mrs Gaposchkin repeated most of her earlier arguments, prefacing them with an account of her 'Herculean labour' in ferreting out the alleged fallacies in *Worlds in Collision.* She chose to disregard the great mass of Velikovsky's evidence and isolate certain quotations from their context, making it appear that Velikovsky had read into them ideas of his own. (See comparison of texts, Appendix 2.) Her audience could conclude only that Velikovsky had been guilty of the most heinous disregard for the rules of scholarship. Towards the end of her address, which was read in her absence, Gaposchkin professed bewilderment: 'Why is it, if scientists are really the open-minded men they think themselves, that they are under so much criticism of the "Science is a Sacred Cow" variety? I confess I do not understand why the revulsion against science takes this form . . .'

Velikovsky was in the audience at the same meeting, and he was permitted to come forward to offer a rebuttal to arguments presented earlier by archaeologists, astronomers, and geologists. The audience listened attentively and responded warmly. But when he requested that his remarks be reproduced along with Gaposchkin's in the society's *Proceedings*,[14] his bid was rejected. Appended to Gaposchkin's paper, however, was a 'quantitative refutation of Velikovsky's wild hypothesis' by Donald H. Menzel, also of Harvard Observatory. '. . . let us make the assumption with Velikovsky and try to determine what would happen if the sun and the planets suddenly acquired gross electric charges.' Menzel calculated that for electric forces to contribute ten per cent of the gravitational attraction between earth and sun equally charged, but of opposite polarities, each must acquire a voltage of 10^{19} volts; the energy necessary to place such charge on the sun would be 5×10^{43} ergs, 'as much energy as the entire sun radiates in 1,000 years'. Menzel then purported to show that the greatest charge a positive sun could retain is 1800 volts. Now, the specification of suddenly acquired charge, which Menzel apparently sought to ridicule by calculating the energy required to emplace it, is wholly arbitrary and misleading; nothing in Velikovsky's thesis suggests that solar and planetary charges are acquired suddenly. Furthermore, Menzel's necessary assumptions as to the dielectric properties of the sun, earth, and space were wholly gratuitous and unsupported by observational evidence. (It has been established in space probes since 1960 that interplanetary space, especially close in to the sun, is filled with plasma. Thus Menzel's assumptions are inapplicable to the situation. Furthermore, in 1960, Prof. V. A. Bailey of the University of Sydney, Australia, reported:[15] 'It has been found possible to account for the known orders of magnitude of five different astronomical phenomena . . . by the single hypothesis that a star like the sun carries a net negative charge . . .' Bailey calculated that the necessary charge on the sun would produce an electric field with a potential at the surface of the sun on the order of 10^{19} volts.)

Walter S. Adams, director of Mt. Wilson and Palomar Observatories, was a rare exception among astronomers who participated in discussions of *Worlds in Collision.* In correspondence with Velikovsky, Adams complimented him on the accuracy of his presentation of astronomical material, though he could not accept the premise that electromagnetism participates in celestial mechanics. Whenever Velikovsky requested information or explanations pertaining to astronomical phenomena, Adams answered courteously and in minute detail. In February 1952 the author of *Worlds in Collision* visited the California astronomer at the solar observatory in Pasadena and discussed with him at first hand some of the problems raised by the historical evidence.

Constructive criticism came also from Professor Lloyd Motz, astronomer of Columbia University, with whom Velikovsky on many occasions discussed problems of celestial mechanics. Motz holds conventional views.

S. K. Vsekhsviatsky, director of Kiev Observatory, has

corresponded with Velikovsky on problems in solar-system phenomena and has cited Velikovsky's works on numerous occasions in support of his own positions in theoretical matters.

Volume I of Velikovsky's *Ages in Chaos* appeared in March 1952. Proceeding from the premise that Egyptian and Israelite histories may be synchronized by equating the upheaval described in Exodus with the catastrophe that befell Egypt at the end of the Middle Kingdom, Velikovsky worked down through the centuries from the fifteenth to the middle of the ninth, highlighting contacts between the peoples of the two lands – Egypt and Palestine. The synchronization is carried almost to the end of the Eighteenth Dynasty in Egypt, to the days of Akhnaton, who thus is revealed as a contemporary of Ahab and Jehoshaphat in the ninth century rather than a precursor of Moses, as in orthodox chronology. Unpublished portions of *Ages in Chaos* must dispose of six apparently superfluous centuries in conventional Egyptian history, and Velikovsky promises that in doing so, his work will show that no enigmatic half-millennium-long 'dark ages' need to be inserted in Aegean, Mesopotamian, or Anatolian histories.

William F. Albright, Spence Professor of Semitic Language at Johns Hopkins University, reviewed and rejected Velikovsky's second book in the New York *Herald Tribune* for April 20, 1952. Albright's only specific argument was that Velikovsky had mistaken the cuneiform plural sign, *mesh*, in some of the El Amarna letters for the name of the Moabite King Mesh(a). But in his text Velikovsky twice called attention to the fact that in several instances in these letters the conventional reading cannot apply, since the grammatical construction definitely pertains to an individual – a rebellious vassal of the king of Samaria (Sumur), well known from the Bible.

Professor Harry Orlinsky of Hebrew Union College echoed Albright's remarks,[16] thus documenting his unfamiliarity with the book he purported to review.

The scientific press did not devote space to analyses of Velikovsky's reconstruction of history, but as Albright described it eight years later in the *Herald Tribune*,[17] there were 'howls of anguish' among the historians.

The Velikovskys moved from New York City to Princeton, N. J., in 1952, and the heretic began to make the acquaintance of scientists in that university community. In October 1953 he was asked to address the Graduate College Forum at Princeton on the subject, '*Worlds in Collision* in the Light of Recent Finds in Archaeology, Geology, and Astronomy'. In the course of this address, in which he was able to cite many items in support of his thesis among discoveries made since the appearance of *Worlds in Collision*, Velikovsky suggested that the earth's magnetic field reaches sensibly as far as the moon and is responsible for certain unaccounted-for libratory, or rocking, movements of that body. He also suggested that the planet Jupiter radiates in the radio-frequency range of the spectrum. [In April 1955, Drs B. F. Burke and K. L. Franklin of the Carnegie Institution startled their audience at a meeting of the American Astronomical Society when they announced their accidental discovery of radio noise emitted by Jupiter. However, when a Doubleday editor wrote to call their attention to the fact that Velikovsky had anticipated just such a finding, one of them replied that even Velikovsky is entitled to a 'near miss' once in a while.] The text of the Forum address was published as a supplement to Velikovsky's *Earth in Upheaval* in 1955.

From about the time of the 1953 Forum address, through 1954, and into 1955 up to the time of Einstein's death, he and Velikovsky carried on a private debate – oral and written – on the issue of colliding worlds and the merits of an electromagnetic solar system. Einstein remained adamant in his conviction that sun and planets must be electrically neutral and space must be free of magnetic fields and plasma. Yet when he learned, only days before his death, that Jupiter emits radio noise, as Velikovsky had so long insisted, he offered to use his influence in arranging for certain other experiments Velikovsky had suggested. It was too late. When Einstein died, *Worlds in Collision* lay open on his desk.

At the same Philadelphia symposium where Gaposchkin's attack on Velikovsky had been read in 1952, I. Bernard Cohen, Harvard historian of science, also spoke. In an abstract of his address released before the meeting Cohen expressed a foreboding that the reaction against Velikovsky might signify that his work was of great importance; it appeared that Velikovsky and his book were to be the principal topics of discussion. By speech time, however, Cohen's theme had been altered considerably, and in the printed version of the address in the *Proceedings*[18] Velikovsky was referred to but once, in an offhand conclusion that Gaposchkin had already discredited him.

In July 1955, *Scientific American* published Cohen's tribute to Albert Einstein, who he had met on just one occasion for an interview. Cohen took the opportunity to ridicule Velikovsky with isolated adjectives allegedly quoted from Einstein. In an exchange of letters with Otto Nathan, executor of Einstein's estate, in the September 1955 issue of *Scientific American*, he conceded that Einstein had compared the reception of Velikovsky with that accorded Johann Kepler and had noted that contemporaries often have trouble differentiating between a genius and a crank. Cohen ended by saying '. . . There is no basis for concluding that Professor Einstein might not have had a friendly feeling for the author in question or that he might not have had some interest in his work . . . Professor Einstein sympathized with the author when he was attacked and disliked the methods used by some of his attackers.'

'EARTH IN UPHEAVAL'

During the same period, Velikovsky himself was completing the manuscript of *Earth in Upheaval*, a book presenting the evidence of recent catastrophes on earth.

Einstein had read portions of the manuscript and contributed suggestions in marginal notes; before his death, according to Helen Dukas, his secretary, he was intending to write a letter requesting the curator of the Department of Egyptology at the Metropolitan Museum of Art to arrange for carbon-14 tests that might check the thesis of *Ages in Chaos*. Despite her transmission of this appeal – and decade-long efforts directed to the British Museum and other institutions by Velikovsky – the New Kingdom and late periods of Egypt, which span more than 1,200 years in conventional chronology, generally have been left out of testing programmes. In more than one instance, however, relics from this period have been adjudged 'contaminated' because they yielded unexpectedly low ages.

Earth in Upheaval appeared in November 1955. Velikovsky examined the century-old principle of Lyellian uniformity by comparing its tenets with anomalous finds from all quarters of the globe: frozen muck in Alaska that consists almost entirely of myriads of torn and broken animals and trees; whole islands in the Arctic Sea whose soil is packed full of unfossilized bones of mammoths, rhinoceroses, and horses; unglaciated polar lands and glaciated tropical countries; coral and coal deposits near the poles; bones of animals from tundra, prairie, and tropical rainforest intimately associated in jumbled heaps and interred in common graves; the startling youth of the world's great mountain chains; shifted poles; reversed magnetic polarities; sudden changes in sea level all around the world; rifts on land and under the seas.

Then Velikovsky took up the question of evolution, arguing that Darwin had rejected catastrophism in favour of Lyell's uniformity because the catastrophists of his day would not acknowledge the antiquity of the earth. But in reality catastrophes suggest the only plausible mechanisms for the phenomenon of evolution by mutation. Thus Darwin's contribution to the theory of evolution, which dates from Greek times, consisted only in the as-yet undemonstrated hypothesis that competition can give rise to new species. In the controversy that followed the publication of *The Origin of Species*, the issue revolved around whether or not evolution was a natural phenomenon, and it was resolved quite properly in the affirmative. But what was obscured in the uproar, argued Velikovsky, was the inadequacy of Darwin's hypothesis; 'If natural selection . . . is not the mechanism of the origin of species, Darwin's contribution is reduced to very little – only to the role of natural selection in weeding out the unfit.' Velikovsky proposed in *Earth in Upheaval* that evolution is a cataclysmic process; '. . . the principle that *can* cause the origin of species exists in nature. The irony lies in the circumstance that Darwin saw in catastrophism the chief adversary of his theory . . .'

It appears that at first scientific journals and reviewers, aware of the adverse effect of their earlier agitation against *Worlds in Collision*, chose to ignore *Earth in Upheaval*. But a few months after it appeared a New York radio station presented a 'Conversation Programme' in which Jacques Barzun, then newly appointed to the position of Dean of the Graduate Faculties at Columbia University, and Alfred Goldsmith, president of the Radio Engineers of America and vice president in charge of research for Radio Corporation of America, discussed the book, with Clifton Fadiman as moderator. All three participants were enthusiastic and affirmative towards Velikovsky's method, scholarship, and convincing manner of presenting his evidence; they considered that his work may be a beginning towards important new concepts in science and history. All agreed that his work deserved objective treatment from scientists.

From this favourable discussion of *Earth in Upheaval* may have come some pressure to discuss it in other scientific media. In March 1956 *Scientific American* presented a review by Harrison Brown. His words, however, were devoted to an apology for the misbehaviour of scientists who had suppressed *Worlds in Collision* and to a restatement of his own earlier position with respect to that book. In a seven-column article, Brown dismissed *Earth in Upheaval* without challenging one of its points. He dealt with the new book in a single paragraph, then reverted to the old controversy. But he again refrained from producing any of the arguments against *Worlds in Collision* which he had claimed would fill thirty pages. [In 1963, Brown declared in a letter to one of Velikovsky's Canadian readers that his review of *Earth in Upheaval* had been directed against the 'abominable behaviour of scientists and publishers.']

In December 1956, when the International Geophysical Year was in the planning stage, Velikovsky submitted a proposal to the planning committee through the offices of Prof. H. H. Hess of Princeton University: '. . . It is accepted that the terrestrial magnetic field . . . decreases with the distance from the ground; yet the possibility should not be discounted that the magnetic field above the ionosphere is stronger than at the earth's surface.' Also, 'an investigation as to whether the unexplained lunar librations, or rocking movements, in latitude and longitude coincide with the revolutions of the terrestrial magnetic poles around the geographical poles' might well be included in the programme. Hess was notified by E. O. Hulburt of the committee that should the first proposition be proven right by experiments already planned, the second might be investigated later. [As it turned out, the most important single discovery of the IGY was that the earth is surrounded by the Van Allen belts of charged particles trapped in the far reaching geomagnetic field.]

Earth in Upheaval came to the attention of Claude Schaeffer, professor at College de France and excavator of Ras Shamra in Syria. Schaeffer's independently conceived theory that ancient Middle Eastern civilizations had suffered simultaneous natural catastrophes on five occasions in the third and second millennia B.C. had been set forth in a 1948 volume, *Stratigraphie comparée et chronologie de l'Asie Occidentale*. [Velikovsky published an abstract of his own thesis in *Scripta Academica* in 1945.] Schaeffer wrote enthusiastically to Velikovsky and the two began a correspondence that has continued ever since. In 1957 Velikovsky met Schaeffer in Switzerland and again in Athens.

Oedipus and Akhnaton, a book that presents Velikovsky's identification of Akhnaton as the historical prototype of the legendary Oedipus, appeared in 1960. It was an outgrowth of the originally planned work, *Freud and His Heroes*, which had been set aside almost twenty years earlier. ['Dreams Freud Dreamed', a reinterpretation of the dreams of the founder of psychoanalysis, was published in the *Psychoanalytic Review* for October 1941.] This work also met with silence on the part of most scholars, although Prof. Gertrude E. Smith of the University of Chicago, one of the nation's leading classicists, wrote a favourable review for the Chicago *Tribune*.[19] In the New York *Herald Tribune*[20] Albright opposed the thesis on the grounds that it was improbable that at such an early time there could have been cultural intercourse between Egypt and Greece; yet Mycenaean ware was found in abundance in the capital city of Akhnaton, and a seal bearing the name of Akhnaton's mother turned up in a Mycenaean grave in Greece. The London *Times*[21] attacked the book anonymously, using a method familiar from the campaign against *Worlds in Collision* in America – discussing the book together with one of doubtful value to establish guilt by association.

Ten years after the abrupt cancellation of Atwater's plans to dramatize *Worlds in Collision* in Hayden Planetarium, U.S. space probe Pioneer V was launched. This experiment was destined to destroy the idea that the earth and other planets are electromagnetically isolated in a near-vacuum space – the position Einstein could not abandon. After Pioneer had been in solar orbit about six weeks, NASA called a press conference to report its findings. As *Newsweek* relayed the news on May 9, 1960, 'In one exciting week, man has learned more about the near reaches of the space that surrounds earth than the sum of his knowledge over the last 50 years. Gone forever is any earthbound notion of space as a serene thoroughfare for space travellers . . . a fantastic amount of cosmic traffic (hot gaseous clouds, deadly rays, bands of electricity) rushes by at high speed, circles, criss-crosses, and collides.' Among the discoveries credited to Pioneer V are space-pervading magnetic fields, electric currents girdling the earth, and high energy charged particles from solar flares.

Between 1954 and 1960 Velikovsky appeared repeatedly before the faculty and students of the geology department at Princeton University at the invitation of Prof. Hess, who recognized the importance of exposing his students to a dissenting view. On April 12, 1961, Velikovsky again addressed the Graduate College Forum, this time on the subject 'How Much of the Great Heresy of 1950 Is Valid Science in 1961?' and offered an extensive list of confirming finds from celestial and terrestrial spheres. Later that same month American radio astronomers announced that the surface temperature of Venus must be 600°F, and scientists began an energetic search for an 'acceptable' explanation of this new aspect of the solar system.

About the time Mariner II approached Venus, late in 1962, Princeton physicist V. Bargmann and Columbia astronomer Lloyd Motz wrote a joint letter to the editor of *Science*[22] to call attention to Velikovsky's priority in predicting three seemingly unrelated facts about the solar system – the earth's far-reaching magnetosphere, radio noise from Jupiter, and the extremely high temperature of Venus – which have been among the most important and surprising discoveries in recent years. They urged that Velikovsky's thesis be objectively re-examined by science.

Also at that time it was announced[23] that ground-based radiometric observations at the U.S. Naval Research Laboratory in Washington and at Goldstone Tracking Station in California had shown Venus to have a slow retrograde rotation, a characteristic that puts it in a unique position among the planets.

Feeling vindicated by these developments and encouraged by the publication of the Bargmann–Motz letter in *Science*, Velikovsky sought to publish a paper showing that the points brought out in that letter were but a few among many other ideas set forth in his books that have already been supported by independent research. The attempt was in vain; Philip Abelson, the editor of *Science*, returned Velikovsky's paper without reading it and published instead a facetious letter from a Poul Anderson, who claimed that 'the accidental presence of one or two good apples does not redeem a spoiled barrelful'.

Mariner II, when its findings were revealed, confirmed Velikovsky's expectations, showing the surface temperature of Venus to be at least 800°F and the planet's 15-mile-thick envelope to be composed, not of carbon dioxide or water as previously supposed, but of heavy molecules of hydrocarbons and perhaps more complicated organic compounds as well.

Retrograde rotation, organic molecules in the envelope, and extreme heat on Venus find no convincing explanation, though they have already caused much deliberation; yet in *Worlds in Collision* two of the three phenomena were claimed as crucial tests for the thesis that Venus is a youthful planet with a short and violent history, and the third (anomalous rotation) supports the same conclusions.

In spite of the clamour against the heretic, his books have found an enthusiastic following in every country of the world. Here and there small study groups have sprung up; Velikovsky's books are required reading in the courses of professors in a number of universities. Letters from enthusiastic readers have poured in upon the author through all the years since *Worlds in Collision* appeared. The British edition of that book is now in its fourteenth printing, and the American edition is regularly reprinted. A German edition went through five printings at the hands of its first publisher, then was attacked and suppressed in 1952 by theologians (*kirchlich-historische Kreise*); after being unavailable for about six years, it is now back in print at the hands of a Swiss publisher.

Seldom in the history of science have so many diverse anticipations – the natural fallout from a single central idea – been so quickly substantiated by independent investigation. One after another of Velikovsky's 'wild hypotheses' have achieved empirical support, but not until December 1962, in the Bargmann–Motz letter to *Science*, was his name ever linked in the pages of scientific journals with any of these 'surprising' discoveries, and never yet by the discoverers themselves. A platitude, repeated on various occasions, has it that any one who makes as many predictions as Velikovsky is bound to be right now and then. But he has yet to be shown wrong about any of his suggestions. Prof. H. H. Hess, who is now Chairman of the Space Board of the National Academy of Science, recently wrote to Velikovsky: 'Some of these predictions were said to be impossible when you made them; all of them were predicted long before proof that they were correct came to hand. Conversely, I do not know of any specific prediction you made that has since proven to be false.'

This record would appear to justify a long, careful look at *Worlds in Collision* by the guild that not only refused to look before condemning it in the past, but actively campaigned to defame its author.

REFERENCES

1. *The Spectator*, London, September 22, 1950.
2. *Zeitschrift fuer Gesammte Neurologie und Psychiatrie*, 1931.
3. Chicago *Tribune*, February 27, 1963.
4. *Newsweek*, March 11, 1963.
5. Indianapolis *Star*, April 9, 1950.
6. Cincinnati *Inquirer*, April 9, 1950.
7. Toronto *Globe and Mail*, April 22, 1950.

8. Los Angeles *Times*, May 14, 1950.
9. *Engineering and Science*, Pasadena, Calif., May 1950.
10. April 22, 1950 (*Saturday Review of Literature*).
11. *Isis*, Vol. 41 (1950).
12. *Amer. Jour. Science*, Vol. 248 (1950).
13. *Science*, April 30, 1951.
14. *Proc. Amer. Phil. Soc.*, Vol. 96 (1952).
15. *Nature*, Vol. 186, May 14, 1960.
16. *Jewish Bookland*, September 1952.
17. New York *Herald Tribune Book Review*, May 29, 1960.
18. *Proc. Amer. Phil. Soc.*, Vol. 96 (1952).
19. Chicago *Tribune*, April 3, 1960.
20. New York *Herald Tribune*, May 29, 1960.
21. London *Times Literary Supplement*, January 20, 1961.
22. *Science*, Vol. 138, December 21, 1962.
23. *Science*, Vol. 139, March 8, 1963; *The National Observer*, December 31, 1962.

AFTERMATH TO EXPOSURE

by Ralph E. Juergens

'Minds in Chaos', reprinted here from the pages of *The American Behavioral Scientist* for September 1963, chronicles more than a decade of controversy over the works of Immanuel Velikovsky. But the story does not end in 1963. Events that have followed – set off in large part by the *Behavioral Scientist* study – shape themselves into additional chapters, and the image of objectivity so cherished by scientists loses even more of its lustre as these later events begin to take on perspective. The story has bright facets as well as shadows, but in the glaring light of new knowledge from many fields the shadows cast by acts of repression and vilification seem darker than before.

To place these events in their proper setting, it is necessary to backtrack a bit. In August 1963 – the month before the appearance of the *Behavioral Scientist's* Velikovsky issue – *Harper's Magazine* printed 'Scientists in Collision', an article by Eric Larrabee, whose 1950 article in the same magazine marked the beginning of the controversy. Now, writing 13 years later, Larrabee chose to point up the case for Velikovsky by citing recent discoveries in astronomy, space science, geology, and geophysics that bring support to the thesis of *Worlds in Collision.*

Like the authors of the articles in the *Behavioral Scientist*, Larrabee called attention to a letter in *Science* (December 21, 1962) in which Valentin Bargmann, physicist of Princeton University, and Lloyd Motz, astronomer of Columbia University, urged their colleagues to recognize Velikovsky's priority in predicting three highly significant discoveries: (1) the high temperature of the planet Venus; (2) the emission of non-thermal radio noise by Jupiter; and (3) the vast reach of the earth's magnetic field in space.

The Bargmann–Motz plea for scientific good sportsmanship won no response in the journals of science,[1,2] even though almost simultaneously Venus-probe Mariner II eliminated all doubt about the reality of the high temperature of Venus and gave strong support to Velikovsky's further suggestion – offered as early as 1945 – that the envelope of Venus consists largely of hydrocarbon gases and dust. After verifying that the editorial lid on discussion of such matters was as tight as ever, Larrabee sought access once more to *Harper's*.

'Science itself,' wrote Larrabee, 'even while most scientists have considered his case to be closed, has been heading in Velikovsky's direction. Proposals which seemed so shocking when he made them are now commonplace . . . There is scarcely one of Velikovsky's central ideas – as long as it was taken separately and devoid of its implications – which has not since been propounded in all seriousness by a scientist of repute . . . His dismissal and suppression by the scientific community require of scientists an act of agonizing reappraisal.'

Almost immediately a reply issued from Donald Menzel, Director of Harvard College Observatory. This highly emotional essay turned up as a free-lance manuscript in the editorial offices of *Harper's*. Hardly had it arrived, however, than it was recalled by its author and replaced with a version less abusive to Larrabee and more abusive to Velikovsky. It was so abusive that before printing it (*Harper's*, December 1963), the editor of the magazine struck one sentence, which read: 'Velikovsky has been as completely discredited as was Dr Brinkley of the goat-gland era or the thousands whom the American Medical Association has exposed as quacks, preying on human misery, by purveying nostrums or devices of no beneficial value whatever.'

Menzel was angered by the Bargmann–Motz letter in *Science*, considering it to be 'uncalled for'. He seemed infuriated that Larrabee in one noncommittal passage had called attention to an ironical situation: in 1952, in the *Proceedings of the American Philosophical Society*, Menzel had offered calculations to show that if Velikovsky were right about electromagnetic forces in the solar system, the sun would have to have a surface electric potential of 10^{19} (10 billion billion) volts – an absolute impossibility, according to the astronomer; but in 1960, V. A. Bailey, Emeritus Professor of Physics at the University of Sydney (Professor Bailey died December 7, 1964, in Switzerland. He was en route to the United States, where he hoped to see experiments carried out in space to test his hypotheses), claimed that the sun is electrically charged, and that it has a surface potential of 10^{19} volts – precisely the value calculated by Menzel. Bailey, at the time his theory was first published, was entirely unaware of Velikovsky's work and of Menzel's repudiation of it.

The idea that his 'quantitative refutation of Velikovsky's wild hypothesis' – Menzel's own description of his contribution to the *Proceedings* in 1952 – should now be brought to Velikovsky's support was intolerable to the Harvard astronomer. So, when he mailed his paper to *Harper's* in 1963, he also sent a copy to Bailey in Sydney and asked him in a covering letter to revoke his theory of electric charge on the sun. That theory was casting doubt on the continuing efforts of Menzel and other American scientists to discredit Velikovsky, and Menzel pointed out what he conceived to be an error in Bailey's work.

Professor Bailey, taking exception to the idea that his own work should be abandoned to accommodate the anti-Velikovsky forces, prepared an article in rebuttal of Menzel's piece and submitted it to *Harper's* for publication in the same issue with Menzel's. Bailey had discovered a simple arithmetical error in Menzel's calculations, which invalidated his argument.

The editors of *Harper's*, evidently taken aback by the heat of the controversy generated by Larrabee's article, rejected Bailey's offering, but agreed to print some of his comments if he would submit them in a brief letter. At the same time, however, Menzel was permitted to correct the arithmetical error pointed out by Bailey, and he did so without acknowledging the effect of the correction on his argument. Larrabee objected to such a use of Bailey's rebuttal paper, and at first Menzel was not permitted to extirpate the evidence of his carelessness; but after more pleading the correction was made.

Insight into the frame of mind of the Harvard astronomer at the time he wrote is to be gained by noting his remarks about Velikovsky's score on predictions. In connection with the radio noise of Jupiter, Menzel wrote that, since scientists for the most part do not accept the theory of *Worlds in Collision*, 'any seeming verification of Velikovsky's prediction is pure chance'. In regard to the high temperature of Venus, the astronomer argued that '"hot" is only a relative term. For example, liquid air is hot [196° below zero, centigrade], relative to liquid helium [269° below zero, centigrade] . . .' Later in his article Menzel referred to this comparison: 'I have already disposed of the question of the temperature of Venus.'

This is all Menzel had to say about the temperature of Venus, although in 1955 he himself revoked his own estimate of two decades earlier that the ground temperature of Venus would be about 50°C. The revocation was explained by saying that the temperature must surely be much lower. In 1959 the ground temperature of Venus was still estimated to be 17°C. Mariner II found it to be at least 430°C, or about 800°F.

As for the extent of the earth's magnetic field, Menzel wrote: 'He [Velikovsky] said that it would extend as far as the moon; actually the field suddenly breaks off at a distance of several earth diameters.'

More than a year before Menzel took it upon himself to answer Larrabee, satellite Explorer X had detected the earth's magnetic field at a distance of at least 22 earth radii and gave no indication that this was its limit. Recently the Interplanetary Monitoring Platform satellites – especially IMP I – have found that the tail of the earth's magnetosphere extends 'at least as far as the orbit of the Moon' (*Missiles and Rockets*, January 18, 1965).

Larrabee, limiting his reply to one page in the same issue of *Harper's*, pointed out that 'where Dr Menzel touches on points of fact he is either misleading or misinformed'. The summation that followed stands as a classic example of the demolition of a scientist's arguments by a non-scientist; it is particularly noteworthy inasmuch as Menzel's main theme was that non-scientists do not understand scientific issues and the scientific method, and therefore should be rebuked for entering into scientific debate before the general public. Just how successful Larrabee's counterattack proved to be is shown in the examples given below:

Menzel claimed that astronomers recognized the presence of electrified gas and magnetic fields in interplanetary space long before Velikovsky. Larrabee quoted Menzel's own words, written in 1953: 'Indeed, the total number of electrons that could escape from the sun would be able to run a one cell flashlight for less than one minute.'

Menzel asserted that the earth's Van Allen belts contain equal numbers of positive and negative particles. Larrabee noted that Dr James Van Allen, who discovered the belts, admits that this is an assumption for which there is no experimental evidence.

Menzel attempted to calculate the electric field in space near the earth that would result from a charge on the sun of the magnitude suggested by Bailey. Larrabee, in reply, observed that the calculation was based on the erroneous assumption that space is a non-conducting medium.

Menzel claimed that satellite motions are not disturbed by electromagnetic forces. Larrabee cited the publications of a number of space scientists to show that both orbital and rotational motions are affected by the presence of charged particles and magnetic fields.

Menzel argued that the disturbance of the earth's rotation by solar flares is attributable to temporary heating and expansion of the earth and is not an electromagnetic effect. Larrabee pointed out that Professor André Danjon, who discovered this phenomenon, evaluated the thermal effect and found it altogether inadequate; Danjon concludes that electromagnetism is the only likely cause.

Menzel insisted on his own earlier position that the envelope of Venus is made up of ice crystals and ridiculed Velikovsky's suggestion of 1950 – actually expressed as early as 1946 in letters to astronomers Harlow Shapley, Rupert Wildt, and Walter S. Adams – that hydrocarbons must predominate in the envelope. Larrabee referred the Harvard astronomer to a number of publications, including the official report of the Mariner II flight to Venus, in which it is stated that the clouds of Venus consist of condensed hydrocarbons.

Summing up, Larrabee wrote: 'Velikovsky offers evidence from numerous other sciences, in particular geology and archaeology. Breaking the barriers between disciplines, he arrives at conclusions which no discipline had reached independently. This is the real nature of his challenge, and it is fundamental.'

In the limited space allotted his letter (*Harper's*, January 1964), Professor Bailey expressed surprise 'that Professor Menzel totally ignores the impressive testimony to the worth of Dr Velikovsky's predictions contained in the recent letter of that outstanding scientist Professor H. H. Hess of Princeton'. Bailey noted that Menzel's challenge to the theory of electric charge on the sun 'is unconvincing since it involves certain out-of-date views about the material contents of interplanetary space as well as the unproved assumption that the earthly laws of the electrodynamic field can be safely extrapolated to bodies such as the sun of unearthly dimensions and temperatures'. In Bailey's view, 'important [new] facts must compel scientists to adopt a cautious attitude towards the astronomical ideas on which they were reared until the powerful new methods of observation developed by space scientists have accumulated more knowledge'.

Earlier, Larrabee's article brought response from astronomer Lloyd Motz, who emphasized that his purpose in writing (*Harper's*, October 1963) was to make clear his own disagreement with Velikovsky's theories. Nevertheless, he stated: 'I do support his right to present his ideas and to have these ideas considered by responsible scholars and scientists as the creation of a serious and dedicated investigator . . . His writings should be carefully studied and analyzed because they are the product of an extraordinary and brilliant mind, and are based upon some of the most concentrated and penetrating scholarship of our period . . .'

The debate in *Harper's* went on in the August, October, December 1963, and the January 1964 issues. During the same period another effort failed to break the editorial barrier.

In the spring of 1963, Velikovsky had reason to suppose that confirmation of so many of his once-heretical predictions, and the even more impressive fact that none of his predictions had gone wrong, might have altered his standing among scientists – that finally he might be granted space in their journals. Despite the fact that a paper, 'Some Additional Examples of Correct Prognosis', had been rejected without being read by Philip Abelson, the editor of *Science*, Velikovsky now prepared an article on 'Venus, a Youthful Planet'. H. H. Hess, who served that year as President of the American Geological Society, offered to transmit the new paper to the American Philosophical Society with his recommendation as a member of the society that it be published in the *Proceedings*.

This simple act of contribution seems to have generated a storm that nearly split the society before calm was restored.

The fortunes and misfortunes of Dr Velikovsky's

paper during the half-year it was held by the Philosophical Society are revealed, in part, in statements made by two men – George W. Corner and Edwin G. Boring – both of whom played earlier, and thus far unrecounted, roles in the Velikovsky story.

In 1952, Corner was chairman of a symposium on Unorthodoxies in Modern Science at the annual meeting of the Philosophical Society. It was he who permitted Velikovsky to mount the platform and offer comments of his own following the reading of a paper in which Harvard's lady astronomer Cecilia Payne-Gaposchkin attacked *Worlds in Collision* in a most violent and irresponsible manner. This bit of fair play on Corner's part later was repudiated by the society's publications committee; Velikovsky's correction of Gaposchkin's misquotations were rejected for publication in the *Proceedings*. (See page 231 for a comparison of texts – *Worlds in Collision* versus Gaposchkin's alleged quotations from the book). By 1963 Corner had become Executive Officer of the Society and Editor of the *Proceedings*.

Velikovsky's Venus paper therefore came directly to the hand of Corner. For several months following the submission of the paper by Hess there was no word as to its disposition. In the meantime, Larrabee's article in *Harper's* appeared, as did the special issue of the *Behavioral Scientist* devoted to 'The Politics of Science and Dr Velikovsky'. Both documents surely came to the attention of at least some of the members of the Philosophical Society's publications committee.

At last, in a letter dated October 15, 1963, Corner reported to Hess. The publications committee, after several sessions in which Velikovsky's paper was discussed 'at great length', was stalemated by 'divided opinions'. The committee split into two belligerent camps, each unwilling to yield to the views of the other. Corner informed Hess that he had been 'directed to seek the advice of several responsible scientists and scholars, all members of the society' but not of the publications committee. He promised to keep Hess informed of later developments.

Along with Cecilia Gaposchkin and I. Bernard Cohen, professor of the history of science, Edwin Boring – a professor of psychology – was a scheduled speaker on the programme of the 1952 symposium on unorthodoxies. Thus the panel was dominated by Harvard professors. Boring, in his talk and in the version later published in the *Proceedings*, did not neglect to make sport of Velikovsky. Two years later, in an article published in the *American Scientist* for October 1954, he classed Velikovsky with those who, bolstered by ego alone, hold to ideas long after evidence turns against them.

Now, however, Professor Boring altered his position. On a visit to the campus of George Peabody College in Nashville in the fall of 1963 he made known his newfound feelings about 'the whole sordid mess' revealed by the *Behavioral Scientist*. He was particularly critical of the role played by Harlow Shapley.

Boring disclosed at Peabody that in stormy meetings of the publications committee there had been heated discussion whether or not to print Velikovsky's paper. Further, he let it be known that he was to be put in charge of a new Letters column in the *Proceedings*. Such a column would provide what Boring described as an 'appropriate vehicle' for the controversial paper, which would be the first item to appear in the column. Handling the matter in this way would permit publication without implying approval by the Society.

As it turned out, however, even this face-saving compromise failed. In a letter dated January 20, 1964, Corner reported to Hess that 'the Committee on Publications . . . completed a long and careful study of the problem raised by the short manuscript of Mr Velikovsky . . . During the past couple of months, at the direction of the Committee, I submitted the paper to an eminent historian of science and an equally eminent sociologist, and an astronomer of very high standing completely outside the circle of Mr Velikovsky's critics.

'After extremely thoughtful discussion, at which every possible way of dealing with this matter was considered, the Committee decided that the Society should not publish this paper . . .'

'The Politics of Science and Dr Velikovsky' appeared in *ABS* in September 1963 and quickly became a subject of intense discussion and debate on college campuses around the country. For the first time the story of the suppression of *Worlds in Collision* had been documented. The initial printing of the issue, itself larger than usual, quickly became exhausted in the face of a surge of orders for additional copies, and a second printing was made.

Reader reaction was predominantly favourable. A number of scholars and foundation officers wrote letters of commendation to the editor, Alfred de Grazia. Others wrote directly to Velikovsky, expressing the hope that recognition for his contributions to human knowledge soon would be forthcoming. One of very few expressions of disapproval appeared in a letter to the present writer from Warren Weaver, a vice president of the Alfred P. Sloan Foundation; Weaver asserted that he was 'amazed, disappointed, and in fact appalled that this serious journal [*ABS*] would devote so much space and effort to a series of articles of this sort'. This was only the first of several occasions when the Sloan Foundation executives constituted themselves a Committee of Public Safety against Velikovsky's ideas.

Professor Bernard Barber of Barnard College, Columbia University, reported within a few weeks of publication that 'I have already used your Velikovsky issue to very good teaching purpose in my Sociology of Knowledge course in connection with my general article on resistance by scientists to scientific discovery'.

Charles Perrow, Assistant Professor of Sociology at the University of Pittsburgh Graduate School of Public and International Affairs, expressed the conviction that the *ABS* Velikovsky issue 'should be required reading in social science courses'.

G. A. Lundberg of the University of Washington

wrote: 'It seems to me that the A.A.A.S., not to mention individual scientists and groups, must now prepare a detailed answer. What is really at issue are the mores governing the reception of new scientific ideas on the part of the established spokesmen for science.'

Indeed, it was tempting for spokesmen of science to take up the charges made by *ABS*. Even though Professor Menzel, taking it upon himself to reply to Larrabee's article in *Harper's*, had, in the opinion of many of his colleagues, fared very badly in the exchange, a more cautious and cleverly calculated reply to the *Behavioral Scientist* might have a telling effect.

Since the issues raised against the behaviour of the scientific community were essentially questions of ethics, a seemingly natural choice of vehicle in which to pursue these issues was the *Bulletin of the Atomic Scientists*, a journal which prides itself on being a medium of expression for 'the conscience of science'. The *Bulletin* has a readership of more than 25,000, including most of the leading scientists of the world. It has prestige among such people and an obligation to undertake inquiries into the politics of science – to demand objective self-analysis on questions of scientific behaviour. Being a platform both for confession of error and for expression of ideas for improving the image of science, it is ideally suited as an arena in which to come to grips with the issues of the Velikovsky case. Unfortunately, however, the *Bulletin* chose to take up arms against the suggestion of fair play for Velikovsky.

As Eugene Rabinowitch, the editor of the *Bulletin*, later acknowledged in a letter to Professor H. H. Hess (September 8, 1964), a widespread reawakening of interest in Velikovsky's theories, and his being championed as a great savant by the *Behavioral Scientist*, required remedial action. Clearly Rabinowitch took it to be his first duty to close ranks with fellow scientists whose conspiratorial acts in suppression of Velikovsky had been publicly charged against them.

Rabinowitch assigned his Washington reporter, Howard Margolis – no part a scientist – the job of wielding the hatchet against *ABS* and Velikovsky. Margolis resurrected techniques employed with devastating effect during the earlier outcry against *Worlds in Collision*. His vulgar and thoroughly irresponsible article, 'Velikovsky Rides Again' (*Bulletin*, April 1964) is filled with misrepresentation and misquotations, jeers and sneers, bald statements of unfounded charges, and dogmatic presentations of received theory as fact.

Margolis chose to discuss matters of philology and Egyptology – fields unfamiliar to him, but having intrinsic appeal in that most *Bulletin* readers could be expected to be little oriented in them and hence dependent upon the integrity of editor and author.

Displaying ignorance even of the elementary French required to read one of Velikovsky's sources, Margolis resorted to bravado – 'Now if you look up the actual inscription . . .' – and launched into a totally confused discussion of Velikovsky's interpretation of a hieroglyphic text found at El Arish in Egypt. This is an inscription in stone telling of storm and darkness and the death of a Pharaoh in a whirlpool. The place name Pi Kirot appears in this inscription, and the name Pi ha-hiroth is given in Exodus as the place where the tribes of Israel crossed the Red Sea; Velikovsky suggested in *Worlds in Collision* – and amplified the argument in *Ages in Chaos*, unbeknownst to Margolis – that both references are to the same place. The name appears only once in the Egyptian monuments and only once in the Bible. And in context, both sources tell of storm and darkness, and of catastrophe befalling a Pharaoh overwhelmed by waters.

From the confused arguments presented by Margolis the only facts to emerge are that he does not understand that Egyptian was written without vowels and that he is not even aware of the use of 'ha' in Hebrew as the definite article. Ironically, the *Bulletin's* Washington reporter elected to challenge Velikovsky on a philological conclusion which had won the acceptance of Professor William F. Albright, one of the world's leading orientalists and a harsh critic of *Ages in Chaos*, as early as 1946.

Rabinowitch printed Margolis's vainglorious essay without comment.

At the appearance of this diatribe in the estimable *Bulletin of the Atomic Scientists*, Eric Larrabee – a past contributor to the journal – contacted the managing editor and was promised space for a reply in an early issue. But when he met the assigned deadline, he was informed that the space was no longer available.

The mere vulgarity and unscholarly quality of Margolis's article did not deter its eager reception in quarters dominated by organized science. For example, L. H. Farinholt, another vice president of the Alfred P. Sloan Foundation, sent a facsimile of the article to Moses Hadas, Jay Professor of Greek at Columbia University. Hadas had remarked in a published book review that 'in our time Immanuel Velikovsky . . . appears to be approaching vindication'. Farinholt thought Hadas should find the Margolis essay 'of interest and perhaps amusing'.

Hadas replied that he had no opinion about the validity of Velikovsky's astronomical theories, 'but I know that he is not dishonest. What bothered me was the violence of the attack on him: if his theories were absurd, would they not have been exposed as such in time without a campaign of vilification? One after another of the reviews misquoted him and then attacked the misquotation. So in the Margolis piece you send me . . . [Hadas gives several examples of Margolis's misrepresentations of Velikovsky's correct quotations] . . . It is his critic, not Velikovsky, who is uninformed and rash . . . The issue is one of ordinary fair play.'

On May 12, 1964, Alfred de Grazia, as publisher of *The American Behavioral Scientist*, wrote to Rabinowitch and demanded that the *Bulletin* editor repudiate the many distortions in Margolis's article. 'Our contributors and our advisors have urged us to take action to remedy the wrong done us. We hesitate to do this since we prefer to rely in the first instance on your scholarly good will.'

Rabinowitch replied to de Grazia on June 23, in a long letter urging him not to go to court; 'the magazine cannot disclaim legal responsibility for any defamatory statements, but I do not see in the article by Mr Margolis any statements of such nature with respect to yourself or to the contributors of your journal'. Thus tacitly admitting that Velikovsky had been defamed, Rabinowitch suggested that 'since Margolis brought up paleographic evidence, fairness requires the *Bulletin* to give space to a letter disputing this evidence (provided this letter is not more abusive than Mr Margolis's criticisms)'. He offered to print an article presenting the views of Velikovsky, should it be written and submitted by a scientist of standing. Rabinowitch concluded: 'It is in this spirit of scientific argumentation that the whole problem should be resolved.'

Velikovsky, informed of Rabinowitch's stand, would not consent to enter into debate with Margolis on matters of Hebrew and Egyptian philology and paleography. The author of the *Bulletin* article had amply demonstrated incompetence in these subjects. But since Rabinowitch had written of the 'spirit of scientific argumentation', Velikovsky thought he might be willing to publish a paper expressing a positive point of view. Professor Hess agreed to submit for publication in the *Bulletin* 'Venus, a Youthful Planet', the paper by Velikovsky which the American Philosophical Society had returned earlier.

On September 8, 1964 (in the letter already quoted in part, above), Rabinowitch replied to Hess: 'I am afraid I cannot offer publication in the *Bulletin* [for Velikovsky's manuscript] – not because we are "afraid" of publishing it, but because the *Bulletin* is not a magazine for *scientific* controversies . . .

'I am not qualified – and have no time – to study Velikovsky's books, or even his article (which I return with this letter), but I know enough of the absence of dogmatism in modern science and its easy acceptance of revolutionary new ideas – including the relativity of time and absence of exact causality in the world of elementary particles – to trust qualified astrophysicists with an unprejudiced judgment about Mr Velikovsky's theories – and so far as I am aware, not a single qualified scientist has raised his voice in favour of [them] (even if you and one of your colleagues from Princeton have felt it their duty to point out in *Science* the remarkable correctness of some of Velikovsky's specific conclusions).'

It is interesting to compare this expression of complacency with comments made by Rabinowitch in his 1963 book, *The Dawn of a New Age*:

'As scientists, we have a common experience – that, in science, free inquiry and untrammeled exploration by individuals are the ultimate sources of the most important progress. The greatest scientific discoveries have come through efforts of non-conformist individuals who have asked heretical questions and boldly doubted the validity of generally accepted conceptions . . . ' (p. 222).

'I believe that the responsibility of scientists in our time is to bring into human affairs a little more of such skeptical rationality, a little less prejudice, a greater respect for facts and figures, a more critical attitude toward theories and dogmas, a greater consciousness of the limitations of our knowledge, and a consequent tolerance for different ideas and a readiness to submit them to the test of the experiment . . . For scientists, there should be no final truths, no forbidden areas of exploration, no words that are taboo, no prescribed or proscribed ideas . . .' (p. 223).

'A scientist must always be prepared to submit his beliefs, findings, and generalizations to the never ending test of observation and experiment. Not that he is entirely without resistance to new theories that would overthrow the principles which he has become accustomed to accepting as valid; but of all groups of men, he belongs to the most open-minded one, the one most ready to accept change. He would be a poor scientist who would refuse to consider new facts and to change ideas to accommodate them. The only thing of which science is intolerant is intolerance itself – claims that certain concepts are sacrosanct, true beyond doubt, and protected from the test of logic and experience.' (p. 323).

In his correspondence with de Grazia and Hess, Rabinowitch admitted that he had not read Velikovsky's books. Furthermore, he displayed an imperfect memory: to de Grazia he expressed a vague recollection that Shapley and Menzel had analyzed Velikovsky's theories, yet Shapley never published any arguments or articles on the subject; in his letter to Hess, Rabinowitch gave evidence of confusion about more recent events, for he mistook Hess for one of the writers of the Bargmann–Motz letter in *Science*. Still, on the basis of no acquaintance with Velikovsky's work, and of hazy memories of what others had said and done, he undertook a campaign against *Worlds in Collision* and put an unqualified journalist in charge of the operation.

Professor de Grazia reproduced the Margolis text in full in the *Behavioral Scientist* for October 1964 and appended an extensive commentary pointing out in detail – 54 examples – its many points of ignorance and misrepresentation. This elicited a letter from Margolis: 'May I merely suggest that before your readers reach a judgment on the matter, they take the trouble to check Velikovsky's assertions, my assertions, and de Grazia's rebuttal against at least one source. I suggest Augustine's *City of God* . . . unlike the El-Arish manuscript . . . the book is available in any library . . .' In a covering letter, Margolis offered to meet de Grazia to establish harmony.

Margolis, still uninformed – many months after his article appeared in print – that the El-Arish document he purported to interpret is an inscription in stone and not a manuscript, suggested that de Grazia's readers inform themselves of what Velikovsky has to say about 'Minerva, Deucalion, Varro, Ogyges, Venus, and so on' by checking references to those names in St Augustine. Clearly he hoped no one would follow through on his suggestion; otherwise he would not have risked such innuendo.

De Grazia replied: 'You claim that Velikovsky misquoted St Augustine's *City of God*, but do not submit any specific reference. In a matter of accuracy in quotations no issue can be settled except by referring to the concrete texts. In the matter of quotations from St Augustine, in your own article, you gave only one example, and on that point your charges were unfounded . . . If you know of texts of ancient literature that contradict the thesis of Dr Immanuel Velikovsky, you will do a service to knowledge by publishing them. But as long as you do *not* quote them, any debate would be built on air. The solid fact is that the *ABS* proved that you have misquoted or misrepresented the writers of *ABS*, the works of Dr Velikovsky, and the two ancient texts mentioned in your article. Please do manifest your professed concern with accuracy in quotations by taking steps to correct this matter.

'Since you are wrong in fifty-four ways already, it ill behooves you to increase your score'.

The issue of irresponsibility on the part of reviewers was brought into focus again in the summer of 1965. *Book Week*, a Sunday supplement to the New York *Herald Tribune*, the Washington *Post*, and the San Francisco *Examiner*, published (July 11, 1965) a review of *Worlds in Collision* by Willy Ley, author of popular works on rocketry and space travel. The occasion for this review, 15 years after the first publication of the book, was its appearance, along with *Earth in Upheaval*, in paperback form (Delta, 1965).

In his essay, Ley wheels to the firing line almost every device used by the earlier reviewers: he dismisses the arguments of *Worlds in Collision* by summarizing them in a manner calculated to make them appear ridiculous; he categorizes Velikovsky's works with those of Hans Hörbiger, a long-discredited catastrophist whose speculations never led to verifiable predictions; he indulges in the same false generalizations about Velikovsky's handling of source materials ('. . . half the time the Bible does not say what it is supposed to say'), but disdains the opportunity to be specific; he objects to a method of scholarly deduction that he does not even attempt to understand ('. . . references to old writings . . . is a peculiar way of establishing proof of physical events'); he flaunts his own ignorance of material Velikovsky assembled in *Earth in Upheaval* ('. . . animal life went through the fateful years of 1500 B.C. without any disturbance'); and he outlines his own mathematical proof of 'the complete impossibility' of the eruption of Venus from Jupiter – showing himself unaware that cosmologist R. A. Lyttleton recently demonstrated mathematically that Venus *must* have originated by eruption from Jupiter or one of the other major planets.

Velikovsky was invited by the editor of *Book Week* to write a rebuttal to Ley's accusations. Taking the opportunity to answer his uncritical critics in general, he prepared a long article, which appeared in *Book Week* for September 9, 1965.

Professor Horace M. Kallen, after reading the rejoinder, wrote to Velikovsky: 'I think you have put Ley in a position he will find it very difficult to wriggle out of.'

The appearance of *Worlds in Collision* and *Earth in Upheaval* in soft covers occasioned another episode that bears recording.

In March 1965 a modest advertisement announcing the Delta editions was submitted by Dell Publishing Co. for publication in *Science* and *Scientific American*. Both periodicals turned down the ad, but were unwilling to put their refusals in writing. Eventually, however, Robert V. Ormes, managing editor of *Science*, wrote to Franklin Spier, Inc., the ad agency: 'As Mr Scherago [advertising manager of *Science*] told you on the telephone, the advertisement you submitted has not been accepted by *Science*.' As the agency reported in a memo to Dell: 'We insisted on a letter giving some reason for the rejection.

So far, just this "answer" from *Science* – which brilliantly avoids mentioning the books that are involved.'

Perhaps inadvertently, *Science* listed the paperback edition of *Worlds in Collision* under 'Reprints' in its occasional department 'New Books' (May 7, 1965).

Throughout the story of Velikovsky's reception by science, one phenomenon occurs over and over again. One prominent scientist after another undertakes to criticize and ridicule the author and his theories; having done this, he states – not without a trace of pride – that he has not read the books.

This trend was established early, when Harlow Shapley, in interviews, and Cecilia Payne-Gaposchkin, in print, spoke out against *Worlds in Collision* before the book appeared. Astronomer Dean McLaughlin of Michigan boasted that he never would read Velikovsky's book, yet he felt no compunction against proclaiming it to be 'nothing but lies'. Philip Abelson rejected Velikovsky's article in 1963 without experiencing any compulsion to read it, and Rabinowitch did likewise with another article, at the same time throwing the weight of his journal's prestige behind a renewal of the campaign to brand Velikovsky as incompetent.

Another phenomenon is the alacrity with which scientist-critics of Velikovsky proclaim their own objectivity by citing their acceptance of Einstein's theories. Again and again the name of Einstein or the theory of relativity has been brought forward in comparisons of Velikovsky and Einstein which are intended to justify the different receptions accorded their works. Einstein's theory, held in highest esteem in spite of the fact that even after half a century there is no indisputable proof of its validity, is held up as a model scientific theory; Velikovsky's theory, on the other hand, although many predictions based upon it have already found vindication, is rejected as unscientific. The logic in this stance – adopted most recently by Rabinowitch – is elusive.

Still another approach to the problem posed by Velikovsky's heresies is to depreciate the evidence or ignore it altogether when it tends to support him. This technique averts discussion and acknowledgment of his successful predictions. *Sky & Telescope*, a journal for amateur astronomers published by Harvard Observatory, reported the findings of Mariner II by reprinting the summary from a book, *Mariner, Mission to Venus*, written by the staff of Jet Propulsion Laboratory – the group which conducted the experiments aboard the spacecraft. Minor ellipses in the text are noted by dots in the reprinted version, but four major deletions are unacknowledged by any sort of mark.

Restoration of the mutilated text requires reinsertion of the following:

(1) 'The rotation might be retrograde . . .'

(2) The clouds of Venus 'probably are comprised of condensed hydrocarbons held in oily suspension . . .'

(3) 'No water could be present at the surface, but there is some possibility of small lakes of molten metal of one type or another.'

(4) 'Some reddish sunlight . . . may find its way through the 15-mile-thick cloud cover, but the surface is probably very bleak.'

Is it just coincidence that these points – which (1) suggest anomalous behaviour in the past, (2) lend credence to a specific prediction made by Velikovsky, (3) challenge long-held notions of water clouds on Venus, and (4) cast an insurmountable barrier across the path of the theory that Venus is heated by a greenhouse-like trapping of sunlight – fell by the wayside in an editorial office at Harvard? Does Harvard University have any responsibility for inquiring into such matters (the question asked by de Grazia in 1963)?

Influential scientists continue to exert pressure against any sort of favourable mention of Velikovsky in popular journals and magazines. The easiest ploy is to impress upon editors that only scientists – and preferably selected members of the establishment – are competent to judge scientific theories. And since science is an important source of news of interest to the general public, editors are not inclined to reject such advice. An article planned in 1963 by *Newsweek* to call attention to Velikovsky's predictions and their fulfilment by Mariner II was abandoned following a telephone conversation between a *Newsweek* editor and Harlow Shapley – the astronomer to whom Velikovsky wrote in 1946 that a crucial test of his theory would be a search for hydrocarbons in the atmosphere of Venus.

In the Soviet Union, a journal of popular science, *Nauka i Zhizn* (Science and Life), in a series of articles continuing since 1962, has been casually presenting Velikovsky's theories, even the parenthetical speculation that in the legend of the sinking of Atlantis one too many zeroes crept into the traditional dating of the event. Velikovsky's name, however, has not been mentioned in the series.

The Italian multi-lingual journal *Civiltà delle Macchine*, in its issue for May–June 1964, underlined the need for eternal vigilance to preserve the spirit of the scientific method, which had been discussed at length in an earlier issue commemorating Galileo's fourth centenary. Professor Bruno de Finetti of the Instituto Matematico of the University of Rome contributed the lead article for the May–June issue.

To illustrate a theme presented by the journal's editors – science must continually guard itself against scepticism that tends to limit its perception to a series of unrelated hypotheses just as it must guard against dogmatism – Professor de Finetti expressed the opinion that the refusal of the large majority in the academic community to even discuss Velikovsky's ideas imparts 'one great teaching above all others': professionalization and departmentalization in science has become a major obstacle to the continuous renewal so necessary to science.

Thus, according to de Finetti, scholars refused to discuss the merits of Velikovsky's studies because their attentions were diverted by a more personal issue – the fact that he challenged 'the right of their fossilized brains to rest in peace' with the skills and problems already established. The defence of such vested interest in the preservation of comfortable interdisciplinary boundaries may transform 'each clan of specialists and the great clan of scientists in general into a sort of despotic and irresponsible mafia'.

Although American scientists and science editors continue to ignore – or rail against – Velikovsky's ideas, impersonal science itself continues to explode its own more conventional theories by turning up new evidence. Much new evidence tends to support Velikovsky; some of it is simply compatible with his views; up to now none of it has refuted them.

In April 1964 an announcement by radio astronomers of evidence that the planet Jupiter suddenly changed its period of rotation made front-page news. The correspondence between the rotational period of radio sources and the rotational period of the body of the planet is entirely inferential, but the time of sudden change noted for the radio sources coincided with a similar change in the period of rotation of Jupiter's red spot. In this connection, it should be noted that in a memorandum of proposed space researches sent by Velikovsky to Professor H. H. Hess at Hess's request in September 1963 the following suggestion is made: 'Precise calculations should be made as to the effect of the magnetic field permeating the solar system on the motions of [Jupiter] which is surrounded by a magnetosphere of an intensity, presumably, 10^{14} times that of the terrestrial magnetosphere. This is basic to the impending re-evaluation of electromagnetic effects in celestial mechanics.'

At a meeting of the International Astronomical Union in Hamburg (1964) the planets Mercury and Venus became topics of intense interest. Australian astronomers reported evidence of temperatures near 60°F on the dark side of Mercury, where temperatures far below zero were expected. According to *Scientific American* (October 1964), 'The explanation advanced for this surprisingly high temperature provides another surprise: that in spite of Mercury's small mass and its exposure to solar radiation pressure . . . it has enough of an atmosphere to transfer some of the sunlit side's abundant heat ration to the dark side.' Perhaps a more reasonable explanation will be found some day in the sequel to *Worlds in Collision*, which deals with earlier catastrophes, at least one of which the human record ascribes to Mercury.

New radar studies of Venus have confirmed its retrograde rotation, first detected at about the time of the Mariner II flyby by scientists at the Jet Propulsion Laboratory's Goldstone Tracking Station. Radar work at Arecibo Ionospheric Observatory in Puerto Rico by scientists from Cornell University and Massachusetts Institute of Technology pinpointed the period of rotation at 247 ± 5 days. The planet orbits the sun in 225 days. British and Soviet workers also have verified the retrograde rotation.

The U.S. Interplanetary Monitoring Platform (IMP) Satellite – Explorer 18 – has detected a magnetosphere around the moon – a teardrop-shaped region reaching at least 68,000 miles into space on the side away from the sun. The same probe has discovered a region of high-energy electrons fanning out and trailing off like a wake on the night side of the earth. K. A. Anderson, who first reported this discovery, believes it likely that the moon encounters this tail on its monthly passages around the earth. Dr N. F. Ness of Goddard Space Flight Center believes the earth's tail may extend well past the orbit of the moon.

The earth's tail is believed to be an elongation of the geomagnetic field in the anti-solar direction. In 1953 Velikovsky suggested that the earth's magnetic field may reach as far as the moon, causing certain unexplained libratory, or rocking, motions of the moon.

In *Book Week* for September 5, 1965, Velikovsky claimed: 'in July, Mariner IV confirmed my picture of Mars as more moon-like than earth-like: "The contacts of Mars with other planets larger than itself and more powerful make it highly improbable that any higher forms of life, if they previously existed there, survive on Mars. It is, rather, a dead planet" (*Worlds in Collision*, page 364) . . . That Mars has crater-like formations, as the moon does, follows from the way these formations were built. Mars was heated and it bubbled; it was pelted by interplanetary bolts; some large meteorites pelted it, too. These events are described on many pages of *Worlds in Collision* as having taken place mainly in the 8th century before the present era . . . the sharp outlines of the formations, in the presence of an atmosphere, speak for their recentness.'

Velikovsky's efforts of more than a decade to induce radiocarbon laboratories around the world to test objects from the New Kingdom of Egypt have yielded their first fruits. The test results are compatible with Velikovsky's chronology and quite incompatible with the coventional timetable.

In 1963 three small pieces of wood from the tomb of Tutankhamen were delivered to the radiocarbon laboratory of the University of Pennsylvania Museum. The Director of the laboratory, Dr Elizabeth K. Ralph, performed the test, using all three samples (total 26 grams). In *Radiocarbon* (1965), a Yale University publication, she reports that the date of the material, based on Libby's estimate of the half-life of radiocarbon, is 1030±50, B.C. (based on the Washington estimate of the half-life, the date is 1120±52, B.C.).

These dates are clearly at odds with accepted chronology, which places Tutankhamen in the fourteenth century. Velikovsky places him in the ninth century. The test results do not confute Velikovsky's chronology because radiocarbon in wooden objects indicates the time when the cells of the wood were actively growing. Only wood from the outer parts of a log yields dates close to the time of cutting, whereas wood from the interior of a log may yield dates hundreds of years earlier. Almost half the wood tested in this case was of Lebanese cedar, a tree famed for its longevity and not usually cut as a sapling. Therefore it is possible that heartwood grown about 1030 (or 1120) B.C. was cut in the ninth century to make objects for Tutankhamen; it is not possible, however, that wood grown centuries after his death furnished objects for a fourteenth-century pharaoh.

No hard and fast conclusions can be drawn on the basis of a single test of this kind. But perhaps now the door has been opened for the further testing that is so urgently needed in the 13 centuries whose chronology Velikovsky has challenged. Up to now this entire period of history has been left out of radiocarbon programmes.

Because of the eminently successful campaign of defamation in the 1950's, the name Velikovsky became anathema among editors and science writers of newspapers and mass-circulation magazines. In large degree this situation is still unchanged. But the article by Larrabee in *Harper's* for August 1963 and the special issue of the *American Behavioral Scientist* in September 1963 initiated a fermentation process in scholarly circles and on college campuses which, up to now, has been unreflected in either the general or the scientific press. Students and young professors are making known their desires to understand the implications of Velikovsky's theories and of their non-reception by science.

The October–November 1964 issue of *Quadrant*, published in Sydney by the Australian Association for Cultural Freedom, carried a ten-page article, 'Velikovsky in Collision', by David Stove, senior lecturer in philosophy at Sydney University.

Stove offers objective criticism of the evidence advanced by Velikovsky in all of his books. '. . . the most striking evidence for Velikovsky's theory remains the historical. The Earth spoke, at least to my ear, very equivocally for him . . . What, then, of the skies? . . . it is the Evening Star herself who has responded to two of Velikovsky's antecedently improbable predictions with an audible and astonishing "yes" . . . [The weight of this evidence] should not be overestimated . . . but I do not see how it could be denied that these two confirmations substantially raise the probability of . . . [the entire thesis] above the value it had in the light of all the previous evidence; and this was by no means negligible.'

Stove attributes the violent reaction to *Worlds in Collision* among astronomers to Velikovsky's forceful reminder 'that astronomy is not a theoretical science, but a branch of natural history . . . The uneventfulness of the history of the solar system is an assumption on which astronomers have placed a tacit reliance it by no means ever deserved. In the house that they knew so well, they had never noticed this door. And Velikovsky did the most infuriating thing in the world: he – a stranger – walked through this open door . . . We should not withhold the highest possible admiration from the first man to suggest that the earth is not only not the centre, not only not still, but not even safe'.

REFERENCES

1. In a letter to *Science* (Vol. 140, p. 1,362), Australian radio astronomer Grote Reber charged that Velikovsky's prediction of the earth's far-reaching magnetic field was 'more in the nature of of ad hoc guess'. His authority for this is science-fiction writer Poul Anderson (*Science* Vol. 139, p. 671), whose childish and facetious comments on the Bargmann-Motz letter (*Science* Vol. 138, p. 1,350) caught the fancy of Editor Philip Abelson. On the basis of his own 1955 speculation that the earth's atmosphere has a disc-like equatorial bulge (not yet discovered), Reber claims prior prediction of the magnetosphere. How this follows is not clear.

2. Norman D. Newell, curator of fossils at the American Museum of Natural History and professor of paleontology at Columbia, offered a theory of 'gradual' catastrophism in *Scientific American* for February 1963. Here Velikovsky's name appears – almost as if it were a late editorial insertion – with that of Charles Hapgood (*Earth's Shifting Crust*), and together the two men are exemplified as writers who 'continue to propose imaginary catastrophes on the basis of little or no historical evidence'. The timing of this reference to Velikovsky suggests that the Bargmann-Motz letter in *Science* may have prompted it.

THE INCONSTANT HEAVENS

by Livio C. Stecchini

The modern system of astronomy is now so much received by all inquirers, and has become so essential a part even of our earliest education, that we are not commonly very scrupulous in examining the reasons upon which it is founded. It is now become a matter of mere curiosity to study the first writers on that subject.
David Hume, Dialogues Concerning Natural Religion (1779), Part II.

Only a few years ago astronomers were unanimous in dismissing as preposterous Velikovsky's contention that the movement of the heavenly bodies is affected by electromagnetic fields. Today creative astronomers are immersed in the study of electromagnetism. The historian finds difficulty in explaining how radical is this change that has challenged three hundred years of cosmological thought and has brought us back to the arguments of William Gilbert (1544–1603) and Johann Kepler (1571–1630).[1] The newness of the revolution is evinced by the Einstein–Velikovsky correspondence wherein the former soon accepted as tenable the hypothesis of global catastrophies and, though originally quite opposed, at last became sympathetic even to the hypothesis of a recent origin of Venus as a planet. However, he persistently rebutted to the end of his life all argument that electricity and magnetism affect the motions of heavenly bodies.

Whereas astronomers are perplexed at the implication of the new picture of the universe as derived from the space probes, Velikovsky has been clear from the very beginning. In one of the first conversations I had with him ten years ago, he summed up this thinking by stating that one of the implications of his work is to reinstate

Descartes as a rightful contestant of Newton in the understanding of the texture of the universe. Velikovsky quoted the following summation by Herbert Butterfield of the results of the famous contest between the two views of celestial mechanics: 'The clean and comparatively empty Newtonian skies ultimately carried the day against a Cartesian universe packed with matter and agitated with whirlpools, for the existence of which scientific observations provided no evidence.'[2] Velikovsky was confident that this evidence would be found, and it has been found. There is reasonable ground to hope that the new investigation which takes electric charges and magnetic field into account will, first of all, succeed in explaining the behaviour of comets especially in the proximity of the Sun. The current explanation, according to which the pressure of solar light drives a cometary tail as a rigid rod at enormous velocities when the head is close to the perihelium, is not much more satisfactory than the one proposed by Newton when he said that the tails of comets turn away from the Sun for the same reason that the smoke from a fire ascends perpendicularly, or in the case of a moving body obliquely, in the atmosphere.[3] Thereafter, the case of planets like Earth or Jupiter, which are surrounded by a magnetosphere and move through the magnetic field permeating the solar system and the plasma winds that sweep through it, will come to quantitative analysis, too.

With new claimants to participation in the mechanism of the solar system, the problem of its stability is brought into new light.

PSYCHOLOGICAL PREMISES

Because of his psychoanalytic training and experience, Velikovsky was able to realize that men tend to shunt off as fables the accumulated memories and records of cosmic cataclysms. Even biblical fundamentalists do not accept at face value what is told in plain language in a book that they purportedly interpret to the letter.

A few hundred years after the last upheaval, as dated by Velikovsky's thesis, Aristotle struggled to refute the cosmology of Heraclitus; and Cicero, when other writers of his century such as Lucretius or Ovid were describing in detail what had happened, proclaimed *ita stabilis mundus est atque ita cohaeret ad permanendum, ut nihil ne excogitari quidem aptius possit* – 'the world is so stable and it holds together so well for the sake of permanence that it is impossible even to imagine anything more fitted to the purpose'.[4] Planets are gods, and because of their divine nature they keep a perfect and immutable order. In another passage Cicero expounds the same view in terms that became a creed both for medieval scholastic natural philosophers and, as I shall indicate, for the followers of Newton:

> In the firmament, therefore, there is no accident, no chance, no aimless wandering, nothing untrustworthy; on the contrary, all things display perfect order, reliability, purpose, constancy ... Wherefore, that man who holds that the astounding orderliness and the incredible precision of movement of these celestial bodies, upon which the support and safety of all things are wholly dependent, are not directed by reason must himself be considered to be utterly devoid of the rational faculty.[5]

But this was a reversal of the older beliefs in the Theomachy, or the struggle among the planetary gods. Critias, the cousin of Plato's mother, in his drama *Sisyphus*, stressed the opposite view, defended by Democritus and his followers, that the belief in the planetary gods was linked with the worst of all human terrors. The following quotation illuminates also the question, with which I shall deal below, that the organization of the heavenly bodies came to be considered the foundation of ethics:

> He [Sisyphus] said the gods resided in that place
> Which men would dread the most, that place from which,
> As he well knew, mortals have been beset
> With fears or blest with that which brings relief
> To their tormented lives – there, high above,
> In that great circuit where the lightnings flash,
> Where thunder's baleful tumult may be heard,
> And heaven's starry countenance is seen

(That lovely work of Time's skilled joinery),
Where molten stones of stars descend ablaze,
And wet rain starts its journey to the earth.
Such were the consternating fears he sent
To men, and such the means by which the gods
Were settled in their proper dwelling-place
(A pretty trick, accomplished with a word);
And thus he quenched out lawlessness with laws.[6]

Modern writers have suspected as much. John Dewey opens *The Quest for Certainty* (1929) with a chapter titled 'Escape from Peril'. He points out that fear is the spring of the search for immutable perfect entities, for the glorification of regularity and invariance at the expense of diversity and change. By rationalizing the beliefs in the heavenly bodies as gods and making them the expression of a higher realm (higher physically and morally) which is rational, regular, and unalterable, Aristotle set up the foundations of classical science.

In a similar vein, Freud[7] asks on what foundation does 'man build the feeling of security with which he armours himself against the dangers both of the external world and of human environment'. In answering he declares: 'Think of the famous dictum of Kant that mentions in one breath the starry heavens and the moral law in our heart. This combination sounds odd – for, what could the heavenly bodies have to do with the question whether a human being loves or murders another – but it touches a profound psychological truth.'

The passage of Kant (1724–1804) to which Freud refers is the conclusion of the *Critique of Practical Reason:*

> Two things fill the mind with ever-increasing wonder and awe, the more often and the more intensely the mind of thought is drawn to them: the starry heavens above me and the moral law within me.

But does the starry heaven inspire us rightfully with the feeling of stability, while it inspired the ancients with an all-pervading fear?

Nicolas of Cusa (1401–64), in his *De docta ignorantia,* denied the qualitative difference between heaven and earth. He also rejected the rest of the related propositions of Aristotelian metaphysics and revived the heliocentric theory, and he stated that the earth is not perfectly spherical and that the orbits of the planets are not perfectly circular.[8] He claimed that heavenly motions do not have stability as an inherent quality, and formulated the hypothesis that some statements of ancient writers may be explained by their having seen a sky different from what was seen in his time. He defined science as 'learned ignorance', because it is impossible to formulate an exact, eternal, and absolute description of the physical universe.

The position of Copernicus (1475–1543) was relatively conservative in that he combined heliocentrism with the traditional conception of circular movements (around the sun) and of a limited universe bounded by the sphere of the fixed stars. The opposition to Copernicus was determined by the realization that by giving mathematical structure to the heliocentric theory he lent support to the subversion of metaphysics that had been associated with it by Nicholas of Cusa.

Questioning of the text of Genesis began as a result of the Copernican theory: if the Earth is nothing but a planet revolving around the Sun, one may doubt that its creation was the result of a providential dispensation. A son-in-law of Osiander, the editor of Copernicus, uttered the first frank challenge to the divine authority of the biblical narrative: *neque mihi quisquam Judaeorum fabulas objiciat.*[9] Scholars began to doubt the notion that the universe had been created once and forever. They started to investigate ancient chronology, and laid down the foundations of geology and paleontology.

In the age of the Reformation some religious apologists argued that a distinction must be made between the creation of the universe as a whole and the creation of the Earth: the biblical text referred to the latter creation.

Giordano Bruno (1548–1600), in his last and greatest work, *De immenso et innumerabilibus*, published just after his imprisonment, made clear the meaning of the assertion of the principle of *indifferenza della natura.* He denied the existence of a providential order in nature and hence of the stability of the solar system which is linked with the doctrine of circular movements; declared that only their imperfect astronomical observations permitted earlier scholars to believe that the heavenly bodies move in circles and in the long run return to their original position (*de vanitate circulorum et anni illius mundani phantasia platonica et aliorum*);[10] and pointed out that astronomical movements are bound to be infinitely complex (*differentias et singularum differentiarum irregularitatem*).[11] The belief in the simple and regular motion of the planets, he continued, is a delusory product of astrological thinking *sub fide vel spe geometricantis naturae*; it is necessary to free mathematical astronomy from Platonic and Pythagorean metaphysical accretions. From the relativity of motion follows the relativity of time; since no completely regular motion can be discovered, and since we possess no records which can prove that all the heavenly bodies have taken up exactly the same positions with regard to the Earth as those previously occupied by them and that their motions are rigidly regular, no absolute measure of time can be found.[12]

The new conception of nature is epitomized in John Donne's poem, *An Anatomy of the World* (1611):

> And new Philosophy calls all in doubt . . .
> And freely men confess that this world's spent,
> When in the Planets, and the Firmament
> They seek so many new; then see that this
> Is crumbled out again to his Atomies.
> 'Tis all in pieces, all coherence gone . . .
> So, of the Stars, which boast that they do run
> In Circle still, none ends where he begun.
> All their proportions lame, it sinks, it swells.

Velikovsky has been scorned for blending the study of astronomy with that of geology, ancient traditions, ancient chronology, and ancient science. But in so doing he has followed the path of Renaissance scholars, since such a course is inevitable once the dogmatic belief in the incorruptibility of the solar system has been questioned. The new astronomy brought forth a series of studies on ancient traditions and chronology, and effected the birth of interest in Egyptian and Mesopotamian science. For instance, Father Athanasius Kircher (1601–80) founded the study of geology with his *Mundus Subterraneus*, while he initiated the study of Egyptian science with his *Oedypus Aegyptiacus*. In *Vicissitudo Rerum* (1600) John Norden refers to these speculations that have been revived by Velikovsky:

> The antique Poets in their Poems telled
> Under their fondest Fables, Mysteries:
> By Phaeton, how heaven's Powers rebelled
> In Fire's force, and by the histories
> Of Phyrrha and Deucalian there lies,
> The like of water's impetuity,
> In part concurring with divinity –
> The Priests of Egypt gazing on the stars,
> Are said to see the World's sad ruins past,
> That had betide by Fire and Water's jars:
> And how the World inconstant and unchaste,
> Assailed by these, cannot alike stand fast.
> Earthquakes and Wars, Famine, Hate, and Pest,
> Bring perils to the Earth, and Man's unrest.

Sir Walter Raleigh in his *History of the World* (1616) wondered how it could happen that the phases of Venus just discovered by Galileo seem to have been known to ancient authors. He listed the authorities who state that at the time of the flood of Ogyges 'so great a miracle happened in the star of Venus, as never was seen before nor in after-times: for the colour, the size, the figure, and the course of it were changed'. The catastrophe associated with the name of Ogyges, a time mark for ancient Greeks, took place simultaneously with Venus' complete metamorphosis. This statement made by Varro, 'the most learned of all the Romans', on the authority of earlier scientists should have provoked interest in the time of Newton, when the working of the solar system was elevated to the state of a most exact science. But, whereas the gleaning of information from ancient authors contributed to more than one discovery of the new age of astronomy (the very heliocentric theory had been advanced on the authority of Greek and Roman writers), Newton pulled down the curtain on the use of ancient sources as an inspiration for astronomical research. The notion that the solar system may have a history, became (in the name of the new religion of science) as sacrilegious as it had been for the scholastics (Saint Augustine, A.D. 354–430, had taken a different position on the authority of classical authors).

On the eve of the establishment of Newtonian cosmology, the speculation on cosmic cataclysms had become so commonplace that in 1672 Molière, in his satire on the ladies who, captured by the new passion for science, studied astronomy, could make a joke of it (*Les femmes savantes*, Act IV, Scene III):

> Je viens vous annoncer une grande nouvelle:
> Nous l'avons en dormant, madame, échappé belle,
> Un monde près de nous a passé tout du long;
> Est chu tout au travers de notre tourbillon,
> Et s'il eût en chemin rencontré notre terre,
> Elle eût été brisée en morceaux comme verre.

> ('I have come to tell you a great piece of news. We have, Madam, while sleeping, had a narrow escape. A world has passed by us, has fallen across our vortex, and if it had on its way met our Earth, it would have broken it into pieces like glass.')

NEWTON

The Renaissance view of life and of the world, which can be summed up by the word *mutability*, was created by personalities of heroic stamina and required the leadership of such personalities for its perservation, for, indeed, it is not easy to live in a world where the only divinity is Fortuna and nothing is certain beyond measurement and probability. As Freud contends, neuroses originate from the failure, due to inferior biological endowment combined with stunted psychic growth, to face the burden of the human condition in a world that owes us nothing.

Some contemporary thinkers were frightened, for the relativism and decentralization of the Renaissance found expression not only in astronomy but also in political theory; furthermore, the impact of thinkers such as Machiavelli was compounded by the geographical discoveries that gave birth to the doctrine of ethical relativism. In England the herald of reaction against Renaissance thought was the theologian Richard Hooker who imagined that a new conservative position could be justified by appealing to nature's laws linked with an absolute reason and an obedience of man to absolute ethics. In the *Laws of Ecclesiastical Polity* (1593–97), he examined the views current at his time:

> Now if nature should intermit her course, and leave altogether, though it were but for a while the observation of her own laws; if those principal and mother elements of the world, whereof all things in this lower world are made, should lose the qualities which now they have; if the frame of that heavenly arch erected over our heads should loosen and dissolve itself; if celestial spheres should forget their wonted motions, and by irregular volubility turn themselves any way as it might happen; if the prince of the lights of heaven, which now as a giant doth run his unwearied course, should as it were through a languishing faintness begin to stand and to rest himself; if the moon should wander from her beaten way, the times and seasons of the year blend themselves by disordered and confused mixture, the winds breathe out their last gasp, the clouds yield no rain, the earth be defeated of heavenly influence, the fruits of the earth pine away as children at the withered breasts of their mother no longer able to yield them relief: what would become of man himself, whom these things now do all serve? See we not plainly that obedience of creatures unto the law of nature is the stay of the whole world?

He proposed the comforting solution that was accepted by Newton and the scientists who followed him:

> But howsoever these swervings are now and then incident into the course of nature, nevertheless so constantly the laws of

nature are by natural agents observed, that no man denieth but those things which nature worketh are wrought, either always or for the most part, after one and the same manner.

Helène Metzger has shown that Newton developed his theory under the influence of this spirit of reaction. She is certainly right when she judges the overall effect of Newton's work which *devait vite devenir une aliée de cette piéte bienséante et bien pensante*;[13] but she has not analyzed in detail what caused Newton to arrive at his conservative conclusions nor what is their technical significance for science. Her pacemaking investigations were cut short by the gas chambeı at Auschwitz.

One of the precursors of Velikovsky as to the general thesis of the catastrophic past of the Earth, to whom he refers in his work, was William Whiston (1667–1752). In 1694, seven years after the first edition of the *Principia*, Whiston, then a fellow of Cambridge University, became a devoted pupil of Newton, and two years later submitted to his master the manuscript of a book entitled *New Theory of the Earth*. The book was intended to replace the then popular *Theory of the Earth* (1681) by Thomas Burnet, and dealt with a theme with which Newton had been concerned for more than a score of years. This book contended that the cataclysm described in the Old Testament as universal Deluge was caused by the impact of a comet at the end of the third millennium B.C., and that up to the Deluge the solar year had the duration of 360 days only, yet the new calendar of 365 days had to wait to be introduced by Nabonassar (in 747 B.C.). These contentions were based mainly on historical evidence, whereas astronomical considerations were the main ground for suggesting that comets may become planets:

Yet comets by passing through the planetary regions in all planets and directions . . . seem fit to cause vast mutations in the planets, particularly in bringing on them deluges and conflagrations, according as the planets pass through the atmosphere . . . Tho' indeed they do withal seem at present chaos or worlds in confusion, but capable of change to orbits nearer circular, and then settling into a state of order and of becoming fit for habitation like the planets; but these conjectures are left to further enquiry, when it pleases the divine providence to afford us more light about them.[14]

Newton was so impressed by Whiston's work that from that moment he established a close scientific relation with him. The book was highly praised also by other contemporaries, John Locke among them. Two years later the Savillian Professor of Astronomy at Oxford, John Keill (1671–1721), dedicated a book to the evaluation of Whiston's hypotheses in comparison to those of Burnet, in which he expressed the following judgments:

> . . . Yet I cannot but acknowledge that Mr Whiston, the ingenious author of the new *Theory of the Earth*, has made great discoveries and proceeded on more philosophical principles than all the theorists before him have done. In his theory there are some coincidents which make it indeed probable, that a comet at the time of the Deluge passed by the Earth.[15]

Keill approved also of the contention that before this upheaval the solar year consisted of 360 days, divided into 12 lunar months of 30 days.

In 1701 Whiston was appointed as a temporary substitute for Newton at Cambridge, and in 1703, when Newton resigned permanently from the Lucasian Chair of Mathematics, he recommended Whiston as uniquely worthy to be his successor. By 1713, when the second edition of the *Principia* was published, Newton's feelings towards Whiston had changed radically. When in 1720 the astronomer Edmond Halley (1656–1742) and others proposed Whiston as a member of the Royal Society, Newton threatened that, should the members vote for Whiston's admission, he would resign from the presidency of the Society. Whiston, who was deeply devoted to Newton, suggested that his candidacy not be pressed; he felt that the ageing Newton was so violently disturbed by the issue that he might die.[16] Halley who one year and a half before the publication of Whiston's *New Theory of the Earth* had read a paper before the Royal Society in which he had explained the Deluge by the impact of a comet, but had not printed it 'lest by some unguarded expression he might incur the censure of the sacred order', reacted to Newton's gesture by publishing with thirty years of delay a memoir in the acts of the Society.[17] Historians of science gloss over this incident, which is vital for the understanding of the evolution of Newton's thought. After 1710, when Whiston was dismissed from his teaching position because of heresy and then formally brought to trial before the body of bishops of the Church of England, he assumed more radical positions and came to disagree with Newton who was becoming more and more conservative.

Whiston's contention was that the creation story told in Genesis should not be interpreted literally, but as referring to a process of progressive creation through several cosmic stages. Newton, who was at first sympathetic to Whiston's religious and scientific views, came to be shocked by his radicalism, and turned towards a fundamentalist position. The concluding words of *Opticks* indicate that Newton, like others of his contemporaries, felt that, if the traditional views of cosmic order were abandoned, the foundations of morality would be undermined.[18] Furthermore, Newton felt that Whiston's hypotheses would end by eliminating what he considered the chief argument for the existence of God, the argument from design, namely, the wise adaptation of the present frame of nature to the needs of living creatures, especially man. In *Opticks* he rebutted Whiston in these terms:

> For it became who created them [the celestial bodies] to set them in order. And if he did so, it's unphilosophical to seek for any other origin of the world, or to pretend that it might arise out of a chaos by the mere laws of nature; though being once form'd, it may continue by those laws for many ages. For while comets move in very excentrick orbs in all manner of positions, blind fate could never make all the planets move one and the same way in orbs concentrick, some inconsiderable irregularities excepted, which may have arisen from the mutual actions of comets and planets upon one another, and which will be apt to increase, till this system wants a reformation. Such a wonderful uniformity in the planetary system must be allowed the effect of choice.[19]

Whereas the first edition of the *Principia* (1687) is essentially rationalistic in spirit and follows a positivistic method, theological preoccupations dominate the second edition (1713). Newton is bent on proving that the machinery of the world is such a perfectly contrived system that it cannot be the result of 'mechanical cause', but must be the result of an intelligent and consistent plan. In order to support further the story of Genesis that the world was created by a single act, he argued also that the world is stable and has remained unchanged since creation. But he could not prove this point, since he admitted that, according to his own theory, the gravitational pull among the several members of the solar system would tend to modify their orbits; hence, he begged the question and claimed that God in his providence must intervene from time to time to reset the clockwork of the heavens to its original state. This point of Newton's doctrine is well known, for it was the object of sarcastic comments by Newton's great rival in the mathematical field, Leibniz (1646–1716). As the latter observed, Newton cast God not only as a clockmaker, and a poor one at that, but also as a clock-repairman.[20]

Jean-Baptiste Biot (1774–1862), the chosen pupil of Laplace, agreed with his teacher in considering the second edition of the *Principia* as highly objectionable. He argued that Newton had ceased to be a creative thinker in 1695 and suggested that this was the result of his mental illness of eighteen months duration.[21] But in truth Newton was hampered by religious preoccupations and not by mental deterioration. The only external evidence that Biot submits for a psychic collapse is Newton's 'infantile' antics in his dealings with Whiston in 1714. In my opinion, the proof that Newton had become fixated on the religious problem, but had not lost any of his intellectual flexibility, is that the few additions that appear in the third edition of the *Principia* (1726), disclose that he came to believe that God reveals himself not in the appearance of things but in the ways of mankind.[22]

Scholars have failed to notice that the refutation of Whiston's doctrine was of major concern to Newton. In the *Principia*, he maintained that comets, far from being a disruptive element, contribute to the providential preservation of the original order: since a certain amount of the water of the Earth is steadily consumed by chemical combinations, the seas would not be preserved in their original state unless new water was provided by the exhalations of comets. The notion of the providential purpose of comets was further expanded in Newton's time: the comets exist also for the purpose of supplying new fuel to the Sun which otherwise would gradually consume itself. One of the important popularizers of Newton's ideas stresses that comets can perform these providential functions, but at the same time are providentially prevented from striking the Earth:

> In the next place, the reason why the planes of their [comets'] motions are not in the plane of the ecliptic, or any of the planetary orbits, is extremely evident; for had this been the case, it would have been impossible for the Earth to be out of the way of the comets' tails. Nay, the possibility of an immediate encounter or shock of the body, of a comet would have been too frequent; and, considering how great is the velocity of a comet at such a time, the collision of two such bodies must necessarily be destructive of each other; nor perhaps could the inhabitants of planets long survive frequent immersions in the tails of comets, as they would be liable to in such a situation. Not to mention anything of the irregularities and confusion that must happen in the motion of planets and comets, if their orbits were all disposed in the same plane.[23]

The writer follows here the reasoning of Newton, who argued that the providential order of the universe required that the comets have beneficial characteristics. In reality, the planes of the orbits of some comets are at a small angle with the plane of the ecliptic, and the chance of collision exists.

Biographies of Newton usually dismiss in a few lines his book *The Chronology of the Ancient Kingdoms Amended* (1728), to which he dedicated the last years of his life. They consider it the product of an irrelevant side activity; yet its purpose is clearly that of refuting Whiston's hypotheses. Newton argues that evidence for the year of 365 days is as old as the year 887 B.C., and that even though this year was 'scarcely brought into common use' before this date, it was as old as the first astronomical observations of the Egyptians. However, these would have started only quite late, in 1034 B.C. The main purpose of the book is to contend that there was hardly any reliable history before the First Olympic Games in 776 B.C. In the first page the point is made that the ancient legends and traditions (the basis of Whiston's argument for a cataclysm caused by a comet) are not a reliable source of information.

Newton believed that his cosmology, which he had summed up in the famous General Scholium of the second edition of the *Principia*, could not be accepted unless Whiston was refuted. For this reason, about three months after the appearance of the second edition, he wrote an essay (that lies unpublished at the British Museum) in which he answered the criticism advanced by William Lloyd (1627–1717), an intimate friend of Whiston, on the ground that the oldest calendars of the ancients are based on a solar year of 360 days. From what is known about this document it can be said that Newton gave a lame answer.[24] He argued that if a calendar of 360 days had been in use without a system of intercalation for the five extra days, the official beginning of the seasons would have moved around the full year in a period of 70 years; since there is no trace of this 70 year cycle, this calendar cannot have existed. But the argument of Whiston and Lloyd was exactly that the solar year was about 360 days long and that therefore no intercalation was needed. Newton was begging the question by assuming that the solar year must have always consisted of 365 days.

In the works of Newton the doctrine of the eternal stability of the solar system is clearly presented as an assumption based not on scientific data but on faith in a providential order. But the flood of popularizations that made Newtonianism the basic doctrine of the eighteenth century claimed that Newton had provided scientific mathematical proof of the marvellous order that he accepted on faith. Carl L. Becker, who has examined this development in *The Heavenly City of Eighteenth Century Philosophers* (1932), concludes that the thinkers of the Enlightenment, while they believed themselves to be anti-Christian or even irreligious, were, in the name of Newton's mechanics (though not his religion), returning to the tenets of medieval theology along with Newton. Not since the thirteenth century had there been such an alliance between faith and reason. It was again possible to lift up one's eyes to the changeless movements of the sky – signs of divine perfection and eternal laws. As Becker remarks, Newtonianism was an immediate success with the educated public, because 'the desire to correspond with the general harmony springs perennial in the human breast'.[25]

Every good textbook of history points out that Newton's astronomy precipitated a religious revolution. Newton was perfectly aware that he had expounded the religious view that was called 'natural religion agreeing with revealed'. The new religion was called theism and its Nicene Creed was the General Scholium of the *Principia*:

> The six primary planets are revolved about the Sun in circles concentric with the Sun, and with motions directed towards the same parts, and almost in the same plane. Ten moons are revolved about the Earth, Jupiter, and Saturn, in circles concentric with them, with the same direction of motion, and nearly in the planes of the orbits of those planets; but it is not to be conceived that mere mechanical causes could give birth to so many regular motions, since the comets range over all parts of the heavens in very eccentric orbits; for by that kind of motion they pass easily through the orbs of the planets, and with great rapidity; and in their aphelions, where they move the slowest, and are detained the longest, they recede to the greatest distances from each other, and hence suffer the least disturbance from their mutual attractions. This most beautiful system of the Sun, planets, and comets, could only proceed from the counsel and dominion of an intelligent and powerful Being.

In the popularizations of Newton theism became deism, and the latter evolved into the mechanistic atheism of La Mettrie (1709–51) and D'Holbach (1723–89). All these views of religion had in common the belief in the perfect regularity of the universe, expressed by the analogy of the mechanical clock. 'The ideal of a clockwork universe was the great contribution of the seventeenth century to the eighteenth-century age of reason.'[26]

There is no doubt that several of our contemporary natural scientists would object that these are metaphysical preoccupations that do not concern an observational science like modern astronomy. But there are no more hardened metaphysicians than those who believe that they do not have any metaphysics, and this can be proved by a timely example.

Venus is the planet closest to the Earth and has a size very similar to that of the Earth, so that it is a sort of twin sister of the Earth. Hence, those who agreed with Newton in believing in the regularity of nature presumed that Venus must rotate in about 24 hours and must be encircled by a moon similar to our Moon. In the eighteenth century a number of astronomers claimed to have seen and tracked this moon; after the solar transit of 1769 Lambert (one of those who advanced the nebular hypotheses) computed the orbit of this moon and its size (28/27 that of our Moon). The subsequent progress in the construction of telescopes made it impossible for astronomers of following generations to see what was not there. According to Newton, Venus has a period of rotation similar to that of the Earth, 23 hours.[27] Jacques Cassini revised the figure to 23 hours 20′, and by the end of the eighteenth century the accepted figure was 23 hrs. 21′ 20″. One more century of observations made the figure of 23 hrs. 21′ acceptable, but in 1877 G. V. Schiaparelli concluded that Venus rotates very slowly, probably once in a Cytherean year. Still, many astronomers published reports of decades of observation that proved the correctness of the Newtonian view that Venus rotates in about 24 hours. In spite of the further support provided by the absence of Doppler effect and of polar flattening, Schiaparelli's view that if Venus rotates, it rotates very slowly, was not accepted by many astronomers until 1963.

Whereas it took two and a half centuries for astronomers to realize that they had been looking into the telescope with the eyes of their mind, the philosopher David Hume (1711–76) recognized the epistemological problem involved in the study of Venus. He presents a Newtonian who declares 'Is not Venus another Earth, where we observe the same phenomena?' And to this Hume in his imaginary dialogue counterposes, by appealing to the authority of Galileo, 'When nature has so extremely diversified her manner of operation in this small globe, can we imagine that she incessantly copies herself throughout so immense a universe?'[28]

The case of the rotation of Venus is a minor example of the intellectual confusion that results when scientists accept all the astronomical doctrines of Newton without discriminating between what is mystical and what is scientific in the modern sense of the term.

In a brilliant and penetrating essay on 'Newton the Man', written for the *Royal Society Newton Tercentenary Celebrations* (Cambridge, 1947), Lord Keynes declared:

> In the eighteenth century and since, Newton came to be thought of as the first and the greatest of modern-age scientists, a rationalist, one who taught us to think on the lines of cold and untutored reason. I do not see him in this light.

The main contention of the essay is that Newton had 'a foot in the Middle Ages and a foot treading a path for modern science'. This contention had been advanced earlier by other scholars, but this time it met with the approval of outstanding historians of science, because Keynes had gained access to the unpublished manuscripts of Newton.

In the case of Newton we meet with the unique occurrence that for three centuries his admirers have fought battle after battle in order to prevent the publication of about nine-tenths of his scholarly work. Whiston was one of the first to clamour for the publication of Newton's manuscripts, since he wanted to have an opportunity to refute his historical theories. Only recently have the efforts to lift the curtain begun to be successful.

If all the manuscripts were published, what has been claimed by some scholars and was granted by Newton himself in some of his letters, would become evident: that science was not his main interest and that he conceived of it as an auxiliary to theology, as *ancilla theologiae*. That he was unusually successful in his scientific endeavours does not disprove that his main aim was to reconcile astronomy with religion. Newton believed that the astronomical revolution linked with the names of Copernicus and Galileo had destroyed the foundations of religious belief and that it was necessary to return to the medieval world view. He was a biblical fundamentalist who tried to prove, among other points, that the Bible contains prophecies of future history. His interest in science was a by-product of his effort to prove that even science does not conflict with biblical religion, conceived by him as the medieval synthesis of biblical religion with Platonic–Aristotelian cosmology.

The voluminous unpublished works of Newton deal with many topics from alchemy to politics, but theology has the lion's share, followed next by ancient history. These unpublished works cannot be dismissed as occasional efforts. To them he dedicated more time than to his scientific writings. They are just as accurately argued and well finished. All his writings constitute a unified stream of thought of which the scientific production was only one aspect.

Recently, Frank E. Manuel in *Isaac Newton, Historian* (Cambridge, 1963), has informed us of the contents of Newton's unpublished historical manuscripts. Manuel has made clear that at the time they were written they dealt with topics that were intensely debated among scholars. But he has not grasped that their purpose was to refute the historical researches of the Renaissance and those of Whiston in particular. Their main object was to discredit all the historical evidence presented for changes in the solar system. For instance, he tried to prove that in Mesopotamia astronomical science did not begin before the era of Nabonassar (747 B.C.).

In substance, Newton was trying to refute the kind of historical evidence that has been brought again to public attention by Velikovsky. It is rather amusing that in the effort to prove that the observation of the heavenly bodies began only at a very late date, he argued that accepted chronology must be lowered and anticipated the conclusions reached by Velikovsky in *Ages in Chaos*. Like Velikovsky, he claimed that Greek chronology must be shortened by four hundred years, eliminating what today we call the Dark Ages of Greece. Like Velikovsky, he claimed that some dynasties of Egypt have been duplicated in chronological schemes. A main contention of Velikovsky is that the Pharaoh Shishak of the Book of Kings, a contemporary of the successor of King Solomon of Israel, is the same person as Thutmosis III of the XVIII Dynasty. Newton, using a similar line of argument, identifies Shishak with the Pharaoh called Sesostris by the Greeks. In giving an account of Sesostris, Greek historians confused the deeds of Thutmosis III with those of Sesostris III of the XII Dynasty. It may be noted that Velikovsky, after a ten year struggle with the committees that administer the carbon 14 tests of archaeological material, has finally succeeded in obtaining at least some tests to prove or disprove his theory and Newton's. These few tests support the contention that the currently accepted dates of Egyptian history must be substantially lowered.

All the pursuits of Newton in theology, history, and science had one purpose. I. Bernard Cohen, the foremost authority on Newton in the United States, concludes (*Franklin and Newton*, Philadelphia, 1956, p. 66): 'Of course, Newton had one real secret, and concerning it he did his best to keep the world in ignorance.' The secret is that he intended to uphold the theology and the cosmology of Maimonides. Cohen agrees with Keynes that this medieval synthesis of biblical religion with the philosophy of Plato and Aristotle, constituted the ideal of Newton. He kept it a secret because he wanted to influence scientific thought without putting the admirers of the new scientific method on the alert. Velikovsky, too, has recognized in *Worlds in Collision* that through Newton he is fighting Maimonides. Maimonides expressly declares that in accepting the story of creation he disagrees with Aristotle, but that he agrees with Aristotle that the cosmos, once created, is permanent and indestructable.

In order to reconcile the cosmology of Aristotle with the text of the Old Testament, Maimonides asserted that all the passages that have been understood as referring to cosmic upheavals and to changes in planetary motions, must be understood as metaphors, not as factual accounts. Velikovsky reports that Maimonides re-examined a long series of biblical texts, establishing thereby a new trend in exegesis. Newton pursued the same line of argument as Maimonides in his exegesis of Greek texts and of what was then known of Oriental documents. In his scientific writings Newton tried to prove that natural science does not contradict this exegesis and the corresponding theology.

LAPLACE

Among those few who had more keenly critical minds than Voltaire and the other so-called *philosophes*, the metaphysics of Newton created an opposite reaction. By questioning it, his contemporaries, Berkeley (1685–1753) and Hume, established scientific empiricism and laid the foundations for our contemporary scientific method. Just as the leading philosophers of England (soon followed by Hegel, 1770–1831) pierced Newton's metaphysical fog, so the leading scientists of France refused to climb the bandwagon of popular Newtonianism and kept in mind the distinction between what Newton had proved and what he had not proved. Historians usually ascribe the reserve of the Academie des Sciences towards Newton to an obscurantist clinging to Cartesian tradition; but these strictures of the French scientists gave the impetus to the studies of Laplace, the greatest genius in mathematical astronomy since Newton. With the emergence of Laplace, gravitational celestial mechanics was more firmly established and the role of providence in sustaining the immutable order was abrogated.

Laplace (1749–1827) was cited throughout the nineteenth century and also has been quoted by opponents of Velikovsky as having provided the mathematical proof that the solar system, and hence nature, is built like a mechanical clock. But this is only one side of his total view. In the *Exposition du systeme du monde* he uses two pages to argue that mankind should learn to accept without obsessive fear the likelihood that a comet may strike the Earth.[29] In his other major work, *Theorie analytique des probabilités*, he insists that the motions of the Earth are not unalterable, being subject to several unpredictable forces, among which is the impact of meteorites.[30] He realized that the resistance to accepting the alterability of the sky springs also from the fear that thereby moral law may be destroyed. For this reason he continues the discussion of this topic by delving into psychology and arguing along lines similar to that of Hume's ethics, that a feeling of sympathy among men can exist without traditional metaphysics.[31] It is worth noting that his treatment of psychology touches upon the importance of childhood memories and upon the role of unconscious thinking.[32]

Laplace observed that from his mathematical formulas it was possible to draw the conclusion that 'nature has arranged everything in the sky to insure the permanence of the planetary system, with the same purpose that it seems to have adopted on Earth for the preservation of individuals and the perpetuation of species',[33] but added that such a conclusion was wrong, even though 'we are naturally inclined to believe that the order by which things seem to renew themselves on Earth has existed at all times and will exist forever'.[34] In reality, the stability of the present order 'is disturbed by various causes that can be ascertained by careful analysis, but which are impossible to frame within a calculation'.[35] He summed up his views in the words: *Le ciel même, malgré l'ordre de ses mouvements n'est pas inaltérable.*[36] He warned specifically that in his mathematical formulas about the solar system he had not taken comets into account, stating, just as specifically, that the motion of the Earth might be affected by meteorites, and one should therefore study the historical evidence, even though this evidence covers only a few millennia.

Laplace stressed that the human race is beset by a great fear that a comet may upset the Earth, a fear that manifested itself dramatically after Lexell's comet in 1770 had passed at only 2,400,000 km from the Earth. Shortly thereafter Lalande published a list of the comets that had passed closest to the Earth.[37] Men should be free from this fear, Laplace argued, for the probability of one striking the Earth within the span of a human life is slim, even though the probability of such an impact occurring in the course of centuries is very great (*très grande*).[38] He proceeded to describe the possible effects of a collision with a comet, painting a picture that is in close agreement with that outlined by Velikovsky. Much in the geology of the Earth and in human history could be explained by assuming that such an impact had taken place. However, if this is true, it must also be assumed that the colliding comet had a mass similar to that of the Earth.[39] Velikovsky conjectures that this comet was Venus, which has the required mass.

Laplace summed up his hypothesis in these words:

> The axis and the movement of rotation would be changed. The seas would abandon their ancient positions, in order to precipitate themselves toward the new equator; a great portion of the human race and the animals would be drowned in the universal deluge, or destroyed by the violent shock imparted to the terrestrial globe; entire species would be annihilated; all monuments of human industry overthrown; such are the

disasters which the shock of a comet would produce, if its mass were comparable to that of the earth.

We see then, in effect, why the ocean has receded from the high mountains, upon which it has left incontestable marks of its sojourn. We see how the animals and plants of the south have been able to exist in the climate of the north, where their remains and imprints have been discovered; finally, it explains the newness of the human civilization, certain monuments of which do not go further back than five thousand years. The human race reduced to a small number of individuals, and to the most deplorable state, solely occupied for a length of time with the care of its own preservation, must have lost entirely the remembrance of the sciences and the arts; and when progress of civilization made these wants felt anew, it was necessary to begin again, as if man had been newly placed upon the earth.

Laplace also wondered whether heavenly bodies might not be affected by forces other than gravitation, such as electric and magnetic forces.[40] He did not exclude such a possibility, even though according to available calculations their effect was not noticeable. Yet, when Velikovsky stated that the members of the solar system have strong electric charges and that these affect their motions, some astronomers objected that this had been proved impossible by Laplace. The first empirical evidence of the present effect of electromagnetic forces on the motion of the Earth is now available.

Scientific literature never mentions the Laplace statements listed above. He won immediate fame for having provided the mathematical proof of the stability of the solar system that was missing in Newton, despite the fact that he had emphatically warned against such an interpretation of his conclusions.

The interpretation of Laplace's theories was influenced by a minor point he made. He felt the need to refute Newton's argument that the fact that all the planets and their satellites rotate counterclockwise is proof of divine providence.[41] After calculating the statistical near-impossibility that such rotation may be a chance arrangement, he concluded that it must be the result of a common mechanical phenomenon.[42] Hence, he proposed the nebular hypothesis which had already occurred independently to the theologian Emanuel Swedenborg (1688–1772), to the philosopher Kant, to the astronomer Johann Heinrich Lambert (1728–77). But Laplace did not yet know of the satellites that revolve clockwise. He would have been pleased by the evidence submitted in 1963 which suggests that Venus rotates clockwise. The uniform direction of the rotation and revolution of the planets and their satellites, far from being a key point of his view, was considered by him to be a stumbling block to his probabilistic view of the universe.

The following quotation indicates to what distortions Laplace's theories were subjected by the interpreters:

> We are naturally led to ponder on the great truth of the stability and permanence of the solar system as demonstrated by the discoveries of Lagrange and Laplace . . . The arrangements, therefore, upon which the stability of the solar system depends, must have been the result of design, the contrivance of that omniscience which foresaw all that was future, and of that infinite skill which knew how to provide for the permanence of His work. How the comets, whose motions are not regulated by such laws, and which move in so many different directions, may in the future interfere with the order of the system, can only be conjectured. They have not interfered with it in the past, owing no doubt to the smallness of their density; and we cannot doubt that the same wisdom which has established so great a harmony in the movement of the planetary system, that the inequalities which necessarily arise from their mutual action arrive at a maximum, and then disappear, will also have made provision for the future stability of the system.[43]

Since Laplace was concerned with eliminating providential order, he proved (within the limits of the formal rigour that was considered sufficient by mathematicians of his age) that the mutual gravitational influence of the planets cannot disrupt the system.[44] But this is an empirical, not a metaphysical, conclusion which is valid only if other factors are excluded, that is, if it is assumed that the solar system is isolated in the universe, that the Sun does not suffer alteration, and that no other matter and no other forces beside gravitation and inertia are present in the space where the Sun and the planets move.

Interpreting Laplace as supporting the theological assumptions of Newton has destroyed the scientific achievements of the Renaissance. We are back at scholasticism, and Aristotle is again *il maestro di color che sanno* on an issue that Galileo considered central to the new thought. In the First Day in the *Dialogue on the Great World Systems*, which is concerned with the refutation of the concept of the immutability of the heavens, the great astronomer formulated his creed in these unequivocal terms:

> I cannot without great wonder, nay more, disbelief, hear it being attributed to natural bodies as a great honour and perfection that they are impassible, immutable, inalterable, etc.: as, conversely, I hear it esteemed a great imperfection to be alterable, generable, mutable, etc. It is my opinion that the Earth is very noble and admirable by reason of the many and different alterations, mutations, generations, etc., which incessantly occur in it . . . I say the same concerning the Moon, Jupiter, and all the other globes of the Universe . . . These men who so extol incorruptibility, inalterability, etc., speak thus, I believe, out of the great desire they have to live long and for fear of death . . .[45]

Galileo is in precise agreement with Dewey's argument and with Velikovsky's psychological assumption.

Laplace was interpreted to meet the psychological need to believe in the eternal stability of the solar system. The following quotations from *An Analytical View of Sir Isaac Newton's Principia* by H. P. Brougham and E. J. Routh are a good example of a general tendency:

> The other changes which take place in the orbits and motions of the heavenly bodies, were found by these great geometricians [Laplace and Legendre] to follow a law of periodicity which assures the eternal stability of the system.
>
> These changes in the heavenly paths and motions oscillate, as it were, round a middle point, from which they never depart on either hand, beyond a certain distance; so that at the end of thousands of years the whole system in each separate case (each body having its own secular period) returns to the exact position in which it was when these vast successions of ages began to roll.[46]

The religious tone of the presentation is obvious. Laplace is construed to be saying that heavenly bodies can have only two types of movements: cyclical movements and uniform rectilinear movements; that is, movements that are equivalent with a state of rest. It is a full return, with some added sophistication, to the Aristotelian doctrine that the heavenly bodies can have only circular motions, motions reconcilable with immobility.

FEAR AND TREMBLING

When one examines the reviews of *Worlds in Collision* written by some one hundred luminaries of our age, he observes that the civil liberty aspects of the affair (the effort to prevent the printing, the academic pressure exercised to keep reviewers in line, and the refusals to publish corrections of misstatements) recede in the face of the frightening realization that the experts to whom is entrusted the human inheritance of scientific thought, our most precious possession, can be the victims of collective hysteria. Scientist after scientist declared that the edifice of science was threatened with destruction by a book which, to hear a number of them, is full of transparent contradictions, written by a 'complete ignoramus' who ranks with the proponents of the flat-earth hypothesis. The atmosphere of panic was somewhat better justified by the opposite contention advanced by a minority of reviewers, that Velikovsky is a hoaxer so unusually well-informed in all technical details and so deft in the subtleties of scientific thinking, that the normal professional expert cannot detect the flaws of his arguments, although these must exist.

The emotional upheaval was such that the *New York Times Book Review* ten years later, in reviewing the literary events of a decade, dwelt upon the fate of 'a book which most contemporary scientists regarded as a publishing catastrophe. It stirred up all sorts of vituperation, especially among astronomers who, it may be recalled, behaved as though they had been stung by a hornet from outer space'.[47] One should peruse the literature of the hundred years that followed Copernicus's work, to assemble an equivalent collection of bizarre and ridicu-

lous arguments used in the refutation of a theory. To cite one of the best publicized instances: a popular argument against Copernicus was that if the Earth moved, human beings would be thrown into space; similarly, the mimeographed memorandum distributed by the Harvard Observatory, and later several other astronomers, contended that if the Earth's rotation had been arrested, as Velikovsky suggested, human beings would have been projected into space along with all objects not anchored to the Earth.[48] This argument completely ignores the possibility of gentle deceleration and attributes gravitational effects, apparently, to the constancy of the Earth's rotation. The natural scientists who gave Velikovsky's evidence the benefit of objective examination were few. Some reviewers, after boasting that they had not read the book, delivered themselves of Catilinarian orations against the crime of Velikovsky.

In spite of the variety of emotional expressions, the greatest number of reviews written by natural scientists, when reduced to the scientifically significant points, repeat monotonously the same general arguments. They appeal to the 'laws of nature', without any further specification, and keep iterating the names of Newton and Laplace, as if they were an incantation, without referring to any specific passage or section of their works. The stereotype is varied only by the late President of the American Astronomical Society, Otto Struve, who in a review entitled 'Copernicus, Who Was He?' (*New York Herald Tribune Book Review*, April 2, 1950), declared that the trouble was that Velikovsky had never heard of Copernicus and was refuted by the Copernican doctrine.

The psychological assumption that gave Velikovsky his original subjective stimulus to investigate ancient traditions, namely that mankind lives in subconscious fear of cosmic cataclysms, could explain the panic and the emotional irrationality of many reviewers. A valuable clue to the cause of such a reaction is given by the professor of philosophy at St Louis University[49] who, while associating himself with the effort of the scientists to suppress the book, complained that they did not fully realize the enormity of the crime committed by the publishing industry, for the book destroyed the foundation of Judeo-Christian beliefs. The article concluded that the Catholic Church should come to the rescue by placing the book on the *Index*. But, after the painful experience with Galileo, the Catholic Church has accumulated more wisdom in scientific epistemology than that revealed by our scientific community.

The Cardinal Bellarmine of this case was Professor Harlow Shapley who was indefatigable in his campaign, started before the publication of the book, to alarm the scientific world of the impending catastrophe. How similar are the two personalities! Cardinal Bellarmine was the epitome of the bureaucratic personality and Shapley has devoted his life to the new Leviathan of scientific bureaucracy. The spirit of the new bureaucracy was revealed by the A.A.A.S. meeting (Dec. 30, 1950) held in response to Velikovsky's book. At that meeting it was proposed that henceforth any publication that presents new scientific hypotheses should not be allowed to be printed without the *Imprimatur* of a proper professional body.[50]

Every bureaucratic organization that wants to be accountable only to itself attempts to base its power on a transcendental absolute, and Velikovsky was threatening the transcendental absolute of the church of scientism. The reaction against Velikovsky's book confirms once more the common observation that the great mass of natural scientists has not yet assimilated the implications of the great scientific transformation that started at the end of the last century (on the foundations laid by Berkeley, Hume, and Hegel), and clings to scientism, the crude mechanical determinism of the eighteenth century, with insufficient awareness of all the knowledge that has been accumulated in two hundred years on the problem of human perception.[51] What has happened is that when science was still operating on scholastic premises, there were developed mechanical clocks. Since early clocks were connected with astronomy and often took the form of orreries, they influenced the interpretation of the cosmological revolution brought about by Copernicus, Bruno, and Galileo. The recent book, *The Myth of Metaphor* (New Haven, 1962), by the philosopher Colin Murray Turbayne, who explicitly appeals to the arguments of Berkeley and Hume, examines the pervading influence of the metaphor of the mechanical clock and observes, in the Introduction, that as a result of it there has been 'founded a church, more powerful than that founded by Peter and Paul, whose dogmas are now so entrenched that anyone who tries to re-allocate the facts is guilty of more than heresy; he is opposing scientific truth'.

In the Velikovsky–Shapley correpondence of 1946, when Velikovsky offered to submit to crucial tests before publishing his book, Shapley took a position similar to that of Bellarmine: one should not test Velikovsky's hypotheses about the physical characteristics of Venus, such as high temperature and atmosphere of hydrocarbon gases, unless he first agreed to frame them within the proper scheme of metaphysical presuppositions. What Shapley had in mind was the dogma of the absolute stability of the solar system.[52] Velikovsky forced the scientists to become well aware that proof of this postulate does not exist.

Scores of reviews were remarkable for the violence of expression and the jejune poverty of the contents. Often columns of denunciation were not followed by a single argument. The case of Harrison Brown is a good example of those who proclaimed that they had peremptory arguments galore, but did not submit a single one. Only a few scientists of note showed a spirit of scholarly cooperation by providing friendly criticism and additional information. Among them were W. S. Adams, G. Atwater, V. A. Bailey, V. Bargmann, A. Einstein, A. Goldsmith, H. H. Hess, H. S. Jones, J. S. Miller, P. L. Mercanton, C. W. van der Merwe, L. Motz, and S. K. Vsekhsviatsky. In contrast with the rational attitude of these men, several other great names affixed their signatures to statements that competent scholars know to be incorrect.

In order to prove the eternal stability of the solar system, scholar after scholar insisted that records document that planetary motions and eclipses have conformed to the present pattern from the origin of writing at the beginning of the third millennium B.C. But this is known not to be so: records proving such assertions do not exist for the period preceding the year 747 B.C. The aforementioned claim is so manifestly incorrect that, when it appeared for the first time in the *New York Times Book Review* (April 2, 1950), Velikovsky for once obtained the satisfaction of a retraction, but the assertion continued to appear in scholarly publications. The most serious effort to prove the basic postulate of Velikovsky's opponents was that of the astronomer John Q. Stewart of Princeton University, who debating with Velikovsky in the pages of *Harper's Magazine* (June, 1951), argued that Venus could not have entered into orbit after the creation of the solar system because this would contradict Bode's Law. What this so-called law amounts to is a mnemonic formula which gives with rough approximation the planets' distances from the Sun, and which has no basis in the gravitational theory.

The almost childish misrepresentations of the available scientific evidence can be explained by the circumstance that many scholars associated Velikovsky's book with their worst personal fears. Astronomers saw the book as a defence of astrology; professors linked it with the McCarthy investigations; a professor at Southern Methodist University declared that it would subvert our traditional way of life more radically than would communism and prostitution combined; and J. B. S. Haldane saw it as fitting into the plans of the American warmongers to start an atomic war.[53]

Leaders in science accused Velikovsky of encouraging belief in sorcery, witchcraft, and demonic possession. Since, however, a good number of his postulates, especially those listed as crucial in the final pages of *Worlds in Collision*, have been confirmed by subsequent discoveries, the new strategy of retreat is the assertion, heard with increasing frequency, that these predictions were lucky guesses: it follows that Velikovsky has gambled and won the longest shot in history. It could therefore be argued that the accusation of witchcraft stands.

On the issue of what constitutes or does not constitute superstitious thinking, natural scientists have had their signals crossed for a long time. 'A true son of the Enlightenment', the great naturalist Buffon (1707–88), in 1749 opened his monumental *Histoire naturelle, générale et particulière*, the most comprehensive effort since Aristotle to gather in one body all scientific knowledge, with a condemnation of Whiston.[54] This ferocious onslaught put the tombstone on Whiston's reputation, whereas up to that point it had been Newton's view of the history of the solar system that had been on the defensive among scholars.[55] Since he believed that the mechanism of planetary motions is so well contrived that its origin could not be ascribed to a series of accidental events, Buffon suggested that it came into existence as the result of the impact of a comet on the Sun; for this reason he could not object to Whiston on mechanical grounds, but resorted to theological arguments. After having presented a mocking summary of his hypotheses, Buffon declared:

> I shall make only one remark upon this system, of which I have given a faithful abridgement. Whenever men are so presumptuous as to attempt a physical explanation of theological truths, whenever they allow themselves to interpret the sacred text by views that are purely human; . . . they must necessarily involve themselves in obscurity, and tumble into a chaos of confusion like the author of this whimsical system, which notwithstanding all its absurdities has been received with great applause.[56]

Whiston was ridiculed for quoting the Old Testament in matters of astronomy and at the same time, condemned for not having taken literally the story of creation in Genesis: 'He says that the common notion of the work of six days is absolutely false, and that Moses' description is not an exact and philosophical account of the origin of the universe.' On the first point Buffon declared that the true naturalist must leave the interpretation of the Scriptures to the theologians, and on the second point he agreed with Newton that the solar system is so exquisitely designed to operate 'in the most perfect manner' that it cannot have changed since its creation. Modern interpreters of the thought of Buffon are perplexed because he appears to be a rank mechanical materialist, whereas he put at the head of the fourth volume a letter to the Faculty of Theology of Paris that begins with this profession: 'I declare that I do not have any intention of contradicting the text of the Scriptures, that I firmly believe all that they report about creation, both in relation to time sequence and to factual circumstances.'[57] In his writings he delved at great length into problems of scientific method in order to maintain that hypotheses must be built solely on the painstaking gathering of facts, monuments, experiences: but apparently, the narratives of mankind's history do not fit into any of these categories, whereas Newton's adaptation of the creation story of Genesis does.

Buffon's intellectual confusion persists among our contemporary scientists: Kirtley F. Mather,[58] Edward U. Condon,[59] and J. B. S. Haldane[60] alleged Velikovsky was a rationalist and an enemy of religious faith; many, among them Otto Struve, accused him of trying to subvert science for the sake of religious superstition and biblical fundamentalism. Obviously, *odium theologale* is not a monopoly of the so-called dark ages.

Frank Manuel came close to the truth in his book, *The Eighteenth Century Confronts the Gods* (Cambridge, 1959), where he acknowledged that Newton was deeply involved in controversies about the significance of ancient mythology (pp. 85–128). Newton championed euhemerism, the theory that myths were based upon the lives of historical personages, for by this doctrine he hoped to discredit the references to astronomical and other natural events in myths – aspects of mythology so frequently cited by his opponents. Manuel has elegantly summarized (pp. 210–27) the ideas of a prominent antagonist of Newton whose views Velikovsky has revived: Nicolas-Antoine Boulanger (1722–59). Author of the entry 'Deluge' for the *Encyclopédie*, Boulanger also wrote *L'Antiquité dévoilée par ses usages, ou examen critique des principales opinions, cérémonies et institutions religieuses et politiques des différens peuples de la terre* (Amsterdam, 1766). In this work he analyzed the cosmogonies and mythologies of several farspread peoples of the Earth, such as Germans, Greeks, Jews, Arabs, Hindus, Chinese, Japanese, Peruvians, Mexicans, and Caribs, concluding that rites, ceremonials, and myths reflect the fact that the human race was subjected to a series of cosmic convulsions for which he also considered the geological and paleontological evidence. He argued that these catastrophes shaped the human mind, causing among other things a deepseated psychological trauma:

> We still tremble today as a consequence of the deluge and our institutions still pass on to us the fears and the apocalyptic ideas of our first fathers. Terror survives from race to race . . . The child will dread in perpetuity what frightens his ancestors. (III, 316)

Boulanger explained by these fears the human tendency to ideological intolerance, and his hypothesis seems to be confirmed by the reactions of the academy to Velikovsky's work:

> We shall there see the origin of the terrors which throughout the ages have alarmed the minds of men always possessed by ideas of the devastation of the world. There we shall see generated the destructive fanaticism, the enthusiasm which leads men to commit the greatest excesses against themselves and against their fellows, the spirit of persecution and intolerance which under the name of zeal makes man believe that he has the right to torment those who do not adore with him the same celestial monarch, or who do not have the same opinion he does about His essence or His cult. (III, 348–49)

When the 'Velikovsky affair' is considered in the light of the history of science it loses its puzzling qualities.

Velikovsky saw what other scholars were not able to see because he relied on pieces of evidence that they had chosen to neglect, namely the accumulated records of human experience. Natural scientists who scorn these records put themselves in the position of the early astronomers who held that no truly respectable scholar should resort to the telescope. In only thirteen years a number of fundamental discoveries, predicted by Velikovsky, have demonstrated the value of his method. And one could have predicted that the academic world would react to his thesis with a most unscholarly fury, even with personal vindictiveness: the record shows that astronomers hold to a peculiar dogma akin to the biblical story of Creation, that the solar system has remained unchanged since it was created eons ago, and their assumption has of necessity determined the views of geologists and historical biologists. This dogma, being basically of theological and not scientific nature, is grounded itself on fear, as Galileo and Laplace have pointed out. The evidence is that the dogma is groundless but the fear real. This was the principal reason for the prolonged emotional outburst in which almost the entire scientific community of the 1950's took part, an outburst of what Soren Kierkegaard termed 'fear and trembling'.

It is now time for a sober and factual reconsideration; William James properly called 'tough minded' those who can face reality and who do not have *a priori* in uniformity and regularity. The scholars, the learned societies, the professional journals which violated, in some cases quite outrageously, the canons of proper scholarly procedure in evaluating Velikovsky's hypotheses, should undo the foolishness of the past by promoting a systematic study of what the records of antiquity can contribute to the natural sciences. Newton himself, by his extensive investigations of ancient accounts and records, recognized that his contention that the solar system has no history stands or falls on the historical record. The crux of the matter is not the validity of Velikovsky's particular historical interpretations, but whether an entire body of scientific evidence can be rejected on dogmatic premises.

REFERENCES

1. The position of Galileo on the question of magnetism is summarized in the following way by Herbert Butterfield, *The Origins of Modern Science* (New York, 1960), 142: 'Galileo at one time was prepared to adopt the more general theories of Gilbert in a vague kind of way, though he did not pretend that he had understood magnetism or the mode of its operation in the universe. He regretted that Gilbert had been so much a mere experimenter and had failed to mathematize magnetic phenomena in which we have seen to be the Galileian manner.'

2. *Op. cit.*, 158.

3. *Principia*, Ed. by Florian Cajori (Berkeley, 1946), 525. This peculiar explanation is already presented in the first edition of the *Principia*, 505: *Ascendit fumus in camino impulsu aeris cui innatat.*

4. *De natura deorum* II, 45, 115. The source of this passage is Posidonius. Whereas the cosmology of Cicero has received great attention and its sources have been traced, the cosmology of Ovid, which is an even richer source of information on ancient scientific theories, has been neglected; but the gap has now been partly filled by Walter Spöerri, *Spathellenistische Berichte über die Welt* (Basel, 1959).

5. *Op. cit.*, II, 21, 56 (Transl. Hubert M. Poteat).

6. Hermann Diels, *Die Fragmente der Vorsokratiker*, 6th ed. (Berlin, 1952), II, 387–88 (Transl. Edward S. Robinson in Werner Jaeger, *The Theology of Early Greek Philosophers* (Oxford, 1947), 187.)

7. Freud's essay has the untranslatable title 'Uber die Weltanschaung', *Gesammelte Werke* (London, 1946), 176. It is Lecture XXXV in *New Introductory Lectures on Psychoanalysis.*

8. *Of Learned Ignorance*, Transl. by Germain Heron (New Haven, 1954), Bk. II ch. XI–XII, 107–118.

9. Johannes Funck, *Chronologia cum commentariis chronologicis ab initio mundi* (Nuernberg, 1545).

10. *Opera latine conscripta*, Ed. by F. Fiorentino (Napoli, 1879), I, 1, 367.

11. *Op cit.*, I, 1, 372.

12. Cf. A. Corsano, *Il pensiero di Giordano Bruno nel suo svolgimento storico* (Firenze, 1940), 249–64.

13. *Attraction universelle et religion naturelle chez quelques commentateurs anglais de Newton* (Paris, 1938), 4.

14. Quoted from William Whiston, *Astronomical Principles of Religion Natural and Reveal'd* (London, 1717), 23. John C. Greene, when he was writing *The Death of Adam* (Ames, 1959)

and was my colleague at the University of Chicago, called to my attention, before the publication of *Worlds in Collision*, the crucial significance of Whiston's writings in the development of scientific thought.

15. *An Examination of Dr Burnet's Theory of the Earth with Remarks on Mr Whiston's New Theory of the Earth* (Oxford, 1698), 177–224.

16. William Whiston, *Memoirs of the Life and Writings of Mr William Whiston* (London, 1760), I, 293.

17. *Philosophical Transactions* XXXIII (1724–25), 118–25.

18. 2nd ed. (London, 1718), 381.

19. *Op. cit.*, 4th ed. (London, 1730), 378.

20. Letter to the Princess of Wales, November 1715, in *Correspondence Leibnitz-Clarke présentée d'après les manuscrits originaux*, Ed. by André Robinet (Paris, 1957), 22.

21. 'Newton, Isaac', *Biographie universelle, ancienne et moderne*, Published by L. G. Michaud (Paris, 1821), 127–94; cf. *Journal des savants*, April 1836, 216.

22. Cf. 'An Historical and Explanatory Appendix' by Cajori to his edition of the *Principia*.

23. Bernard Le Boyier Fontenelle, *Conversation on the Plurality of the Worlds*, Transl. from French, 2nd ed. (London, 1767), 466.

24. Quoted in *Gentleman's Magazine*, XXX (1755), January, p. 3.

25. (New Haven, 1932), 63.

26. Butterfield, *op. cit.*, 118.

27. *Principia*, 534.

28. *Loc. cit.*

29. *Oeuvres complètes* (Paris, 1884), VI, 234.

30. VII, p. cxx.

31. VII, p. cxxiv.

32. VII, p. cxxx.

33. VI, 478.

34. VII, p. cxx.

35. VII, p. 121.

36. *Ibid.*

37. VI, 235.

38. VI, 234.

39. *Ibid.* (The following translation by Kenneth Heuer, *The End of the World*, New York, 1953).

40. VI, 347.

41. VI, 479.

42. *A Philosophical Essay on Probabilities*, Transl. by F. W. Truscott and F. L. Emory (New York, 1951), Part II Ch. IX, 97.

43. David Brewster, *Memoirs of the Life, Writings, and Discoveries of Sir Isaac Newton* (Edinburgh, 1855), Vol. 1, 359–60.

44. Several reviewers stated or intimated that the Newtonian theory is absolutely confirmed by the ephemerides. But, as every

student of astronomy is taught, the Newtonian theory, in spite of the contributions of Laplace, is only nearly confirmed. The discrepancy between the predictions and the events may be explained by the inadequacy of our mathematical equipment in matters of three-body or n-body problems, or by the inadequacy of the theory, or by the possibility (which is extremely rarely mentioned in the texts of celestial mechanics) that a third factor may be at work besides gravitation and inertia.

45. *Dialogue on the Great World Systems*, Ed. by Giorgio de Santillana (Chicago, 1953), 68–9.

46. (London, 1855), 122, 124.

47. Russell Lyne, 'What are Best-sellers Made of?', November 27, 1959.

48. C. Payne-Gaposchkin, *The Reporter*, March 14, 1950; F. K. Edmondson, Indianapolis *Star*, April 9, 1950.

49. Thomas P. McTighe, *Best Sellers*, August 15, 1950.

50. *Science*, April 30, 1951.

51. Most leaders of science, except for the very top layer, reveal themselves as being naive realists without any knowledge of scientific epistemology. An expression of this is that some of them declared that Velikovsky's earlier activity in neurology and psychiatry disqualifies him from discussing questions of cosmology. However, it was just from an interest in neurology and psychiatry that Kant moved to his investigation of the phenomenology of space and time, which is the foundation of non-Euclidian geometry and Einsteinian physics; cf. F. S. C. Northrop, 'Natural Science and the Critical Philosophy of Kant', *The Heritage of Kant*, Ed. by G. P. Whitney and David F. Bowers (New York, 1962), 37–62. The fruitfulness of Kant's background is indicated by the circumstance that, in his very first essay published in 1753, he declared: 'A science of all the possible kinds of space would undoubtedly be the highest enterprise which a finite understanding could undertake in the world of geometry', and continued by considering the possibility of conceiving a space of more than three dimensions.

52. Shapley, *Flights from Chaos* (New York, 1930), 56–7, declares that the Earth has 'a quiet predictable behavior' and that 'not many catastrophes happen to the Earth, except those of its own making, like floods, earthquakes, and sudden continental shifts'. According to him the destruction caused by the impact of a small comet in the Tunguska uninhabited area of Siberia on June 30, 1908, was a unique event in history. On this occurrence, cf. V. G. Fesenkov, *Meteorika*, XX (1961), 27–31.

In the introduction to *Of Stars and Men* (Boston, 1958), 2, Shapley sums up his philosophy in these terms:

> It is a good world for many of us. Nature is reasonably benign, and good will is a common human trait. There is widespread beauty, pleasing symmetry, collaboration, lawfulness, progress

– all qualities that appeal to man-the-thinker if not always to man-the-animal. When not oppressed by hunger or cold or manmade indignities, we are inclined to contentment, sometimes to lightheartedness.

Like other militants, he seems to have identified dialectical materialism with the optimistic mechanical materialism of the eighteenth century, which rehashed the position of the most dogmatic among the scholastics. Such a position would have been too extreme even for the more critical of the scholastics, such as the nominalists. It would have been too extreme even for Plato and Aristotle. It occurs only in the more literary passages of Plato, as *Gorgias* 508 A:

> Friendship, orderliness, harmony, and justice hold together heaven and earth, and Gods and men, and because of this the whole is called an order (*kosmos*) and not disconnected chaos. Cf. G. P. Maguire, 'Plato's Theory of Natural Law', *Yale*

Classical Studies, X (1947), 178. John Wild, *Plato's Modern Enemies and the Theory of Natural Law* (Chicago, 1957), 117, observes how these passages of Plato inspired *The Laws of Ecclesiastical Policy* by the Anglican theologian Richard Hooker, a work which, as I have indicated, framed the foundations of the Newtonian ideology of the eighteenth century. But Plato deals at length with the astronomical changes and related physical disasters that have befallen the human race.

53. William A. Irwin, *Journal of Near Eastern Studies*, April 1952; Haldane, *New Statesman and Nation*, November 11, 1950.

54. *Oeuvres complètes* (Paris, 1858), I, 96–100.

55. The last time that Whiston's view was given serious consideration was in 1754 when the Berlin Academy of Science offered a prize for an essay on the question: 'Whether the Earth since its origin has undergone a change in its period of rotation, and whence this fact could be established.' Kant submitted an essay for this competition (*Werke*, Ed. by Ernst Cassirer, Berlin, 1912, I, 189–96); but, since he was an ardent Newtonian, he refused to answer the question as it was stated: 'One could investigate the question historically by considering the documents of the most ancient period of the ancient world that concern the length of the year and the intercalations . . . But in my proposal I shall not try to gain light with the help of history. I find these documents so obscure and so little trustworthy in the information that they could provide on the question before us that the theory that would have to be built on them in order to make them agree with the foundations of nature, would sound too much like an artificial construction.' He then proceeded to outline the nebular hypothesis which implies the stability of the solar system.

56. Transl. by William Smellie (London, 1791), I, 108.

57. *Oeuvres philosophiques de Buffon*, Ed. by Jean Piveteau (Paris, 1954), p. XVI.
58. *American Scientist*, Summer, 1950.
59. 'Velikovsky's Catastrophes', *New Republic*, April 24, 1950.
60. *Loc. cit.*

CUNEIFORM ASTRONOMICAL RECORDS AND CELESTIAL INSTABILITY

by Livio C. Stecchini

To prove that there are ancient records which document that in recent times the earth underwent a cataclysm of extraterrestrial origin which is precisely described and should be taken into account as an empirical datum by those whose task is to construct astronomical and cosmological theories, I shall quote the opinion of a recognized major authority on Babylonian and biblical astronomy, chronology, and mythology, Father Franze Xavier Kugler (1862–1929).

Kugler had a strictly scientific bent of mind. He started his academic career as a university lecturer of chemistry, but, after the death of Joseph Epping (1835–94), a fellow member of the Jesuit order and the founder of the study of cuneiform astronomical texts, Kugler decided to take over and continue his work and to this end became an outstanding expert on ancient astronomy and cuneiform philology. Most of his life was dedicated to the interpretation of cuneiform texts dealing with astronomy and with the related topics of chronology and mythology; the main characteristic of his method was a mathematical rigour for which he is considered still unsurpassed today.

In the latter part of his life he applied the knowledge developed in the field of cuneiform documents to the solution of related problems of biblical interpretation. His greatest contribution to the study of ancient astronomy was his approach, by which he built only from the most painstaking interpretation of specific texts and thereby cleared the field of *a priori* presuppositions and hasty generalizations.

The decipherment of cuneiform materials had produced from the very beginning an overwhelming mass of novel data which compelled thoughtful scholars to question most of the accepted notions about the development of civilization in ancient times. However, this wealth of revolutionary evidence drove a number of highly competent specialists of cuneiform philology to raise too many general questions at the same time and, in their enthusiasm for the new data before their eyes, to commit themselves to general theories without adequate empirical backing. It is true that many of these general theories were presented as merely tentative, with the purpose of stressing that most of our assumptions need to be totally revised; but the concrete result was that the debate shifted to controversies about generalities, obscuring thereby the more meaningful aspect that cuneiform texts provided a new exact historical documentation, more reliable than most of those that had been hitherto available.

Kugler insisted that one should suspend judgment and concentrate on the careful study of specific groups of documents. For this reason, only at the end of his life did he feel ready to come forth with a general theory, and less than two years before his death, he published a rather slim book entitled *Sybillinischer Sternkampf und Phaëthon in naturgeschichtlicher Beleuchtung*, 'The Sybilline Battle of the Stars and Phaethon Seen as Natural History', (Münster, 1927).

He who rested his fame on tomes which, in spite of their intrinsic clarity, are comprehensible only to the few who can understand both mathematical astronomy and cuneiform philology, issued this book as part of a series called *Zeitgemässige Beiträge*, ('Essays of Current Interest'), because, as he explains, he felt that he had a message that should affect contemporary society, since it had a great meaning for the history of culture. Kugler well understood that great innovating ideas can be made to prevail by presenting them to a public wider than the narrow specialists, who have a tendency to become prisoners of the general conceptions they have learned together with the technical routines that they have spent their lives to master. But even though Kugler intended to address himself to the general public, he could not help following his usual method, which consisted in proving a general point by concentrating on the exact technical interpretations of a few texts.

Werner Jaeger was fond of repeating to us students that the most important rule he had learned from the great Wilamowitz, was that in philology a few univocal texts have more compelling force than one hundred ambiguous ones. The trouble with this method is that it leads to the formulation of conclusions meaningful only for the wise who can understand that the revision of the interpretation of a single text may automatically imply the revision of a host of similar ones. What Kugler submitted was intended to be dynamite that should have shaken the entire field of ancient chronology and historical astronomy, but the fuse was not lit because the general public did not understand what was implied, and those who were competent to understand the implications were not psychologically ready to draw the inevitable conclusions.

The 'pressing warning' that Kugler wanted to communicate to the public was summed up by him as:

> the momentous doctrine that ancient traditions, even when they are dressed as myth and saga, cannot be dismissed lightly as fantastic, or worse, meaningless fabrications. It is particularly proper to avoid this pitfall when dealing with serious reports, especially those of religious nature such as those that occur in large number in the Old Testament.

He applied this general theory to the interpretations of the ancient texts that deal with the Battle of the Stars. He observed that these texts have been dismissed by scholars as:

> completely nonsensical and that nobody has succeeded in explaining them as a meaningful allegory, if it is not possible to interpret them as references to true cosmic occurrences . . . I have to confess that in my first occasional attempts I did not succeed any better. But, many years of experience with the

decipherment of cuneiform documents that concern the astronomical and astromythological conceptions of the Babylonians, have taught me that, in the system of ideas of the Easterners and of the ancient Orientals in particular, there is much that seems nonsensical to us Occidentals, but is in reality within the realm of factual foundations and sound logic.

When in 1966 I published a first version of the present essay, I stressed that pronunciamentos such as the two just quoted, were intended to sum up an entire life of research on ancient astronomical documents. It was the intention of Kugler that they should be taken as statements of fundamental importance for the understanding of ancient science (which is relevant to history) and for the gathering of actual empirical data of astronomy (which is relevant to natural science).

After this brief, but final and comprehensive, publication of Kugler was rescued from oblivion, it was quoted by several supporters of Velikovsky. Yet it has been ignored by his opponents, which is regrettable since I heartily desire to hear their interpretation of the astronomical records submitted by Kugler.

My essay of 1966 stimulated a writer friendly to Velikovsky's theories, Malcolm Lowery, to dedicate a learned article to the contents of Kugler's book. This article is a valuable contribution. First published in England, it was then published again in the United States in a revised form.[1] It is remarkable that the latter version of Lowery's article (which is the one I shall quote), in spite of its effort to summarize what Kugler intended to convey, had to dedicate 25 compact pages to Kugler's 52 pages. In spite of this, Lowery missed several points made by Kugler. This is not to be taken as a reflection upon Lowery's learning, which is of the highest level: for instance, he has translated well some Greek texts of astromythology which have challenged even the professional classicists. The root of the problem is that, although Kugler meant to address himself to the general public, he knew that he was uttering momentous statements and therefore tried to document every single step:

for this reason, in many cases, instead of presenting an argument in his own words, he limited himself to citing the text of ancient documents. The result is a booklet that is comprehensible only to those who are familiar with his previous publications of an extremely specialized nature.

Kugler published his booklet when he was sixty-five years old, because what he intended to issue was actually a manifesto announcing a new line of solutions for problems which had been debated since scholars first began to read the astronomical clay tablets found in Mesopotamia. Kugler had wrestled with these problems all through his scholarly life. A manifesto is a declaration of opinions and of related objectives to be pursued. In his manifesto Kugler was considering what had developed in the study of ancient astronomy in the preceding half century, and was setting aims for future research to be pursued by the next generation.

Unfortunately Kugler's manifesto was ignored by the generation that immediately followed it. This is not a unique case. Thomas S. Kuhn (*The Copernican Revolution*, Cambridge, Mass., 1957, pp. 185–6) relates that Copernicus had been 'widely recognized as one of Europe's leading astronomers' for twenty years, before he published his revolutionary book on point of death (A.D. 1543):

> Many advanced astronomical tests written during the fifty years after Copernicus' death referred to him as a 'second Ptolemy' or 'the outstanding artificer of our age'; increasingly these books borrowed data, computations, and diagrams . . . Authors who applauded his erudition, borrowed his diagrams, or quoted his determination of the distance from the earth to the moon, usually either ignored the earth's motion or dismissed it as absurd.

Today, if what Kugler stated in his booklet was put into the hands of a writer with some journalistic talent, it would be the source of a runaway bestseller. It would be expedient that this writer reserve to himself the copyright to the film version, because Hollywood would be most likely to make a bid for it. But Kugler belonged to a different generation and to a different world: he spent most of his life within the walls of Jesuit training institutions, carrying on, as a practical sideline to his reading of Sumerian and Assyrian tablets, the teaching of mathematics to his brothers of the Order.

The pivotal idea in Kugler's book is that the myth of Phaeton, one of the best known but also oddest Greek myths, was based on an actual physical occurrence which can be dated historically around 1500 B.C. According to Kugler it was at this time that there appeared in the sky a body which was more brilliant than the light of the sun and finally made an impact on the earth: 'There really were at one time simultaneous catastrophes of fire and flood.'

The myth narrates that Phaeton (The Shining One) borrowed and drove the chariot of the Sun, but was forced by the steeds that were pulling it to drive it off course through the sky and finally to drive it disastrously close to the surface of the earth. The gods had to put an end to the calamity. Phaeton was struck by a bolt of lightning and fell to earth dead. Kugler concentrates upon this myth in order to establish the principle that, if such a 'highly fantastic' story must be taken as scientific truth wrapped 'in the veil of poetry', there are other ancient myths which must be understood as having a similar basis.

Before Kugler many scholars had recognized that the myth of Phaeton refers to an event of physical nature, but they had tried to explain it as an ordinary recurring phenomenon. Some had maintained that it describes the fiery glow of particularly brilliant sunsets, and some, as the coming out of Venus as the morning star. Lowery has translated in full from the original German the pages in which Kugler lists these interpretations, in order to show how forceful Kugler was in scorning them as preposterous. This is a quotation from Lowery's translation:

> So simple, ordinary and peaceful a phenomenon as the evening sky could not provide the basis for a legend which patently

describes complicated extraordinary and violent natural events. And yet neither, on the other hand, could the appearance of Venus as the morning star awaken the idea of a universal catastrophe – even in the wildest imagination.

According to Kugler, the reality behind the myth, is that the earth was enveloped by a stream of meteorites, a stream of 'enormous width' and containing meteorites of such 'giant' size that they could cause 'great fires and violent flood waves'. He also indicated that the impact must have been preceded by the appearance in the sky of a body larger and more brilliant than the sun. He left the definition of this body open for reasons that I shall explain later.

According to Kugler, the fire of Phaeton which according to the Greeks had its main impact on Africa (some poets claimed that it caused the Africans to turn black), refers to the same event which in Greek mythology is called the Flood of Deucalion (the name by which the Greeks called the man who supposedly survived it and repopulated the land). Having identified the Fire of Phaeton and the Flood of Deucalion, Kugler proceeded to document that ancient chronologists had assigned specific dates to these two events, such as 610 years before the founding of Rome or the 67th year of Moses. Actually, Greek chronologists state that the period for which we have certain dates begins with this event. They date as contemporary the Flood of Deucalion or Ogyges in Greece, the Fire of Phaeton in Africa, and the Plagues of Egypt. Kugler left out of his account of the ancient information the detail that the foundation of Athens, that is, the city of Athena (who was the planet Venus), was made contemporary with these events. In the chronology set up by the Greek historian Ephorus (fourth century B.C.) the cataclysm took place in the year 1528/7 B.C.[2] This chronology was accepted in the chronological studies of Eratosthenes (third century B.C.) which in turn were incorporated into those of Castor of Rhodes (first century B.C.). Varro quotes Castor as his source for the information that at the time of the Flood of Ogyges 'so great a miracle happened in the star of Venus, as never was seen before nor in aftertimes: for the colour, the size, the figure and the course of it were changed. Adrastus of Cyzicus and Dion of Naples, famous mathematicians, said that this occurred in the reign of Ogyges'.[3]

Kugler concluded his quotations of the chronological texts with these words: 'Even though we do not get the notion of ascribing certain chronological value to these dates and of accepting the old chronological tables based on them (e.g., Petavius, *de doctrina temporum*), we do not have any right to deny that these traditions have a core of historical truth.' Like Velikovsky, Kugler studies both the ancient writers of chronology and the chronological investigations of Renaissance scholars. Velikovsky quotes a number of Renaissance writers who stress that ancient sources make the cataclysm contemporary with the appearance of the comet Typhon, and observe that, although this was called a comet, it had a circular shape. These Renaissance writers quote, among others, a passage of Pliny (II, XXIII, 91–92) from which one can gather that it had been disputed whether Typhon was a comet or a planet. The passage reads:

> Some comets move like planets, but others remain stationary . . . A terrible comet was seen by the people of Ethiopia and Egypt, to which Typhon the king of that period gave his name. It had the nature of a fire, twisted like a spiral, but it was dismal in appearance. Rather than a comet it was some sort of conglomeration of fire. Occasionally both planets and comets spread out a coma.

Wilhelm Gundel, a specialist in Hellenistic astromythology, in his review of Kugler's book sharply rebuked Kugler for not mentioning that all the texts similar to those examined by Kugler ascribed the catastrophe to a comet, and specifically to the comet Typhon.[4] Gundel denied to Kugler the merit of originality by remarking:

> Kugler arrives at the conclusion that the saga of Phaethon has as its historical core the appearance of a comet that was followed by a partial world fire and a flood. In support of this Kugler provides a complete detailed analysis of the saga. I can

observe that this interpretation has been already offered several times in antiquity. Probably it is based on an old Pythagorean theory of comets. The first references to it are in Plato and Aristotle, but it is presented in detail by later commentators.

It would seem that Kugler refrained from using the term *comet* because he was puzzled by the role of Venus and because the texts mention a globular body similar in apparent size and brightness to the sun. He used the term 'sunlike meteor' which sounds strange except to those who are familiar with ancient terminology. Aristotle, in order to defend the immutability of the heavens, distinguishes astronomy from meteorology and defines the latter as the study of 'the appearance in the sky of burning flames and of shooting stars and of what some call torches and horns' (*Meteor.* I 341 B). It is significant that, after having described the general topic of meteorology, Aristotle begins the treatment of it by refuting those who say that 'the comet is one of the planets' (342 B).

Gundel's criticism is not justified, because even though it is clear from Kugler's explanation of the ancient accounts that he was suggesting answers in terms of the appearance of a comet and of the impact of the comet's tail, he refrained from committing himself because he was puzzled by the role assigned to Venus in the entire event.

Having dealt with the myth of Phaeton, Kugler, in order to prove further that ancient texts that touch upon heavenly occurrences and are dismissed as fantasy or gibberish contain precise scientific information, picks as a test case the last lines of the Fifth Book of the *Sybilline Oracles*. He chose these lines (512–31) because F. W. Blass, the editor of the text of the *Sibylline Oracles*, had referred to them as 'the insane finale' of the Fifth Book, and the historian of ancient science, Edmund Hoppe, had declared that, no matter from which angle they are examined, they prove 'entirely nonsensical'.

Kugler concluded that to him, as an expert on ancient astronomy, these lines have a clear meaning, since they contain 'an elegant dressing of real natural events according to a fully unified plan'.[5]

The lines purport to describe the circumstances of the coming end of the world; they were written in the century before the birth of Christ by Greek-speaking inhabitants of Egypt, when the ancient world was agitated by the Messianic expectation of a cosmic upheaval. But the lines give an account that is so exact and technical that it must be something more than a mere mystical vision of coming destruction. Such precise astronomical details are given that, calculating by the position of the constellations around 100 B.C., the crisis began in September and reached a climax in seven months and 2.7 days, after the 7th or the 8th of April. Velikovsky has concluded on the basis of the agreement of Egyptian, Hebrew, Athenian, and Aztec traditions that the earth was hit by the tail of a comet on April 13. According to Kugler, the crisis described as the Battle of the Stars began with the appearance in the eastern sky of a body as bright as the sun and similar in apparent diameter to the sun and the moon. The light of the sun was replaced by long streams of flame crossing each other.

After the mention of these streams of flame that replaced the sun as a source of light, there follows the line, 'the Morning Star fought the battle riding on the back of Leo'. Kugler observed that this association of Venus with Leo must have had a momentous meaning for the ancients, since the several goddesses that represent Venus, such as the Phrygian Cybele, the Greek Great Mother, the Carthaginian Coelestis, had the lion as an inseparable companion. Coelestis was portrayed as riding a lion while holding a spear in her hands. In Babylonian mythology Venus as Evening Star was a goddess of love and motherhood; but as Morning Star she was a divinity of war, leader of the army of the stars, associated with the lion 'as a symbol of a power that overthrows everything'.

The Battle of the Stars ends when the attacker is defeated, falling into the ocean and setting the entire earth on fire. Kugler explained these events by bringing to bear another prophecy of the same book of the *Sibylline Oracles* (line 206–13) where, after mentioning the same positions of the stars, warning is given to the Indians and the Ethiopians to beware of a coming 'great heavenly fire on earth and a new nature from the fighting stars, when the entire land of the Ethiopians will be destroyed in fire and wailing'. The emphasis on Ethiopia is comprehensible when one considers that these texts were written in Lower Egypt.

Kugler concluded that the details of the world disaster prophesied in the *Sibylline Oracles* are materials taken over from the reports of past events, which among the Greeks were presented as the story of Phaeton.

Lowery has stated that in dealing with the Sybilline oracle Kugler retreated from his former position that some major catastrophe of extraterrestrial origin took place at the middle of the second millennium B.C., because Kugler analyzes the oracle according to the normal movement of the heavenly bodies in the year 100 B.C. In spite of his diligence and familiarity with the Greek originals, Lowery has missed the drift of Kugler's argument. First of all, it is a good guess to assume that this oracle was written in the first century B.C., the age in which the Mediterranean countries were most agitated by expectations of a messianic end of this world.[6] In the second place, Kugler wanted to indicate that the writers of the oracle were so preoccupied with solid astronomical facts that they described the successive phases of the episode of Phaeton according to what they knew about the position of the heavenly bodies in the several months of the year. It is his contention that the writers of this oracle, far from being maniacs breathing gibberish, were trying to make their prediction (based on a past historical occurrence) credible by framing it in an accurate astronomical timetable. Kugler left no doubt that he was not thinking of an ordinary movement of the heavens according to the yearly unfolding of the seasons, when he put emphasis on the line of the oracle that reads, 'the Morning Star fought the battle, riding on the back of Leo', and linked this line with the fact that, in several ancient cults of the planet Venus, the goddess was portrayed as riding on a lion.

Followers of Velikovsky may find fault with Kugler for having left the role of Venus hang loosely as an unexplained item. They do not understand that Kugler did not intend to compile a treatise of cosmology: he was broadcasting a manifesto on how texts of astromythology should be interpreted. Perhaps one can explain his approach by referring to his first academic position as a teacher of chemistry: by testing two pieces chipped out of a mountain, he proved that there was an entire gold mine to be dug out.

Lowery criticizes Kugler for not having raised the issue of catastrophism versus uniformitarianism; but Kugler was not trying to construct an astronomical theory: he was stating less and stating more, in that he was arguing that there was an entire world of astronomical knowledge to be explored. In any case, Kugler was more clearminded on the theoretical aspects of the problem than Lowery has proved to be. The latter regrets that at the end of his presentation Kugler took a stand against 'catastrophism'; that is, he dismissed as without historical significance all those passages of Greek philosophers, from Plato in his late writings to the Roman Stoics, in which mention is made of universal destructions by fire and flood, despite the fact that these passages take some elements from the myth of Phaeton.

Kugler was scientifically correct, but in a peculiar sense: these ancient writers failed to see the episode of Phaeton as a unique event. This group of philosophers was fathering modern uniformitarianism, because they were fitting the historical tradition of 'catastrophes' into a cyclical pattern of phenomena recurring at fixed intervals of time, past and future, according to an absolutely unchangeable and predictable order of the heavenly cosmos. It was *their* way of moving from a disorderly universe, now often admitted, to an *orderly progression of disorders*, which was a first step towards dropping *disorders* entirely and leaving the history of science with simple orderly progression of the ages.

PANBABYLONIANISM

Since Kugler's booklet on the myth of Phaeton has been ignored, his reputation rests on his monumental work *Sternkunde und Sterndienst in Babel*, 'Astronomical Science and Astronomical Observations at Babylon'. The first volume was published in 1907 and the second volume in 1909; supplements were issued up to 1914. The contents consist essentially in the edition, interpretation, and numerical analysis of cuneiform astronomical records. Even today it is quoted as an invaluable source of data; but those who draw from it do not mention that it was written in order to solve problems of astromythology. The two published volumes were intended to be followed by a third volume dealing with mythology; but this volume was not issued for reasons that I shall explain.

In the period that goes from the beginning of our century to the First World War, the field of ancient studies was agitated by debates about the value of a theory to which there was given the misleading name of Panbabylonianism. In order to explain how their theory came to be formulated, one would have to review the entire history of the decipherment of cuneiform languages, but here I shall limit myself to a few points. The reading of the clay tablets that were excavated in Mesopotamia after 1842 provoked a revolution in biblical studies, since it was found that many of the accounts of the Old Testament had close parallels in cuneiform narratives. A typical example is the story of the Deluge and of the Ark. To explain these parallels was a complex task which was rendered even more arduous by the circumstance that the Old Testament is sacred literature to Jews and Christians (divine revelation to the more conservative ones). The problem became extremely difficult and at the same time of utmost importance when it was realized that episodes which are common to the Old Testament and to cuneiform literature occur in the mythologies of the most diverse areas of the globe. The case of the Deluge story is the best known one. To this day scholars have not yet agreed on an explanation for these astounding parallels. Velikovsky's hypotheses constitute an effort to arrive at the solution of the problem, which obviously is central to the understanding of the development of any civilization and of civilization in general.

The decipherment of the cuneiform signs (particularly of the original Sumerian ones) had relied in part on the study of mathematics; documents dealing with measurements had been particularly useful. In the process it was found that, at the time the Sumerians were developing the art of writing, they had already established a scientific system of measures linking length, volume, and weight; the very fact that these units were sexagesimal indicates their connection with time units. Even before one began to read cuneiform tablets, it had been surmised that the measures of the ancient world derived from Mesopotamia. A highlight in the growth of cuneiform studies was a paper submitted by C. F. Lehmann-Haupt to the International Congress of Orientalist held at Stockholm in 1889; 'The Old Babylonian System of Volume and Weight as the Foundation of the Ancient System of Weight, Coinage, and Volume'. Since the notion that a single system of measures spread through the world by *diffusion* from Mesopotamia was then generally accepted, it was reasonable to infer that scientific thinking spread from the same area by *diffusion*.

Friedrich Delitzsch (1850–1922) thought of applying these notions of *diffusion* in the mathematical field to the solution of the problems of the similarities between the mythologies of the world. This scholar who was one of the most powerful minds in the field of cuneiform studies, developed a comprehensive theory which centres on two main contentions. The first is the common elements of mythologies. The second is that very early in Mesopotamia there was developed an advanced astronomical science which was carried by *diffusion* to the rest of the world in the form of mythological stories. In substance mythology would have been used as a medium for *coding* astronomical information. According to this interpretation the mythological dress would have helped in *remembering*. (According to Velikovsky's interpretation the memory of some astronomical occurrences would have been clothed in a mythical dress because a direct recollection was too traumatic.)

The reason why the Panbabylonists were hurrying to formulate a comprehensive theory, even before all the available evidence was gathered, was that cuneiform scholars were under pressure to answer to statements made by students of the Old Testament; this category included a broad range of writers, from biblical scholars to religious zealots. The discovery of the similarities between Old Testament narratives and cuneiform accounts had caused a commotion among interpreters of the Bible, whether scholarly or not. Much of what was published was irrational or irresponsible, and there was some outright exploitation of the interest of the general public. The excavation of the Tower of Babel which was then being planned by German archeologists, seemed to be symbolic of the situation; in Germany one spoke jokingly of *Babel und Bibel*, a phrase which in English was expanded into 'Babel, Bible, and babble'. The German scholars, who were the world leaders in developing the new field of cuneiform studies, felt they had the responsibility to come out with some clearcut formulation that could put an end to this confusion of tongues.

Delitzsch and his many supporters among the experts on cuneiform philology would have been on solid ground if they had stuck to their own area and investigated the assumed high level of early Mesopotamian astronomy. Instead they over-extended themselves in a sort of imperialist enthusiasm for their own discipline. For instance, they engaged in an unnecessary, and in my opinion misguided, campaign to belittle the achievements of Egyptian mathematics and astronomy. They rushed to explain the great riddle of the similarities among the mythologies of the world.

Panbabylonianism became so well established among German scholars that in 1902 Delitzsch was asked by them to present his ideas in two solemn public lectures in the presence of the Emperor. The latter was so impressed that he asked Delitzsch to repeat them for the Emperor and his court. The text of these lectures was immediately translated into English: *Babel and Bible, Two Lectures Delivered before the Members of the Deutsche Orient-Gesellschaft in the Presence of the Emperor*, (New York and London, 1903). In England too the Panbabylonist theory received so much public attention that the London *Times* of February 25, 1903, printed a letter in which Wilhelm II answered those who wondered whether he had performed his imperial duty of upholding the Christian faith.

THE ERA OF NABONASSAR

Kugler at first was sympathetic to Panbabylonianism, but later rejected it, because he became convinced that any serious astronomy could not have existed in Mesopotamia before the era of Nabonassar.

Late Mesopotamian and Hellenistic astronomers reckon the years by a chronological system called 'era of Nabonassar', which begins on February 26, 747 B.C. This era gets its name by the circumstance that, in the initial centuries, the years are counted according to a list of the years of reign of the Kings of Babylon; the first of the kings included in the list, is Nabonassar. At the time of Nabonassar, Babylon was under foreign rule and the power of its king was only nominal; in any case, as Kugler observed, no significant political event occurred during the reign of Nabonassar. Nevertheless, starting with the reign of Nabonassar there began to be kept a yearly record of outstanding political events, known as the *Babylonian Chronicle*. Since Ptolemy calculated the years by the era of Nabonassar, it continued to be used by astronomers until the Julian era was adopted as the scientific era during the Renaissance.

The common explanation for the adoption of the era of Nabonassar, which is still repeated today in standard textbooks, is that at that time in Mesopotamia there was introduced a new luni-solar calendar, which gradually was adopted in the neighbouring countries, including Greece. But Kugler realized that the introduction of this calendar was not the cause, but the result of whatever caused the adoption of the new era.

In the very first pages of the Introduction to his *Sternkunde*, Kugler states that only with the beginning of the era of Nabonassar did Babylonian and Assyrian astronomers feel the urge 'to ascertain and record the heavenly motions according to space and time by measurement and number'. Before this era the astronomers of Mesopotamia would have been only 'stargazers' (the German word *Sterngucker* has a humorous connotation which may be rendered by 'starpeeper') who were 'exceptionally inclined to fantasy' (*ausserördentlich phantasiereich*). This is indeed a strange claim, but Kugler dedicated the entire body of his *Sternkunde* to justifying it by facts and figures. In the supplements to it there is a chapter entitled triumphantly, 'Positive Proofs for the Absence of a Scientific Astronomy before the Eighth Century B.C.'

The proofs are basically of two types. First, after the beginning of the era of Nabonassar, the astronomers of Mesopotamia, for a period that lasted about two centuries, worked laboriously to ascertain some basic pieces of numerical information without which any rational study of the heavens is impossible, as, for instance, the exact day of the spring equinox. Second, the earlier astronomers of this group developed elaborate calculations which begin with basic figures set through a rough approximation. For instance, computations of the oppositions and conjunctions of the sun and the moon, made for the purpose of calculating the beginning of the new moon, would have been based on a value of the longest day which is in excess by more than ten minutes. Since some of these data could have been obtained by a minimum of diligent observation, he concluded that these astronomers liked to play with numbers and enjoyed calculations that had little to do with reality. Still he had to admit that at times one comes across figures of breathtaking accuracy.

According to Kugler there are two specific pieces of proof that astronomy began to be based on exact calculations in the era of Nabonassar. The first is that, because the list of eclipses available to Hellenistic scholars begins with the year 721 B.C., one can infer that Mesopotamian astronomers had not kept a record of eclipses before this date; any serious study of the heavens would start with such a record. Kugler was not aware of the fact, called to our attention by Velikovsky, that the Chinese list of eclipses begins at the same point of time. The second is that before the age of Nabonassar the Mesopotamian calendar appears to have been based on irregular lengths of the year and month; obviously the establishment of a reliable calendar is a prerequisite even of elementary astronomy.

Kugler fails to provide a consistent evaluation of the method of pre-Nabonassar astronomers: at times he describes them as totally oblivious of numerical data and at other times as occasionally careless. At the beginning (p. 25) of the second volume of the *Sternkunde* he hedged the statement he had made at the beginning of the first volume, by declaring that the collecting of observational data 'at least was not administered systematically'.

Kugler tried to establish why at the time of Nabonassar there would have been a striking change in the attitude towards astronomical records. At first he suggested that 'perhaps Nabonassar promoted it'; but later he recognized that Nabonassar contributed only a name to the dating system. He concluded that observers must have been influenced by some momentous astronomical occurrence. Kugler could not trace anything more significant than that, at the time, Jupiter, Venus, and Mars were in conjunction. On December 12, 747 B.C. Venus and Jupiter were at a distance of 1′ 30″ and on February 26, 746 B.C. Mars and Jupiter were at a distance of 23″. In reality these conjunctions do not provide an explanation for a total reform in the art of astronomy. If they prove anything, they give some support to Velikovsky's hypothesis that Venus, having been originally ejected from Jupiter, came to interfere with the orbit of Mars on February 26, 747 B.C. According to astrophysics, if there was a near collision, the present orbits, retrojected to the assumed time of the near collision, should indicate proximity.

Kugler had his doubts about the meaning of the era of Nabonassar, but these were assuaged by the statement of the Byzantine chronologist Syncellus that, 'Beginning with Nabonassar the Chaldeans made precise the times of the movements of the heavenly bodies'. What Kugler did not consider is that Syncellus drew on the Greek chronologists that I mentioned in the first chapter of this essay. These chronologists indicate that whatever change took place in the methods of measurement was not limited to Mesopotamia.

In my doctoral dissertation I studied the role of Pheidon, King of Argos, in Greek chronology.[7] Greek chronologists divide their system of dates, which begins with the Flood of Deucalion, into a first period called *mythikon* (period of the myths) and a second period called *historikon*. The dividing line is the date of Pheidon of Argos which was originally set in 748/7 B.C.[8] Other dates of early Greek history, such as the supposed date of the First Olympiad (776 B.C.), were calculated from this assumed date of Pheidon, who would have interfered with the Olympic Games (cf. Herodotus VI, 127). According to Greek tradition Pheidon of Argos would have invented measures of lengths, volume, and weight; but this tradition puzzled the same Greeks who reported it, since, as they say, 'measures existed even earlier'.

However, I proved to the satisfaction of my academic readers that Pheidon was an imaginary character whose name is derived from the verb *pheidomai* 'to reduce'. The earliest texts do not speak of Pheidon, which in Greek is a nickname for one who gives scanty measures, but of *pheidonia metra*, 'reduced measures'. Since in successive investigations I established that the basic units of length, volume, and weight were not changed from the Mycenean age, the only units that could have been changed would be time units.

Greek historians report that the first basis for a yearly record of events was the list of the priestesses of the Temple of Hera outside Argos. Excavations show that this temple may well have been founded in the eighth century B.C. One point can be accepted as proven, namely, that Greek chronologists set a break in the calculation of time at the middle of the eighth century B.C., independently of anything that may have happened in Mesopotamia, and that this break was connected with the units of measurement.

Possibly similar developments had occurred independently in Rome. The foundation of Rome is dated by the earliest annalist, Fabius Pictor, in 748 B.C. The foundation of Rome was ascribed to an imaginary character called Romulus after the name of the city, Rome. Romulus was followed by another imaginary character called Numa; this name is derived from an Italian modification of the Greek word *nomos*, 'norm, standard'. We are told that Numa was the second founder of Rome; his birthday was April 21, which was the supposed date of the foundation of Rome by Romulus. Numa was the first to establish a calendar 'according to exactness':[9] he would have calculated a luni-solar calendar according to the correct length of the solar year and the lunar month. Before him the Romans would have used erroneous figures for the length of the year and the month. Finally, it must be observed that, up to the second century B.C., the Roman year began on March 1, and hence we say September, October, November, December. The beginning of the era of Nabonassar has been calculated as beginning on February 26, 747 B.C., at a point which, as Kugler related, had no particular significance in the Babylonian calendar and which does not mark any turning point in the unfolding of the seasons.

Kugler probably did not know that Newton too had argued, on the basis of the Greek and Latin authors available to him, that the science of astronomy began with the era of Nabonassar. The purpose of Newton was to silence those who disputed the stability of the solar system since creation. Newton's contention that astronomical science was a late historical development, was challenged by a scholar who anticipated some of the views of the Panbabylonists, Nicolas Fréret (1688–1749), the first permanent secretary of the Academie des Inscriptions. Fréret, who is properly described as *l'un des savants les plus illustres que la France ait produit*[10] in a series of monumental studies published in the acts of this academy, foresaw the immense advances that could be made in the study of ancient history by combining linguistics, mythology, chronology, geography, astronomy, and history of science in general, taking into account the information that was beginning to be available concerning the civilization of Mesopotamia, Persia, India and China. He realized that with this material there could be obtained conclusions that not only are revolutionary, but also particularly reliable. This point is summed up in his essay, *Réflexions sur l'étude des anciennes histoires et sur le degré de certitude de leurs preuves*. He saw that the data of ancient history were in conflict with the theory of Newton. He challenged Newton's views about mythology and ancient science by which the latter tried to dismiss the evidence for changes in the solar system before the era of Nabonassar. A number of scholars of the time wrote heatedly for and against his *Défense de la chronologie fondée sur les monuments, contre le système chronologique de Newton* (Paris, 1758). The strongest argument, however, against Newton's contention that the ancient evidence on astronomical events is unreliable, is contained in Fréret's essay on ancient geodesy, in which he maintained not only that the length of circumference of the earth was well known in early times but also that the Egyptians knew the length of their country almost to the cubit.[11] In 1816, Jean-Antoine Letronne (1787–1848), after reviewing the entire documentation on the subject in a work crowned by the Académie des Inscriptions concluded that, given the precision of the Egyptian methods of geodetic surveying the declaration of Fréret 'is verified or at least ceases to be too exaggerated'.[12]

In 1972, I published the figures used by the Egyptians in calculating the length of their country at the beginning of the dynastic period and showed that they calculated the size of the earth according to a polar flattening of 1/297.75.[13] At present, I have ready for publication the Mesopotamian figures for the size of the earth, which are based on a polar flattening of 1/298.666. There are accounts that concern the discrepancy between the two sets of figures. In our own age, before the launching of satellites, it was believed that the flattening is 1/297.1. With the help of satellites it has been established that the earth flattening is 1/298.25. Using this figure and an equatorial radius of 6,378,140 metres, it has been calculated how each area of the globe is above or below the level indicated by a geometrically perfect spheroid. It happens that Egypt and Mesopotamia are among the few areas in which the actual sea level agrees with the spheroid of reference. Even before the figures of our space age were published, on purely empirical grounds I had reached the conclusion that the ancient calculations of distances within Egypt agree best of all with a flattening of 1/298.3.

In conclusion, Kugler was right in documenting that a new age in the reporting of astronomical data began with the era of Nabonassar, but the aberrant astronomical data reported for the earlier period cannot be explained by a lack of interest in precise measurements.

Kugler's criticism, which concentrated on the specific issue of the era of Nabonassar, had a sobering effect on some leading members of the Panbabylonist school. Hugo Winckler (1863–1913) and Alfred Jeremias (1864–1935) withdrew from the emotion laden debates about the value of the biblical testimony. In 1907 they began to publish a series of monographs aimed at refuting Kugler. This Series was entitled *Im Kampfe um den Alten Orient; Wehr- und Streitschriften*, 'On the Field of Battle about the Ancient Orient; Writings of Defence and Attack'; but in spite of their flamboyant heading, these monographs concentrated on what their authors knew well, cuneiform philology. General questions of comparative mythology were introduced only as far as it was necessary to interpret cuneiform texts.

In their counteroffensive Winckler and Jeremias tried to prove their case by focusing the attention on one specific item: 'the entire manner in which Venus is handled by mythology'. They observed that all the astromythologies they considered reveal consistently three features: there is a paramount concern with Venus which is described as the Queen of Heaven; the planets are listed as four, whereas Venus is grouped together with the sun and the moon; mention is made of the phases of Venus. In their opinion the last feature must have been the determining one: Venus was grouped with the sun and the moon because it has phases like the moon and was the object of particular attention because of these phases. Only advanced astronomers would have been able to observe the phases of Venus. Hence, it should be inferred that an advanced level of astronomy was reached so early in Mesopotamia as to have an echo in the mythology of distant countries.

The phases of Venus became the kingpin of Panbabylonist theory. Winckler stated that one should not be surprised at discovering that the astronomers of Mesopotamia were acquainted with them since unquestionably these astronomers had seen four satellites of Jupiter, 'which are much more difficult to observe than the phases of Venus'.

At this point Kugler felt that he could score a crushing victory over his opponents. In March of 1909 he published in *Anthropos*, an international magazine of anthropological and ethnographic studies, an article entitled *Auf den Trümmern des Panbabylonysmus*', ('On the Wreckage of Panbabylonism'). The following year he expanded it into a book.[14] His main contention was that to assume a knowledge of the phases of Venus was a patent absurdity. He remarked sarcastically (p. 58 of the book): 'The phases of Venus! If this discovery is authentic, then, oh Galileo Galilei, your fame is turning pale.' According to Kugler the Panbabylonist should have refrained from any further publication until they were ready to submit a special excursus on the physiology of the eyes of the Babylonians.

In reality Kugler was treading on slippery ground, because when in 1611 Galileo announced the discovery of the phases of Venus, some of his contemporaries immediately remarked that they seem to have been known to the ancient Greeks (I have mentioned what Sir Walter Raleigh wrote in 1616). The contemporaries of Galileo who were familiar with classical literature wondered whether Greek mythology hinted at the four satellites of Jupiter, which Galileo saw in 1610 with a telescope that enlarged thirty times. For this reason the four satellites were given the name of four mythological figures closely associated with Zeus: Io, Europa, Ganymede, and Callisto.

For that matter, the contemporaries of Galileo did not know that in Babylonian mythology the god Marduk is accompanied by four dogs. They did not know that the planet Jupiter is portrayed with satellites in the art of the Near East. Kugler did not deny that the Babylonians were acquainted with the satellites of Jupiter, but he dismissed this point as unimportant (p. 61): 'Only this is true: in most rare cases and under most favourable conditions one could have observed the satellites of Jupiter – in any case they could have been seen only for a few minutes.' They would not have been seen well enough to permit listing their appearances in astronomical tables, and only such a listing could be a proof of scientific astronomy.

On the central issue of the special treatment of Venus, Kugler granted readily that this planet forms a 'triad' with the sun and the moon. He even submitted pictures from Babylonian monuments in which Venus is grouped with the sun and the moon. But, according to Kugler, all of this can be explained by the elementary fact that occasionally Venus is bright enough to cause a pointer to cast a shadow, as the sun and the moon do, and often is bright enough to be seen during daylight. In reality, neither the Panbabylonists nor Kugler could account for the cuneiform texts in which Venus is referred to by phrases such as the 'diamond that shines like the sun' or 'lordly miraculous apparition in the middle of the sky'.

The very title of the book that Kugler published in 1910 indicates how confident he was that he had succeeded in laughing his opponents out of the scene of cuneiform studies. But their ranks received reinforcement in the person of a young recruit, Ernst Friedrich Weidner (born 1891), who was not only like them a master of cuneiform languages (he was respected as an authority throughout the following half century of his life), but was also well versed in astronomy and mathematics. Winckler and Jeremias, like other distinguished Panbabylonists such as F. E. Peiser, had declared that they were philologists whose task was merely the deciphering of the texts and that they intended to leave the task of solving the problems of astronomy to experts of that discipline.

The arguments lined up by Weidner hit Kugler so hard that in reacting he lost his balance. He stated that the texts that mention that a star was seen as being near the 'right' or 'left' crescent of Venus, really referred to the crescent of the moon (waxing or waning moon) behind which Venus was concealed at the moment; then, a short time later, he printed a special sheet in order to withdraw this interpretation. The debate between Kugler and Weidner had become so heated that their publications were dated not only by the year, but also by the month and the day.

In March 1914 Weidner published a monograph entitled *Alter und Bedeutung der babylonischen Astronomie und Astrallehre* ('Antiquity and Import of Babylonian Astronomy and Astrological Conceptions'), which was intended to be a refutation of Kugler's main contention, as stated in the Preface. Weidner felt so sure of himself that, in spite of his young age, soon after, in 1915, he issued the first instalment of a comprehensive manual of Babylonian astronomy.[15]

In the mentioned monograph Weidner saved his best argument for the last pages where he refuted Kugler on the interpretation of texts which mentioned the 'crescent' of Venus. The very last sentence of the book reads: 'Henceforth nobody will try to shake the solid fact that the Babylonians were acquainted with the phases of Venus.' But this forceful and positive statement is followed, at the bottom of the page, by the following elusive footnote: 'One may also mention that well-known staffers of astronomical observatories have assured me that, in the clear sky of the Orient, it is definitely possible to follow the phases of Venus with the naked eye.'

The quarrel between Kugler and the Panbabylonists had reached a dead end. Kugler could not deny that the phases of Venus and the satellites of Jupiter, had been observed; but his opponents could not explain how this feat had been accomplished. It was pointless for them to cite alleged expert opinions, unless they could produce living individuals who had actually seen such features of the heavens with the unaided eye. Both sides had declared that they were interested in establishing the textual record and that they did not intend any personal rancor, but in fact their exchanges had deteriorated into unconstructive vituperation. Kugler, years later, expressed regret for the asperity of his attacks on the Panbabylonists. Both Kugler and his opponents took advantage of the pause forced upon them by World War I to drop the matter entirely. However, although silence about what had been aired in the controversy may have been advantageous in terms of academic respectability, it did not contribute to the advancement of knowledge.

ON THE WRECKAGE OF PANBABYLONIANISM

Since the 'Panbabylonists' were the innovators and Kugler proved that some of their contentions were incorrect, their silence was interpreted by the academic community as a confession of defeat. But Kugler too had been forced into a corner, and kept silent after 1914. Scholars who chose to avoid thorny problems on their way to achieving academic prestige acted as if the 'Panbabylonists' had been totally refuted. Yet, even assuming that Kugler had made a 'wreck' of Panbabylonism, one should ask whether in this wreck there were pieces of valuable salvage.

A distorted view of the status of the controversy was created by the circumstance that Delitzsch, in 1920, at the age of seventy, two years before his death, aimed a Parthian shaft at his religious opponents, in which he reiterated and broadened some of the original positions of Panbabylonism. The claim that many of the most striking accounts of the Old Testament must be interpreted as astronomical information and that this information was derived from Mesopotamian scientific astronomy was presented in the context of a book entitled *Die grosse Taüschung*; the title 'The Great Fraud' refers to Old Testament religion. This book stirred a furor in Jewish and Christian religious groups and aroused all sorts of suspicion in less committed circles. Delitzsch even felt compelled to write an article in the popular press, in which he reviewed his life in order to prove that he had not been motivated by antisemitism.[16]

A standard German encyclopedia, *Brockhaus Enzyklopädie*, in the edition of 1972, in the entry 'Panbabylonismus' states the following: 'Today Panbabylonism survives only as a subject of historical interest, because in a onesided manner it reduces the history of religion to diffusionism.' This evaluation may be justifiable in relation to Delitzsch, but not in relation to the other 'Panbabylonists' who tried to avoid theological topics and concentrated on the interpretation of cuneiform records.

In 1914 they withdrew from the battle because they did not know how to respond to Kugler's documentation of the 'gross errors' in early Babylonian records. Weidner tried to answer by pointing out that there are errors of a few degrees in Ptolemy's list of the positions of fixed stars;[17] but this is a poor way of defending the high scientific level of early Mesopotamian astronomy. He might have made his point, if he had had the courage to infer from the records that Mesopotamian astronomers made use of some means of optical enlargement. But the Panbabylonists were intimidated by Kugler's statement of 1910 that, 'At the start one must relegate to the realm of illusions the assumption that the Babylonians were already acquainted with the telescope'.

They appeared ridiculous when they ascribed unusually good eyesight to the Babylonians. There is a consensus among those who deal with measurements, that the human eye cannot perceive intervals of less than a minute. It has been argued that this practical reason explains why the degree was divided into 60 minutes. An object which, because of its size and distance, subtends an arc of less than a minute of degree is perceived as a point without any recognizable shape. The apparent diameter of Venus varies from less than 10″ to 63″ when she is closest to the earth (inferior conjunction); but at the latter point she shows us her dark side (being between the Sun and the earth like a new moon), so that she is hard to observe even with a telescope. For an amateur astronomer the best time to observe Venus is about a month before and after inferior conjunction, when she appears as a thin crescent. The four satellites of Jupiter *per se* would be in the range of visible objects, since they have a brightness of stars of the fourth or fifth magnitude, but what is decisive is their angular distance from the body of Jupiter. We perceive as one light two stars that are less than 3 minutes apart.

Supporters of Velikovsky could argue that the phases of Venus were seen because there was a time when Venus came closer to the earth. In this spirit Lynn E. Rose, with the help of mathematicians and astrophysicists, has been conducting investigations aimed at establishing what may have been the orbits of the earth, Mars, and Venus before the age of Nabonassar.[18] He has gone so far as to consider the possibility that there had been a period of time in which Venus was an outer planet and Mars an inner planet. But, even if these investigations were to arrive at a wellgrounded conclusion, they could not solve all the problems raised by the Panbabylonists.

There has been a general neglect of one problem which in my opinion should be the first one to be asked in dealing with ancient astromythologies: how could Jupiter have been conceived as ruler of the gods, when the planet Jupiter, although by far the largest of the planets, appears to the naked eye as a not particularly brilliant point. However, with an enlarging tool of modest power one can see that Jupiter surpasses all other planets in apparent diameter; this diameter varies between 30″ and 50″. I do not claim that the apparent diameter of Jupiter is the only explanation for the role assigned to Jupiter by mythology, but I suggest that it may be a part of the explanation.

Since the great debates of the period that preceded World War I, scholars of ancient astronomy have avoided difficult problems. Father Johann Schaumberger in 1935 published an addition to Kugler's *Sternkunde* based upon the notes that Kugler had left unpublished at his death. Upon noticing that Kugler did not reply to Weidner's statement of 1914 about the phases of Venus, he supposed that Weidner had been refuted by implication.[19] The argument of Weidner was that cuneiform documents refer to the left and right 'horn' of Venus, using a Sumerian symbol which is used to refer to the shape of the waxing or waning moon. Schaumberger observed that there have been found texts in which the same symbol is used in relation to Mars; since the phases of Mars undoubtedly cannot be observed with the unaided eye, the symbol should not be understood as referring to a moonlike shape. He left out of consideration that Mars when in quadrature (that is, just before and after its closest approach to the earth) shows a contour similar to that of the moon in second and third quarter, and that this fact was first noticed in 1636 by Francesco Fontana with the help of a poor telescope.

The total evidence suggests to me that the astronomers of Mesopotamia made use of some sort of enlarging device.[20] But, even if one chooses to let the investigation of this possibility hang suspended in limbo, it remains that the astronomers of Mesopotamia were acquainted with the phases of Venus and Mars and with four satellites of Jupiter, and must have had some notion about the huge size of Jupiter. The question whether Mesopotamian astronomy had an influence on the astromythology of other countries may also be ignored for the time being. The essential point is that the early astronomers of Mesopotamia cannot be dismissed as fantasts who had no concern with empirical reality and lacked scientific spirit; here the Panbabylonists were right.

But, on his side, Kugler was right in pointing out that in the early cuneiform records there occur figures which seem to be gross errors, and that after the beginning of the era of Nabonassar Babylonian astronomers were conducting investigations aimed at ascertaining basic data without which any scientific study of the heavens is impossible. It must have occurred to Kugler that the explanation of these discrepancies may have been some shift in the heavenly motion in the period preceding the era of Nabonassar.

It is a fact that after 1914 Kugler suspended the publication of his major work which had given him a world-wide reputation. From the beginning he had announced that the first two volumes, which dealt with observational data, would be followed by a third volume dealing with mythology and cosmological concepts. This third volume was never published, and one must understand that the booklet of 1927 on the myth of Phaeton, in a real, if limited, sense, replaced it. The message of this booklet is not so much that the myth of Phaeton refers to a cosmic catastrophe which took place at the middle of the second millennium B.C., but that in general astro-mythologies are based on astronomical occurrences. Kugler would have granted to Velikovsky that it is perfectly legitimate to use mythological materials as a source of information about astronomical events.

In substance Kugler accepted one of the major contentions of the Panbabylonists. It may not be true that Mesopotamia was the centre of diffusion of astromythologies, but the Panbabylonists were right in pointing out that in Mesopotamia one comes across data which are superior as sources of astronomical information. The information is not only couched in the form of mythological stories, but also in the form of numerical records.

The cuneiform astronomical tablets dating before the era of Nabonassar must be taken at face value. It is no longer possible to speak of careless measurements. Since the publication of Kugler's writings these tablets have been almost completely neglected, with the result that only a fraction of what is available has been published. The collections of cuneiform astronomical tablets that are stored in some museums have been gathered from the excavation of entire astronomical libraries of Mesopotamia. The wealth of material that is available is such that it should occupy scores of scholars for several generations. But the effort would be well justified, because these tablets contain more than general accounts of the events, such as those studied by Velikovsky; they contain exact quantitative data on the basis of which it will be possible to establish on empirical, not metaphysical, foundations the history of the solar system.

REFERENCES

1. The article first appeared under the title 'F. X. Kugler – Almost a Catastrophist', in the second *Newsletter* of the Interdisciplinary Study Group, now *I.S.G. Review*. It appeared in revised form under the title 'Father Kugler's Falling Star', in *Kronos*, II (1977), No. 4.

2. Felix Jacoby, *Das Marmor Parium* (Berlin, 1904), 136–37.

3. Augustine, *City of God*, XXI, 8.

4. *Gnomon*, 1927, 449–51.

5. The Greek text of this particular oracle with an English translation and commentary, has been now provided by Lowery in *Appendix I* to his mentioned article. It must be noticed that, although the academic world has generally ignored Kugler's book, when Alfred Kurfess, *Sybillinische Weissagungen* (Berlin, 1951), published an authoritative translation with commentary upon the entire body of *Sybilline Oracles*, in relation to this particular oracle he followed Kugler's interpretation.

6. Lowery objects that Kugler was arbitrary in choosing the date of 100 B.C. for the composition of this oracle. Kugler would have just chosen a point of time in which the sky fitted the text of the oracle, although the book called the *Sybilline Oracles* most likely was put together in the second century A.D. But the date of the gathering of the oracles in a collection has no relation with the date of composition of this particular oracle.

7. *The Origin of Money in Greece* (Harvard, 1946).

8. Jacoby, *op. cit.*, 93, 158.

9. Plutarch, *Life of Numa*.

10. *Grand Dictionnaire Universel*, ed. by Pierre Larousse (Paris, 1866–90), VIII, 818, s.v. 'Nicolas Fréret'.

11. *Mémoires, Académie des Inscriptions*, XXIV (1756), 507–522.

12. *Recherches critiques, historiques et géographiques sur les fragments d'Héron d'Alexandrie* (Paris, 1851), 133.

13. *Notes on the Relation of Ancient Measures to the Great Pyramid*, published as Appendix to Peter Tompkins, *Secrets of the Great Pyramid* (New York, 1971).

14. *In Bannkreis Babels: Panbabylonistische Konstructionen und religionsgeschichtliche Tatsachen* (Munster, 1910).

15. *Handbuch der babylonischen Astronomie*, Vol. I (Leipzig, 1915).

16. 'Mein Lebenslauf', *Reclams Universum*, 36 (1920), Heft 47, 241–46.

17. *Alter und Bedetung*, 13.

18. A good sample of these investigations is provided by Lynn E. Rose and Raymond C. Vaughan, 'Velikovsky and the Sequence of Planetary Orbits', *Pensée* IV (1974), No. 3, 27–34. Cf. also *Velikovsky Reconsidered*, by the Editors of *Pensée* (Garden City, 1976), 100–133.

19. *Ergänzungsheft* 3, 302.

20. One of the few Orientalists who pays attention to this problem is H. W. F. Saggs, *The Greatness that was Babylon* (New York, 1962), 432. But Saggs assumes that the solution must of necessity be the discovery of lenses in excavations. Saggs indicates that some lenses were found. Sir Flinders Petrie too was always on the lookout for lenses in his excavations in Egypt, and reported that once he found an object that might have been a lens. I must observe that a simple glass container of the right shape, filled with water, can perform the function of a lens. Furthermore, the written and archeological evidence suggests that in the ancient world enlargement was obtained by the use of mirrors. Mirrors provide simple and powerful enlarging devices.

ASTRONOMICAL THEORY AND HISTORICAL DATA

by Livio C. Stecchini

Jupiter: 'Ah Venus, Venus! Is it possible that you will ever consider our condition even once, and yours in particular? Do you think that what humans imagine about us is true, that he among us who is old is always old, that he who is young is always young, that he who is a boy is always a boy, and thus we eternally continue as we were when first taken into heaven; and that just as paintings and portraits of ourselves on earth are always seen unchanged, so likewise here our vital complexion does not change again and again?'

GIORDANO BRUNO, *Spaccio della bestia trionfante*,
First Dialogue, First Part. Translation by Arthur D. Imerti.
(New Brunswick, 1964), 98.

In the September 1963 issue of the *American Behavioral Scientist*, my essay, 'The Inconstant Heavens', dealt with the Velikovsky controversy only tangentially and intended to limit itself to a mere gathering of its historital antecedents. The substance of what I said was that the doctrine of the eternal stability of the solar system since its creation eons ago is a theological dogma for which there has never been presented scientific evidence and that, hence, it must be concluded that the 'contention that the solar system has no history stands or falls on the historical evidence'. Yet my essay, in spite of its antiquarian intent and tone, happened to touch a most sensitive point, since it dealt with a controversy about the nature of science that has been fought for more than two thousand years.

In his last treatise, the *Laws*, Plato declares that the most dangerous and subversive doctrinaires are those who deny the eternal regularity of the heavenly bodies. According to him, no intellectual, political, or moral order can exist unless it is believed that the stars (in Greek the terms refer to the heavenly bodies in general) 'behave always in the same way according to rules of action established long ago, at some distant time beyond human understanding, and that these rules are not altered up and down, so that the stars at times change nature and now and then act in a different way with wandering and change of orbits'. (*Epinomis* 982 C.) Although Plato here states his general principle, his choice of words intimates that he had concretely in mind the contention which Aristotle too (*Meteor*, 1343A) tries to refute, that a planet may become a comet or a comet may become a planet.

On the basis of this view of astronomy Plato states that there are two conceptions of science, one that we may call *noumenic* and the other that we may call *phenomenic*. According to the first, the physical order is the manifestation of an ordering mind, a *nous*; he sums it up in these words (X 903 C): 'the ruler of the universe has ordered all things with a view to the excellence and preservation of the whole'. The essential proof of this is the system of heavenly motions.

The opposite view, which was represented by Democritus's theory of atoms and celestial bodies in collision, is summed up by Plato in these terms (X 889 B):

> They say that fire and water, and earth and air, all exist by nature and chance, and none of them by art, and that as to the bodies that come next in order – Earth, and Sun, and Moon, and stars – they have been created by means of these absolutely inanimate entities . . . After this fashion and this manner the whole heaven has been created, and all that is in heaven, as well as all animals and plants, and all the changes of seasons, having had their origin not by mind, not from any god or art, but, as I was saying, by nature and chance.

For those who uphold this second view of science, Plato recommends (X 909 A) that they be imprisoned for five years in a House of Better Judgment to be brainwashed and that, if they do not change their minds within that period, they be put to death.

This recommendation was not lost to history, for, in fact, Giordano Bruno was subjected to such treatment for seven years and, when it was seen that in spite of the repeated tortures he would not agree even to a partial recantation, he was finally put to death. It must be kept in mind that in the famous passage (*De immenso*, VI, 19; Op. lat. I, 2, 229) in which Bruno sums up his cosmology with the motto *veritas temporis filia* (a motto that was later adopted by Galileo), he refers to the mentioned passage of Artistotle about comets and takes his stand with the opponents of Aristotle. In the work entitled *Spaccio della bestia trionfante* (which means 'The Expulsion of the Triumphant Beast', that is, Platonic and Aristotelian cosmology) Bruno propounds an interpretation of ancient astromythology that is similar to that followed by Velikovsky.

The reactions to the publication of Velikovsky's books prove that those who agree with Plato are still with us. The case of the curator Gordon Atwater, who was summarily dismissed without trial from his position as Chairman of the Astronomy Department of the American Museum of Natural History and prevented from ever practising his art, indicates that the supporters of the perfection of the solar system went as far as they could in the use of repressive measures and missed only the help of the secular arm of the state.

Animistic thinking will always be with the human race and, therefore, the battle for the defence of phenomenic science will never be ended. This is well documented by a letter that the editor of the *Bulletin of Atomic Scientists*, Eugene Rabinovitch, wrote (September 9, 1964) to Professor H. H. Hess, in which he tried to justify the attack of his magazine against the contributors to the *American Behavioral Scientist*. In this letter he condemns Velikovsky, while boasting, as other scientists of his faction have done, of having never studied any of his writings, and dismisses those who advocate a free discussion on the value of Velikovsky's hypotheses as being 'behavioural scientists' who do not understand the nature of science. The fact that Rabinovitch claims a monopoly on the definition of what is science and uses the term 'behavioural scientist' as an abomination, indicates which kind of science he is upholding.

Behaviouralism is a movement which aims at introducing the scientific method propounded by Galileo, the phenomenic method, in the area of the so-called social sciences, an area infested with dogmatic, theological, metaphysical, and rhetorical thinking. Against the behaviouralists, Rabinovitch resorts to arguments *ad hominem*, imputing to them malice and obscure ulterior motives; it is a variant on the old Platonic accusation, repeated today even by many social scientists, that the use of the behavioural approach destroys necessary human certainties and subverts moral values. One could have expected from Rabinovitch, at least for the sake of rhetoric, a statement to the effect that, having examined the arguments of his opponents, he found reasons for not accepting them. But he felt the need to state that his condemnation is based on major premises and not on the study of the evidence. The alternative to such medieval scholasticism would have been to accept the method of phenomenic science.

The editors of *ABS* well know that, by dealing with the attitude of some scientists toward Velikovsky's hypotheses, they were risking the wrath of well-entrenched academic power organizations. What they wondered was whether raising this issue was worth the trouble in relation to their general aims of scientific enlightenment. The results prove that in publishing the special issue they made a wise decision, in that they struck at the roots of the opposing position.

Since this year marks the fifth centenary of the death of Nicolas of Cusa and the fourth centenary of the birth of Galileo, it is timely to remind the reader that the preservation of the scientific method established by them requires eternal vigilance. The same need for eternal vigilance has been underlined by an international magazine written in several languages and published in Italy, *Civiltá delle Macchine*, which is concerned with the problem of the role of science in contemporary society. In celebration of the fourth centenary of Galileo, this magazine came out with a special issue (May–June 1964) dedicated to the problem of scientific method. In presenting the special issue the editors stated on the first page:

> Precisely today, because the progress of science seems to shine with particular brilliance, there is a tendency to neglect some obscure forces that affect scientific progress from the inside and the outside. If it is easy to identify, at least historically, the external obstacles to scientific research (the case of Galileo is just an obstreperous example of it), one often forgets that some resistances come from the inside of science itself . . . To the obstacles that are often set by the closed-mind attitude of the humanists there is added, with more harmful consequences, the immobilism resulting from *a priori* and absolutist tenets held by some of the very people whose task is to cultivate science. This problem is treated with breadth and profundity of analysis in the article by Bruno de Finetti, who reminds us that scientific thought is 'unitary and in perpetual renewal, not fragmentary and final'.

The main article is by Professor Bruno de Finetti of the Instituto Matematico of the University of Rome, a specialist in probability theory whose main contribution to scholarship has been the analysis of the interplay of mathematical method with psychological attitudes in the structure of quantitative science.

The editorial of the magazine,[1] under the title 'Truth in Expansion', remarks that modern science was born by proclaiming the independence of science from theology and metaphysics, but that this claim of science to be a complete and autonomous source of knowledge 'has two enemies that are never tired and never defeated: on one side, there is dogmatism, which may come from inside science itself, that pretends to give absolute value to what has been already acquired to such a point as to make difficult or even impossible the introduction of new concepts, and on the other side there is scepticism which pretends to limit the cognitive aspect of science to a series of unrelated hypotheses'.

In order to illustrate this point, Professor de Finetti, in his article 'Brakes on the Path of Science',[2] gives a good deal of attention to the Velikovsky case. In his opinion, the refusal of the large majority of the academic community to discuss objectively how much is acceptable about Velikovsky's hypotheses, in the light of the present state of the empirical evidence, imparts 'one great teaching above all others', namely, that the professionalization and departmentalization of the several branches of science have become an obstacle to the necessary continuous renewal of science itself.

Scientists forget that the division of science into disciplines exists for the sake of science and come to think that science exists for the preservation of the boundaries of the several disciplines and the related academic organizational structures. In de Finetti's opinion, the uproar against Velikovsky resulted from his trying to relate the art of interpreting historical memories and documents to astronomical and physical research. What was felt as a threat was the possibility, for instance, that the space probes might help to solve problems in the field of the history of ancient civilizations. Scholars refused to discuss the merits and demerits of Velikovsky's studies, because they were concerned with a larger issue, the fact that he challenged 'the right of their fossilized brains to rest in peace' with the skills and problems already established. The defence of this vested interest in the preservation of disciplinary boundaries may transform 'each clan of specialists and the great clan of scientists in general into a sort of despotic and irresponsible mafia'.

Here we are reminded of one of the distinctive contributions to behavioural science made by Harold D. Lasswell, who has demonstrated that the conflict for money, power, and prestige among different skills, and in particular for the preservation of old skills against new skills, can be as explosive in society as the class struggle is according to Karl Marx.

AGAINST HISTORICAL SCIENCE

Professor de Finetti makes us realize that the ideologists who planned the opposition to Velikovsky, even before his first book was published, were successful in their efforts to mobilize the academic community because they were raising what politicians call a bread-and-butter issue, the fear of natural scientists that they might be compelled to learn something about historical evidence. The ideological issue of denying that the solar system has a history becomes intertwined with the issue of denying the significance of historical evidence.

As I demonstrated, the scientific evidence for the non-historicity of the solar system does not exist: if this evidence existed, the opponents of Velikovsky could simply point to it and the debate would be closed. But, since this evidence does not exist, the supporters of the stability of the solar system have been forced to carry the battle into the field of history itself. They are engaged in the strange manoeuvre of denying the historicity of the solar system by denying the value of historical science. This is clearly indicated by the fact that, in the campaign against Velikovsky of fourteen years ago, at the meeting of the American Philosophical Society which was intended to dispose of the issue forever, the performer was the astronomer Cecilia Payne-Gaposchkin, who did not discuss astronomy, but made a mockery of historical science.

Rule number one of this discipline is that one must quote the texts correctly and she demonstrated *ad abundantiam* how this rule can be violated. Similarly, the renewed onslaught by the *Bulletin of the Atomic Scientists* was concentrated on the field of historical science. In the field of physical science the supporters of the Newtonian theology of the solar system not only cannot find proofs, but find themselves confronted with a steadily increasing number of discoveries (many of them predicted by Velikovsky) which flatly contradict it. The space probes have an effect on this theology that is as devastating as that exercised by the telescope on the similar theology defended by the opponents of Galileo.

Therefore these dogmatists are forced into the position of defending scepticism. As de Finetti observes, they are forced to deny the unitary character of science. In the area of natural science they have to claim that astrophysical data, such as magnetic fields, radio noises, hot temperature and hydrocarbon gases of Venus, gases in the moon, and geological data, such as Worzel layer, tektites, the recent origin of at least some oil deposits, the results of paleomagnetic analysis, are isolated phenomena. In the field of historical science they have to prove that this discipline is not science and cannot provide reliable data of any sort. This is the reason why Margolis in the *Bulletin of the Atomic Scientists* followed in the footsteps of Madame Payne-Gaposchkin in presenting an outrageous caricature of historical documentation. He showed his contempt by stating that in a few hours of study of Egyptology he could contradict an interpretation laboriously arrived at by Velikovsky and supported by the authority of William F. Albright. Margolis trampled on the most precious tenets of historical research: he misquoted passage after passage, referred to statements that did not exist, submitted erroneous translations, and subverted the most elementary rules of linguistics.

But his quarrel is not with Velikovsky, not with me, not with the *American Behavioral Scientists*; it is a quarrel with an entire scientific tradition that dates from the revival of scientific learning in the Renaissance. In my essay, having assumed that any person who enters into discussions of scientific method is familiar with at least the main work of Galileo, I limited myself to quoting the complementary opinions expressed in less known works of other major figures of science. But, since there has been an effort to muddy the waters, I am willing to rest my case on this passage in which Galileo expressed, with superb lucidity of thought and expression, the epistemological conflict between his spokesman and his Aristotelian opponent:

> *Salviatus*: But to give Simplicius yet fuller satisfaction, and to reclaim him, if possible, from his errors, I affirm that we have in our age new occurrences and observations and such that I doubt not in the least that, if Aristotle were here today, they would make him change his opinion. This may be easily gathered from the very way he argues, for when he writes that he esteems the heavens unalterable because no new thing was seen to be born there, or any old one to be dissolved, he seems to imply that, if he were to see any such accident, he would then hold the contrary and put observation before natural reason (as indeed is right); for, had he not made any reckoning of the senses, he would not have then argued immutability from not seeing any change.
>
> *Simplicius*: Aristotle deduced his principal argument *a priori*, showing the necessity of the unalterability of heaven by natural, manifest, and clear principles, and then established it *a posteriori* by sense and the traditions of the ancients.[3]

The astronomical question, whether the solar system is unalterable, cannot be settled *a priori*, but must be settled *a posteriori*, by examining 'the traditions of the ancients'. Galileo stated that astronomical theories about the structure of the solar system must stand or fall on the historical record. I have shown that even Newton, although he did not like what he found in the historical record, granted as much. One cannot defend Newton's cosmology without defending also the conclusions of his historical studies. Hence, the astronomer who wants to pronounce himself today on the mechanics of the solar system cannot ignore the historical documentation and must depend on the results of historical scholarship.

The writer of the *Bulletin* tries to reduce a controversy on the nature of scientific method to arguments *ad hominem*. He asserts that Velikovsky is a person of dubious morality, a peddler of hokum, and hence those who advocate investigations in the same direction are equally tarnished. Similarly, Eugene Rabinovitch, on the one side, in his letter to Professor Hess explaining the editorial policy of the *Bulletin*, accuses the 'behavioural scientists' of unconfessed invidious intents, and, on the other side, in his letter (June 23, 1964) to the editor of *ABS*, asserts that historical evidence is 'inevitably tentative and often controversial matter'.

Indeed, any phenomenic science, any science which is not based on noumenic premises dogmatically accepted, is bound to be 'inevitably tentative and often controversial matter'. If one reads the record of the trial of Galileo, one sees that this was the main argument against him. This appears to be the reason why he chose to sign a recantation; he granted that to those who were asking for absolute certainty his science was of no avail.

History (unless one believes in a dogmatic and scholastic Marxism which today is outmoded even in the Soviet Union[4]) is an empirical science, a behavioural science, indeed, *cum pace Rabinovitchi*. As such it cannot produce the apodictic certainty to which the *Bulletin*, with Plato, would like to restrict the name of science; but it can be shown that history can produce a body of information that is specific and positively significant, even in the area of celestial phenomena. Historical science, properly used, achieves the same results as any other science. The only limit that is specific to this discipline is that it depends on the records of the past that happen to be preserved and it cannot manufacture them if by chance they have been destroyed. Hence, the problem is the factual one of assessing how many and which kind of documents are available. In the following pages I shall address myself to this problem, relying on the opinion of scholars other than Velikovsky and stressing the significance of documents that do not constitute the major element of his argumentation.

REFERENCES

1. Page 17. The editorial is signed by the Director, Francesco d'Arcais.

2. Pages 19–24.

3. Dialogue on the Great World Systems, ed. by Giorgio de Santillana (Chicago: U. of Chicago Press, 1953), p. 59.

4. The likelihood of recent shifts in the structure of the solar system, with resulting catastrophes upon earth, has been discussed over the past three years in the general science magazine, *Nauka i Zhizn'* (*Science and Life*). The articles quote both physical and historical evidence, similar in kind to, and at times identical with, material adduced by Velikovsky.

THE SCIENTIFIC RECEPTION SYSTEM

by Alfred de Grazia

When a scientist writes a book of his controlled experiences, a publisher ponders its audience, and a colleague weights its value, the special order of human relations called science is in being. Their patterns of motive and behaviour emerge from and return to the larger sphere of social behaviour. They are different from, yet the same as the general social order.

Perhaps then never can it be said that 'this could only happen in science'; in a scientific sense science cannot follow laws uniquely its own. Also it would be exceedingly risky to reason that, though possessed of a basis of generally understood behaviour, science receives from somewhere a unique moral code that cannot be evaluated by general moral codes.

THE CONCEPT OF RECEPTION SYSTEM

There is, in every social order, a reception system. In the sub-order of scientific behaviour, the reception system consists of the criteria whereby scientists, their beliefs, and their practices are adjudged by scientists as a community to be worthy, true, and effective.

The importance of a reception system in every social order is manifest. The reception system shapes the character of new recruits to the order and therefore forms the product of the order. If the term itself is new, the reception processes in themselves are well known. Whenever a scientist concerns himself with the training methods and the curriculum of his field, or with its system of publications and the criteria for evaluating work, he contributes to the building or enforcement of the order.

Political parties and mass movements, religious groups, business enterprises, bureaucracies, and a host of voluntary associations have similar reception systems, and of course there is little difference between the natural and social sciences in this regard.

The principal elements of the reception system are doctrines and an operational formula with typical tactics of acceptance and rejection. Thus, 'truth according to empirical principles' constitutes a doctrine of the science reception system. It is generally believed that some criteria satisfying this goal must be extracted from those who contend for acceptance. The operational formula sets forth a number of methods by which behaviours are to be tested to determine the degree to which they fulfill the obligation of 'empirical truth'. And a set of tactics is employed to admit or reject offerings determined to have succeeded or failed according to the formula. For instance, a journal will return a manuscript with a polite note of refusal or fit an article meeting its criteria into its publishing schedule. Ultimately the social and scientific consequences of this reception system must be discovered and analyzed in order to pass judgment upon the system and to enable an applied science of science to revise and reform doctrines, formulae, and tactics.

Such a reception system may be postulated to operate when a person, belief, or practice is projected upon the perceptive and cognitive screen of scientists with an implicit or explicit demand for acceptance. We therefore view Dr Velikovsky, his theories, and his practices as a case relevant to the study of the reception system of science.

The interpretation of the science reception system may be facilitated by fitting its activity to assumed models. Models of social behaviour in a given setting can be numerous, since the construction of any single model depends only on the perception of a patterned dynamic of actions, and since the validity (and utility) of such models is theoretical and statistical, not absolute. The number of principal models may be reduced to one in the case of purely-motivated and purely-acted behaviour, or to several in the case of the usual complicated performance of social institutions. In the case of the scientific reception system the problem is to determine what postulated pattern or complex of motives and behaviour best accounts for what happens in most cases coming before the reception system for consideration. What accounts for the favourable or unfavourable reception of men, beliefs and practices?

The historical sociology of science is obliged, in the long run, to provide materials and analysis in a large enough number of cases to verify empirically that one or several given models explain in great part and usefully the vast majority of relevant actions. A single case, as the one of Velikovsky, can contribute to an ultimate historical sociology of science, but cannot in itself prove the validity of the models used.

However, if there is support from materials already known to us, and from such writings as the preceeding article by Livio Stecchini, we would be inclined to credit the hypothetical model with somewhat more validity than the single case would warrant *per se*. Moreover, in order for a rule of law to characterize the behaviour of social groups, justice has ultimately to be defined in relation to singular parties. Therefore a finding of injustice in a single case is sufficient to provide grounds for remedial action then and there, without resort to laws of averages, or the 'long run'. If a postulated model of the scientific reception system fits a case well, and is believed to be either personally unjust[1] or socially (scientifically) harmful, then the question will naturally arise whether the case should be reheard, as well as whether this condition is typical, this model is normal, and the public or social policies (rules) of scientific behaviour should be revised.

Four models appear to explain a good deal of scientific reception-system behaviour. They may be called the Rationalistic Model, the Indeterminacy Model, the Power Model, and the Dogmatic Model.

The rationalistic reception system is openly displayed by scientists in general as the 'scientific method'. It is considered in proto-thought[2] to be the exclusive determinant of admission policies to the corpus of science. Its goal is truth, enlightenment, knowledge, or just simply 'science'. It postulates a purity of science, namely that the propositions and methods of scientists are arrived at only by efficient, logico-empirical operations. Personal animosities, psychopathology, politics and other social conditions are ignored, reduced in importance, or denied a place in the scheme of science.

The rationalistic model, defender of the purity of science, requires that the 'scientific method' be pursued in validating fact and proposition. It demands control, prefers quantification, and honours prediction as marks of scientific work. It asserts that new material offered for scientific examination and appraisal will be fairly and openly dealt with, will be communicated freely to whoever may be in a position to judge its merits, and will, upon approval, convey credit to its author. It resembles the rule of law in court systems in that a set of procedures for arriving at truth are to be required of all men regardless of their degree of authority, their previous record, and the resources they command.

These are some of the doctrinal, procedural, and tactical elements in the rationalistic model. The socio-scientific consequences that are deemed valuable are 'truths'; by the operation of this process more and greater 'truths' will be discovered. The truth will be communicated. As its value becomes apparent, the truth will be used in all applied fields that are related.

Those who operate in the name of this model tend to deny a sociology of science. The concept of sociology implies that men are conditioned in their behaviour by social factors lying outside of the intellect. The scope of the psychology of science is similarly reduced, creating a constant tendency to believe in absolute realities. Furthermore, since those under the rationalistic spell claim that after all 'there is an objective method of testing reality and any reasonable person can see the truth when it is presented to him', they tend to dismiss political problems as irrelevant, and to dismiss power as a factor in the building of the corpus of science.

In detailing the rationalistic model, some of the behaviour of scientists in the Velikovsky case that exemplify the use or non-use of the rules of the model can be described. To be noted first of all is that the model is itself used as a mode of attack upon Velikovsky. This is immediately apparent when articles and correspondence dealing with his work are examined. Perhaps the most indignant published attacks against Velikovsky occur at the hand of Professor Cecilia Payne-Gaposchkin. She precedes them, however, with a statement of the rationalistic doctrine of science, for she says:

> In these days of loyalty oaths, scientists may congratulate themselves that they are not, as such, required to swear to anything. Nonetheless, every scientific man, every man who devotes his life sincerely to the advancement of knowledge, commits himself to certain loyalties. His loyalties are to principles, not to dogmas; to respect for evidence – all the evidence, not merely such as fulfills his expectations, and respect for those formulations that embody the evidence. We who are engaged in research are not concerned in preserving the existing framework of theories. We spend our lives searching for the wherewithal to modify and supplant them. The discovery of discordant facts is cause for rejoicing, not consternation. If Velikovsky had adduced any real evidence that compelled a revision of the laws of celestial mechanics, astronomers would have accepted the facts, and the challenge, with delight. His supporters imagine that we are shaking in our shoes. This is partly true: we *are* shaking, but with laughter . . . Our critical faculties have not been developed only by dealing with cranks, for there is plenty of loose thinking and misinterpretation of evidence within the fold. The outsider might be surprised to learn how little mercy we have on, or ask from, our fellow scientists.[3]

The *Scientific Monthly*, which was later incorporated into the magazine *Science*, also printed an article by a professor of philosophy that endeavoured to explain to the public the criteria that distinguish scientists from cranks. We quote the rationalistic doctrine as carried there:

> We have already said that there is hardly a scientific theory that is not questioned by some scientist of repute. This is so because science is unfinished business, an inquiry into the habits of nature where all the evidence is not in and where much of the evidence that is in has not been digested. Under these conditions there is room for minority opinions, some of which will, no doubt, turn out to be correct. There is a parallel here, though, with horse racing: long shots run in the races, and some will no doubt win. But a sports commentator who expected a long shot to win in almost every race would be open to suspicion. In the same way, the man who accepts one or two scientific 'long shots' is perfectly reasonable, but when a man accepts too many of them, his scientific standing becomes suspect. The crank is one who tries to force nature into his own selected pattern; the evidence of strain resulting from this practice is divergence from currently accepted views.[4]

Harrison Brown, reviewing Velikovsky's work in the *Scientific American*, similarly asserts several rules of the science reception system:

> . . . In the world of science the individual research worker usually subjects his results and theories to his fellow scientists for searching criticism and checking before making his results known to the public. If he is at a university he first solicits the criticisms of his local colleagues, following which he shows his results to scientists in other institutions. When he has thus satisfied himself that his results or ideas make sense, he submits a paper to a scientific journal. The paper is sent to anonymous referees for criticism, and if they judge it worth publishing it is published in that journal.[5]

Earlier, writing in *The Saturday Review*, Brown had this to say about the Velikovsky hypotheses:

> . . . Modern science can . . . marshal far more convincing evidence – evidence which possesses mathematical rigor as distinct from interpretations of what human beings may or may not have done, observed, or said thousands of years ago.[6]

In each case, following upon or included in the doctrinal statements are assertions that Velikovsky has failed to fulfil the conditions. The doctrinal statements reveal how aware the scientific community is of the need to precede strong criticism by a credo.

In the rationalistic doctrine the rule of *publication* holds primary importance. It says that any would-be scientist should make known the results of his investigations, and, by inference, should have the right to publish his work. It also is expected that a scientist's work will be discussed before publication by those capable of evaluating it. These obligations were, of course, fulfilled by Dr Velikovsky. He consulted many specialists, among them the historian Pfeiffer and astronomers Adams and Motz. The book was examined carefully before publication. Macmillan held it for three years, and then was subjected to pressure from leading scientists not to publish or stop selling it after it was brought out. His work was subjected to double the regular scrutiny by experts prior to publication because of these pressures. It was read by at least six experts and emerged with a favourable verdict. His book was removed from one firm and transferred to another because of the threat to the publisher of loss of reputation and sales. Whereas the first article by Larrabee in *Harper's* was a responsible piece of journalism, and those of Atwater and Oursler were respectable presentations, a portion of the popular press distorted some of the features of his work, creating an image of it that many scientists could use to discourage other scientists from writing about the work seriously. The scientific journals would not subsequently publish articles by Velikovsky which adduced further proof of his thesis or responded to criticism.

A second canon of the rationalistic model is that *works will be read* before a judgment is passed. This promise is not always fulfilled. Yet the principle of reading offered material must be upheld lest the whole rationalistic model collapse. If the new work cannot be guaranteed some degree of expert reading it must naturally fail to make its mark. Science is a communication system as well as a method of advancing truth. Several of the most severe attacks against Velikovsky can now be shown to have been made by scientists who had not read the book.

Perhaps as many as half a million American have read *Worlds in Collision.* Among them are relatively few of the scientists – astronomers, geologists, paleontologists, historians – who are directly affected by the ideas treated in the book.

Reviewing is one step beyond reading. The review is necessary to pinpoint the audience of a book, to enlighten others as to its contents, and to suggest considerations of its truth or falsity. Hundreds of reviews were written of Velikovsky's book, *Worlds in Collision.* The popular reviewers tended to be favourable. The scientists were hostile. If there is such a thing as an ideal book review, whether favourable or unfavourable, it is not to be found in the story of *Worlds in Collision.* The question may be raised whether not only Velikovsky but also other scientists are subjected to the same inadequate treatment of their work and whether thereby this principle of the rationalistic model is continually being violated.

Another rule is that *theories offered should be tested,* not only by the author but his critics. This rule again turns out to be unobserved in many instances.[7] Velikovsky, whose behaviour throughout the controversy was that of a person committed to the rationalistic model, began to ask for tests of his theories four years prior to publication of his work. He reasonably claimed to have performed all tests within his power (the historical tests) but sought other tests requiring the use of equipment that he did not have access to. For instance, over a ten-year period he corresponded with several institutions – universities, museums, laboratories – trying to persuade someone to perform radiocarbon tests on Egyptian artifacts of the New Kingdom, without success. He also sought unsuccessfully to have the spectrogram of Venus analysed for heavy molecules of hydrocarbon. One wonders here, as in the case of other 'folk heroes', whether a condition of accepting with grave seriousness the rationalistic doctrine is to be innocent of experience of the world wherein the doctrine operates. Velikovsky, having had no university appointment or foundation grant, was more tenacious in his adherence to the rationalistic myth than his detractors.

Honesty and fairness are cardinal tenets of the rationalistic credo. Unless scientists are willing to admit the source of their knowledge and theories, and willing to grant a fair hearing and test to ideas brought forth, they contribute to the collapse of the rationalistic reception system. The honesty of Velikovsky was frequently called into question by natural scientists, in a manner so strong and unbalanced as to constitute libel. Yet no single case of mis-stated fact was proven in any of the four books of Velikovsky, and it would be untrue to assert that his works are too vague to assail; they are, in fact, exceedingly detailed and specific.

The 'ruthless honesty' that both Gaposchkin and Brown asserted as the hallmark of science in relation to self-criticism and appraisal of new works was quite ruthless, it is true, but directed entirely at Velikovsky. The degree of honesty in the appraisal of Velikovsky's studies can be judged in some of the evidence presented in these papers.

The appraisal of works by specialists, we have said, is a necessary ingredient of the rationalistic model. And specialists were brought to bear upon the work of Velikovsky. However, it would appear that the specialists' functions in the Velikovsky case were primarily to proclaim their competence and to disperse the vulgar masses who claimed to see revelations of value in Velikovsky's writings. Instead of specialism being used as a positive weapon of analysis, it tended to be used as a negative weapon of destruction: 'Anything un-narrow must be bad.' Professor Boring wrote in an article on unorthodoxies of science that agreement by trained scientists is the critical determinant of truth.[8] His theory, itself unorthodox, and not part of the rationalistic model, was used to show why Velikovsky was wrong even by those scientists who were operating in the name of the rationalistic credo: since the specialists said Velikovsky was incorrect, he *must* be incorrect.

Open discussion is supposed to characterize the rationalistic model. The social settings provided for the discussion of Velikovsky's work were mostly arranged for and administered by hostile critics or intimidated moderators. He was excluded from discussions of his own work and, when he succeeded in participating under a special dispensation, his words were not subsequently published. Several scientists and intellectuals who attempted his defence were silenced or sanctioned severely. I. Bernard Cohen, Professor of history of science (Harvard University), wrote sympathetically, almost enthusiastically, of Velikovsky's work in the advance summary of his address before the American Philosophical Society in April 1952, but changed his approach markedly in the published version of his address in the *Proceedings of the American Philosophical Society* (October 1952).

Radical innovation, declared Dr Gaposchkin, *is no bar* to the reception of new science. This is part of her testimonial to the rationalistic reception system. More in keeping with the facts of the reception of Velikovsky by herself and the scientific order is the statement by Bernard Cohen that 'Any suggestion that scientists so dearly love truth, that they have not the slightest hesitation in jettisoning their beliefs, is a mean perversion of the facts'.[9]

Nor should radicalism in method be a deterrent to the recruitment of ideas. Yet one of the glaring features of the Velikovsky case is the humanistic ignorance of natural scientists. A reading of the Velikovsky record should be part of the proceedings of any group considering the revision of curriculum for students of the natural sciences. Soon a century will have passed since the beginnings of the scientific investigation of myth, folklore, and primitive psychology. It has been many years since a theory of the unconscious has found a place in the instrumentation of social science. The science of linguistics, of symbols, of the sociology of communication, has progressed. It would appear that a more broadly educated or at least philosophically trained scientific class would have been able to perceive the relevance, validity, and unique capabilities of Velikovsky's method to key problems of natural science.

But the passage of time has relegated the natural sciences principally to hardware instrumentation. The natural scientists are still dwelling mentally in the hollow rationalistic universe of the 19th century. Indeed such a statement is unfair to the 19th century, which was far richer in mental constructions than its impoverished and dependent epigoni. They were victims of the fallacies that the present writer came to list in a previous article as common among natural scientists.[10]

The rationalistic model naturally assumes that sincerity is a hallmark of scientific work. Harlow Shapley called Velikovsky a fraud,[11] without having read the book. Thereupon Shapley engaged in collective action to prevent the publication and use of Velikovsky's book, actions which he then denied upon being accused of them. He declared in the *Harvard Crimson* (Sept. 25, 1950):

> The claim that Dr Velikovsky's book is being suppressed is nothing but a publicity promotion stunt. Like having a book banned in Boston; it improves the sales. Several attempts have been made to link such a move to stop the book's publication to some organization or to the Harvard Observatory. This idea is absolutely false.

The model of rationality demands that *the populace be barred from scientific proceedings*. Sales of a work to laymen does not disprove the validity of a work yet this seems to have been indicated by critics of Velikovsky. We even note that Velikovsky was criticized negatively for having found people to buy his book, the implication being that unless a work has the previous blessings of the scientific establishment, it has no right to exist.[12]

The rational model holds that *imprecision is a defect of scientific work*. An ideal is quantification, though many of the sciences fall short of this ideal in most of their propositions. Without foundation in fact, Gaposchkin says of *Worlds in Collision*: 'It contains no scientific arguments; not a formula, not a number (save for arbitrarily assigned dates) presents itself for analysis.' Dr Donald H. Menzel's appendix to her critique, sturdily entitled 'The celestial mechanics of electrically-charged planets', goes on to show quantitatively that a planet or sun charged to the potential demanded by equations based on Velikovsky's theory, amounting to 10^{19} volts, 'would be violently unstable . . . trying to put such an electric field on the sun resembles trying to hold back the entire mass of water in Lake Mead by a Boulder Dam made of tissue paper sheets'.[13] Recent space probes led Professor V. A. Bailey to the conclusion that the sun must hold a net negative charge with a potential of the order of 10^{19} volts.[14] The coincidence is only that, for even Menzel's arithmetic was faulty. The main point is that in astronomy and other sciences, natural and social, to make quantification a rigid condition for the admission of new theory, even in areas where qualification today rules, can promote dysfunctional rigidities.

'*Reject appeals to authority*,' affirm the rationalistic rules of procedure. Presumably, nothing is made true or false by the character of its supporters. However, science has not yet discovered a set of techniques for superseding authority, and the corpus of science would be a skeleton if this rule were seriously followed. We have more to say about that shortly, but meanwhile it is well to note that in no respect was the scientific movement against Velikovsky so much at variance with the rationalistic model as in its reliance upon authority.

The rationalistic model, when it is sociological at all, remembers history, warns against the blind opposition to new science, and as insurance that it can no longer happen in our secular and non-magical age, offers the assertion that *when at first, ideas are rejected, they may return with additional proof for admission and will be cordially reexamined.* On December 21, 1962, Prof. V. Bargmann of the Department of Physics of Princeton University and Prof. Lloyd Motz of the Department of

Astronomy of Columbia University published a letter in *Science* magazine claiming Velikovsky's priority of prediction of the hot surface temperature of Venus, of the existence of the magnetosphere around the Earth, and of the radio noises emanating from Jupiter. We quote from their letter:

'On 14 October 1953, Immanuel Velikovsky, addressing the Forum of the Graduate College of Princeton University . . . concluded the lecture as follows: "The planet Jupiter is cold, yet its gases are in motion. It appears probable to me that it sends out radio noises as do the sun and the stars. I suggest that this be investigated." . . . In April 1955 B. F. Burke and K. L. Franklin of the Carnegie Institution announced the chance detection of strong radio signals emanating from Jupiter. They recorded the signals for several weeks before they correctly identified the source.'

'This discovery came as something of a surprise because radio astronomers had never expected a body as cold as Jupiter to emit radio waves (1. See also the New York *Times* for 28 October 1962.)'

'In 1960 V. Radhakrishmah of India and J. A. Roberts of Australia, working at California Institute of Technology, established the existence of a radiation belt encompassing Jupiter, "giving 10^{14} times as much radio energy as the Van Allen belts around the earth".'

'On 5 December 1956, through the kind services of H. H. Hess, chairman of the department of geology of Princeton University, Velikovsky submitted a memorandum to the U.S. National Committee for the (planned) IGY in which he suggested the existence of a terrestrial magnetosphere reaching the moon. Receipt of the memorandum was acknowledged by E. O. Hulbert for the Committee. The magnetosphere was discovered in 1958 by Van Allen.'

'In the last chapter of his *Worlds in Collision* (1950), Velikovsky stated that the surface of Venus must be very hot, although in 1950 the temperature of the cloud surface of Venus was known to be −25°C on the day and night sides alike . . . By 1961 it became known that the surface temperature of Venus is "almost 600 degrees [K]" (4. *Phys. Today* 14, No. 4, 30, 1961). F. D. Drake described this discovery as "a surprise . . . in a field in which the fewest surprises were expected". "We would have expected a temperature only slightly greater than that of the earth . . . Sources of internal heating [radioactivity] will not produce an enhanced surface temperature. Cornell H. Mayer writes (5. C. H. Mayer, *Sci. Am.*, 204, May 1961), "All the observations are consistent with a temperature of almost

600 degrees," and admits that "the temperature is much higher than anyone would have predicted".'

They urged 'that his other conclusions be objectively re-examined'. Following the publication of this note, Velikovsky on January 29, 1963 submitted to *Science* magazine a more complete presentation of recent empirical evidence of the correctness of some of his statements. On January 31, the article was back in his hands with a formal letter of rejection.

In connection with reports of the Venus probes, *Newsweek* magazine was independently developing a story about Velikovsky at the time. The Editor of *Science*, Philip Abelson, stated to the *Newsweek* reporter in the course of a telephone inquiry that he had not read the Velikovsky manuscript before returning it.

Both as a document in the present case and for its intrinsic significance, the Velikovsky note, as submitted to *Science* and rejected, is printed below (see page 215). In the months since its submission to *Science*, additional corroborative finds have occurred. The paper was written and submitted before the results of the Mariner II probe of Venus were announced on February 26, 1963. The probe further confirmed Velikovsky's claims concerning the great heat of Venus (800°F) and the hydrocarbons (or organic compounds) of its envelope.

It was upon an occasion shortly after reviewing the memorandum of Velikovsky that Professor H. H. Hess, Chairman of the Department of Geology of Princeton University, wrote to Dr Velikovsky:

> I am not about to be converted to your form of reasoning though it certainly has had successes. You have after all predicted that Jupiter would be a source of radio noise, that Venus would have a high surface temperature, that the sun and bodies of the solar system would have large electrical charges and several other such predictions. Some of these predictions were said to be impossible when you made them. All of them were predicted long before proof that they were correct came to hand. Conversely I do not know of any specific prediction you made that has since been proven to be false. I suspect the merit lies in that you have a good basic background in the natural

sciences and you are quite uninhibited by the prejudices and probability taboos which confine the thinking of most of us.

For nearly a decade, Professor Hess has encouraged a hearing for Velikovsky and a testing of his ideas.

On February 15, *Science* carried a letter by Poul Anderson that lampooned Velikovsky and criticized the Bargmann–Motz letter on grounds that jokers and science-fiction writers had also made fantastic assumptions that were later verified. When Eric Larrabee, managing editor of *Horizon* magazine, protested to Dr Abelson against the exclusion of Velikovsky's article and the publication of Anderson's letter, Abelson thanked him and replied that:

> Velikovsky is a controversial figure. Many of the ideas that he expressed are not accepted by serious students of earth science. Since my prejudices happen to agree with this majority, I strained my sense of fair play to accept the letter by Bargmann and Motz, and thought that the books were nicely balanced with the rejoinder of Anderson.

When the Reverend Warner Sizemore, a Philadelphia minister, wrote to *Science* to show that the very cases that Anderson cited might be construed in favour of Velikovsky he received in reply a letter from Dr Abelson that declared:

> Science can exist and is useful because much of the knowledge in it is more than 99.9 percent certain and reproducible. If science were based on suggestions that were true 50 percent of the time, and all were free to make predictions which were only that reliable, chaos would result. I have repeatedly seen men of brilliance with fertile imaginations make all kinds of suggestions. Ideas are easy. They are cheap. It is the proving of a suggestion beyond a reasonable doubt that makes it valuable.
>
> At least half of Velikovsky's ideas have been proved wrong and he has done little to substantiate the remainder. In view of this, he is not to be taken seriously.

Yet, a few months earlier, Abelson was proclaiming the role of ideas in a *Science* editorial:

> The synthesis of xenon tetraflouride and related compounds ... makes necessary the revision of many chemistry textbooks ... For perhaps 15 years, at least a million scientists all over the

world have been blind to a potential opportunity to make this important discovery. All that was required to overthrow a respectable and entrenched dogma was a few hours of effort and a germ of scepticism. Our intuition tells us that this is just one of countless opportunities in all areas of inquiry. The imaginative and original mind need not be overawed by the imposing body of present knowledge or by the complex and costly paraphernalia which today surround much of scientific activity. The great shortage in science now is not opportunity, manpower, money, or laboratory space. What is really needed is more of that healthy scepticism which generates the key idea – the liberating concept.[15]

We must question whether the P.H.A. who wrote these lines stands for Philip H. Abelson.

This was not the first time Dr Velikovsky had difficulties entering the pages of professional journals. *The Proceedings of the American Philosophical Society*, which in 1952 carried extensive attacks upon him, would not suffer his reply. In 1956, the *Scientific American* carried a strong attack on both *Worlds in Collision* and *Earth in Upheaval* by Harrison Brown. (The magazine had refused to carry advertising of Velikovsky's book.) When Velikovsky asked for permission to rebut, the Editor, Dennis Flanagan, wrote:

. . . I think you should know my position once and for all. I think your books have done incalculable harm to the public understanding of what science is and what scientists do. There is no danger whatever that your arguments will not be heard; on the contrary they have received huge circulation by scientific standards.

Thus I feel that we have no further obligation in the matter.

This quotation reveals that the Editor has picked up a common sociological misapprehension among scientists. It is that the media of the general public can substitute for the media of science. They cannot. Furthermore, most scientists, when they reflect, realize that they themselves insist upon a distinct separation of the two types of media.

Science magazine has a subscription list of 90,000. Its sponsoring body, the A.A.A.S., includes 71,000 individual members and 298 affiliated scientific societies, academies, and other professional organizations. The *Scientific American* sells a quarter of a million copies. They can reach fully the diversified audience of scientists who are concerned with Velikovsky's work. Or they can serve as a block to the admission of new material. If the *American Behavioral Scientist* prints accounts of Velikovsky's theories, it does so in the pursuance of its commitment to treat with the sociology of science and scientific freedom. If *Science* magazine carries or does not carry the developments of the substance of Velikovsky's work, it acts out of its obligation to present new scientific propositions and theories to the scientific world.

At this point the discussion of the rationalistic system of science may be concluded. Its doctrine, formulas, and tactics have been only feebly exercised in the Velikovsky case. It has furnished a poor fit. A few scientists – in conversation, by letters, and rarely by public statement – asked for the rules of rationalistic science to be observed. The behaviours of almost all scientists involved, with the expected exception of Dr Velikovsky who acted in accord with the rules of seeking admission, must be fitted to some other model. Perhaps it will be that which is called here the indeterminacy model.

THE INDETERMINACY MODEL

The Indeterminacy Model postulates a scientific order that is not replenished according to any scheme that is instrumentally rational. Rather it almost randomly absorbs or refuses. The lightning of discovery can strike anywhere. The pattern of science forms and becomes recognizable out of a vast collection of accidents. The truth value of the scientist and his product are alleged to have very little to do with their chances of success in being incorporated into science. Nor are they kept out by skilful managers of power and arbiters of claims.

The indeterminacy model differs from the rationalistic in that it postulates deliberate activities that are distributed so as to nullify and cancel out each other, thus giving the total system an unplanned effect. Its rules therefore are not rules of conduct but rules of effects.

The very first rule of the indeterminacy model is that 'truth' about reality has as much chance of rejection as of acceptance. Truth is an irrelevant trait of candidates and material.

Let us pause for a moment to contemplate this radical expression. It does not say that truth is non-existent. It can still hold to the theory that statements can be distinguished as to their relative correlation with facts, patterns of fact, predictions of events, and control of events. However, for truth to exist does not imply truth will be admitted – even to its own domain of science. Like the proverbial prophet, it can be without honour in its own land.

To conceive of this situation, let us assume that all men are scientists, even if some are more so than others. They have problems that might be solved by logico-empirical procedures. Taking into account all that men allow into their body of convictions, all the statements about the world and about the future to which they grant their assent, can it be said now, or ever, that the bulk of these statements are true? Perhaps not, at least not by logico-empirical standards.

Now, moving from the common man to the scientist, can it be said that scientists take in more correct statements than incorrect ones? To affirm such, one would have to believe that they have attained omniscience. He would say, as men usually have said through history, that those who went before had mental closets packed with the shabby clothes of superstition, wrong theories, and unempirical ideas, whereas today, most of what men know is true.

If pressed, one would be forced to justify his pride by the known effects of specialization. A worn witticism says that the scientist as specialist is one who knows more and more about less and less. This may be granted, in which event one would have to resort to a collectivist theory of knowledge: knowledge is a corporate possession; apart from the question of whether most of what is known is true, more is true today than before, despite specialization, because science is a set of wonderful pools connected by communicating pipes.

If this is so, then everything depends upon communications. If the pipes are not working, truth is forever partial and in a worse condition than when the lesser sum of it was more generally distributed. Is this the case today? It may be. It may be becoming so. The indeterminacy model postulates that it *is* so. Error is not only as common as truth; but truth is fragmented for being uncommunicated. When a truth is admitted only to a small part of the realm of science, it does not exist except for that portion of the realm.

Probably the extent of the admission of error into science is underestimated by those scientists who have high morale or rigid unconscious self-doubts. Probably also truth today does not enter a reservoir of science but only a separate pool. Therefore the indeterminacy model can affirm that truth does not enter as a matter of course – not because it is deliberately excluded, but from logical, social, and psychological conditions beyond current means of control.

The model suggests that the spirit of the times and customs dictate what will and will not be science. Few or many people will acquire the habits of inquiry. They will produce results, theoretical and practical, and they will be accepted or rejected partly by chance, partly by favour or patronage, partly by publicity, partly by the use to which their work may be put.

Scientists operate under the indeterminacy system by various myths – primarily of rationality, of causation, and of power of choice – but in fact do not know what they are seeking, what is available, or what are solutions. That their compensation, whether in esteem, position, or money, is related to performance is only an illusion. What is accepted and what is rejected are therefore only a product of chance encounters of purpose and provision.

Under these circumstances, scientists follow the laws of nonrational collective behaviour. They think in stereotypes (e.g. the eternal harmony of the spheres, uniformitarianism, catastrophism). They circulate ideas via popularization and texts.[16] Thus have Newton, Galileo, Darwin, Freud and Einstein been conveyed. Scientists are at the mercy of popularizers. Their own minds are formed by simplistic ideas, try as they will to evade their grip.

A new theory spreads as a rumour, simplified, overly precise, and success comes as a surprise. No two persons understand its extended meanings quite alike. It is resistant to rational counterargument. And it persists until it is stale and a more vibrant report originates. It seems to be specific and operational until it is shown to be blind and vague; such is the fate of most past statements about the universe.

We would expect more scientists to dislike the indeterminacy model than the rationalistic or power models. It negates the rationalistic model. And the power model, though disliked, entrusts judgments to 'qualified authorities', as we shall see. The indeterminacy threatens the whole order. It can be fully expected that among various kinds of scientists, statisticians and sociologists will be least offended by it, astronomers most offended, because of their own methodology. Physics and individualistic psychology, it may be noted, have in recent years been prone to demand complicated systems of priorities in giving scientific credits. Quarrelling over datelines of reports and property in 'findings' has sometimes occurred. This, it may be assumed, is in part a reaction against surrendering to indeterminacy. Much greater nervousness, verging on trauma, is approaching as scientists will consign their work to the anonymous maw of the electronic information storage apparatus of the future.

Under the indeterminacy model, in the jargon of avant-garde statistics, the man/material 'takes a random walk'. The random walk signifies that *for control purposes* (including predictive and tactical behaviour) there is no pattern except randomness. Only behaviours of a low level of typicality can be discovered, and these are too weak to determine directions. In the light of this theory, the Galileo case reads understandably. One cannot escape the feeling that the treatment afforded Galileo was produced by a host of non-rational, inconsistent incidents and intrigues leading up to his condemnation. A hierarchical or power system was at work, but its instrumental rationality was inept. The Church did not behave as a fully-aware, clearly organized, accurately aimed body. Galileo's punishment seems in retrospect almost to have been an accident, though an understandable one.

The following rules prevail:

(1) There are no prescribed scientific procedures. The rule of creative hypothesis is great and scientists 'monkey around'. Science fiction, magic, astrology, and half-rationalized ideas are joined to logico-empirical procedures and facts, creating an environment from which practical accomplishment emerges. There is a chaos of communication. A person working in science applies himself to whatever comes to him through his peculiar interests and *situs*, and casts forth a product whose destination and fate are unknown.

The indeterminacy model stresses the chance reception of discoveries. Poincaré recites how he solved a theorem of Fuchsian functions while walking across a street.[17] Karl Gauss after working for years on proof of a theorem succeeds and writes: 'At last, two days ago, I succeeded, not by dint of painful effort, but so to speak by the grace of God. As a sudden flash of light, the enigma was solved. For my part, I am not in a position to point to the thread which joins what I knew previously to what I have succeeded in doing.' Where is Velikovsky's method, more than one of his reviewers asks in anguish. There is a method, not highly selfconscious, *not always* exposed. It is much more clearly recognizable to social scientists than to natural scientists. Sometimes the method is concealed by an easy style that separates empirically-tied ideas while allocating them to short sentences. Of course, a number of the rational propositions, which lend the work its distinction, are only as explainable as the leaps of Poincaré and Gauss. The social psychology, much less the neurology, of such events is little known.

The indeterminancy model, in this regard, offers in place of the rationalistic model a description of 'normal' science as a quasi-administrative routine.[18] It affirms the *idea* over the *process*, as in the letter from Professor H. H. Hess to Velikovsky (2, Jan. 1957) that refers to the memorandum he was sending to IGY:

> ... I will pass your ideas on to Dr Kaplan in the IGY organization ... Scientific discoveries and ideas are produced by the intuition, creativeness and genius of a man. Dollars of themselves don't produce this any more than they could be expected to produce another Mona Lisa. This is something which I believe you can readily understand ...

(2) There are no rules for the form in which material is submitted, nor rules for publication. Whatever is offered is admitted or rejected for reasons largely mythical. The works of Velikovsky are actually high in the scale of adduced proof and formality, by the standards of all past useful scientific production. Much of science is passed down as lore. The procedures are habitual and not rationally and consciously prescribed or learned. Much that is communicated passes via devices and hardware inventions that elude the literature of science.

The true inventor has to be dissociated from the accredited inventor. Every famous scientist rests on the back of hundreds of unknown inventors. Even if credit were to be assigned by a laborious objective research process, it would not be well enough informed to do justice to the process of discovery.

The indeterminacy model fits the inefficiencies in maintenance and replenishment of the *corpus scientiae. Much more is discovered and forgotten than is known. Much that is known is unused or known in a partial form.* In Velikovsky's works are found numerous discoveries of the past that became essential parts of his theory. The theory that a comet created destruction on Earth was itself once propounded in various forms by distinguished scientists, as Dr Velikosvky and Professor Stecchini have shown. Whenever a new scientific discovery or invention is made, its predecessors can be unearthed. Sometimes the ideas may be shown to be in a causal sequence. At other times they are apparently aborted and unrelated. And occasionally they are independently invented in the same idological epoch.

(3) A work penetrates into the body of science by the machinery of publicity, through acquaintanceship circles, by accident, by unconscious exposure and the creation of frames of mind (subliminal stimulation). It enters also by parallel practical operations independently derived from the same sources or from the same, different and related sources. It joins science by 'creative misunderstanding' or by 'anticreative misunderstanding'.

(4) The rationalistic modes of presentation, as treated above, become unreliable and the scientific establishment turns out to be wicked, foolish, or ineffectual. There really are heroes, whom the people adore as *the Heroes of Science*, but the scientist does not learn from the heroes and cannot know the origins of their knowledge. The heroes are really hallucinations arising from the troubled mass mind that cannot rest with an anonymous and uncontrolled world. Subscribing to the ideal system of rational science, the public performs rituals and makes obsequies to an order which they believe to exist (but which is only fantastic and invisible) and which they believe guides the destinies of science. The representatives of the public act like the member of Parliament in J. H. Poincaré's story who, when asked about the value of geodesy, would answer, 'I am led to think that geodesy is one of the most useful of sciences, for it is one of those that cost us most money'.

To conclude, a reasonably satisfying history of science and of the Velikovsky case might be written from what might be called a purely phenotypical perspective. This would decommission all the personalities of science. It would consider only the massive output of symbols. It would reveal the patterns by which certain applied operations, of considerable practical value, emerged from the nodules or clusters within this communicative system. It would conclude that there is little control over the reception of new science. It would conclude that other models for organizing and incorporating new knowledge are either practical myths sustaining the morale of scientists, and/or weak determining systems having at best a mild effect on scientific advance and almost no effect on the use to which science is put.

This set of problems is familiar to history, if not to the history of science. Did Napoleon win his battles or did the French Revolution pre-conquer Europe for him? Would science be largely the same if Newton or Galileo or Einstein had not lived? Does not the readiness of people – few in the case of science and many in the case of politics – to perceive, to believe and to use new materials, ideas and instruments constitute the deterministic, inevitable, and overpowering structural force? Are not all the actions of the powerful in the personalized drama of science, like the personalized drama of political history, a glossing upon reality, a personalizing of events not less natural for being human?

The documents of the Velikovsky case explain in this light some of the behaviours that take place. They point to the immense practical impact of science while revealing the chaotic conditions of the reception system. Scarcely any scientist appears to have read Velikovsky properly. Practically all of the mechanisms for appraisal of his work failed. Yet his findings appear to be increasingly validated, if not recognized. The science of the future may be heavily conditioned by the existence of Velikovskian natural and historical science, even though many of the sources of that science might have been incubating independently of Velikovsky.

Probably some thousands of natural and social scientists might have been among the readers of Velikovsky's works – which are written clearly, deal with important problems, and are controversial – were it not for the curse of superstition and fakery called down upon it. Nevertheless, through the indeterminacy system, Velikovsky's works were kept alive and read. His ideas could become part of a frame of thought among a mass of people, and to some unknown degree, help them develop a new vision of history, science, and nature.

THE POWER MODEL

Still a third reception system presents itself for consideration. It is the power model. Its pure dynamics posit as an exclusive goal the admission of scientists and their works to the establishment and corpus of science only as means to the preservation or enhancement of the power and prestige of the ruling group.

In this model science is organized as a hierarchy operating by power principles in the name of the rationalistic myth. The rationalistic doctrine is embraced, formulated, and controlled as dogma by the hierarchy, which employs it as circumstances dictate. As keepers of the sacred corpus of science, the hierarchs define ethical practices. They accept or reject men and material, and inflict sanctions, all according to their own power interests.

The power model presupposes one or more power elites. It foresees a possibility of factual conflict among elites and also of dissension through ineffective control systems. It also admits the possibility of economic and political alliances that may be employed to affect the internal power structure of a science.

In the beginning are the hierarchs of the scientific establishment. As in all political situations their existence can be proven by observation of their activity, by effects of their interventions and by correct prediction, either in the present case or by transfer of evidence in other similar situations. Thus, if Professor X, head of a famed University department and incumbent of numerous professional and public specialized offices, agitates against Dr V. and sways others to do so; if typical sanctions of non-appointment, non-promotion, non-discussion, non-publication, and negative prestige result from this for Dr V. and friends; if certain correct predictions are made about the negative response of the establishment to projected actions of Dr V.; and if the impressive positions, connections and behaviour of Professor X in other situations are of a nature similar to his behaviours towards V.: then Professor X is a hierarch and the setting in which he operates can be said to be hierarchical and those with whom he cooperates are co-leaders and those to whom he delegates the same power tasks are subordinate hierarchs, and the whole establishment is a power structure to the extent to which all of these behaviours are typical and exclusive.

An authority sanctioned doctrine is called dogma. It is the set of beliefs about how events occur and their rightness or wrongness. In science, the major dogma of method is the rationalistic model. And a minor dogma about authority is contained here in the power model, so that it is permissible to claim 'authority' even if authority must bow down before the 'proof' of the rationalistic model.

If a doctrine prevails in a social order, such as is science, it cannot be ignored by the holders of power. They must rule in its terms. They must control it. Naked power is difficult to achieve and hold. Man can no more live by power alone than by bread alone. This is especially true of ruling groups such as scientific ones, that lack the sanctions of physical coercion.

The control of dogma or doctrine rests on an original legitimacy of rule and then upon control of means. In science, appointment to leading universities, designation to honours and esteem by prior designees (co-option) confer legitimacy inside and outside the establishment.

The control of dogma enables the hierarchs to dominate a controversy in that correct dogma may be attributed to oneself and violations of dogma, hence illegitimacy, to the opposition. As indicated above, the establishment leaders were not remiss in their tasks; Gaposchkin, H. Brown, Lafleur, Stewart, *et al.* enunciated the code before passing judgment upon Velikovsky and his works.

At the same time, they were equally careful to state, even if without confirmation, that Velikovsky violated the code of science in salient respects. He was accused of writing for money.[19] He was accused of a hoax. In numerous varying terms, he was labelled as incompetent to discuss his topics.

Velikovsky's detractors were vulnerable, actually, on dogmatic grounds. But only in the public press could they be attacked thereupon. *Newsweek* and *Harper's* carried the chief pro-Velikovsky statements, alleging the failure of the hierarchs to conform to their asserted belief-system.

Naked power is a shameful thing in science. Members of the establishment, realizing the vulnerability of naked power, were quick to defend themselves against accusations of arbitrariness, suppression, and censorship. One reason why their reviews and letters seemed short on literary and scientific quality was that in them they were conducting a three-fold operation – they had often to assert their control over dogma, effectuate their power, and act out the model of a rationalistic reception system, all at the same time and in the same place.

There can be no ruling group without an institutional base. The preferred situs is a university of high prestige, funds, fellowships, staffs, and expensive, collectively controlled apparatus. Holding the chief position in astronomy at Harvard is in these regards like controlling the New York State delegation at a Presidential nominating convention. From such a position come honours and other positions as well. In the 1952 *Who's Who in America*, Harlow Shapley, Professor of Astronomy and Director of the Lowell Observatory at Cambridge, listed himself as an officer or member of 41 professional associations. In this case, as happens in most power situations, the network of influence extends outward through former students, new appointments, and professional rewards, and also overlaps and is reinforced by affiliations of other kinds – sometimes of a political and ideological nature, at other times of family, of money, etc.

The tactics of power normally operate to suppress undesired opinion and manipulate favourable opinion. In the scientific reception system, this involves action in two spheres, professional opinion and public opinion. The points where control can be exercised are in the specialized and public publishing media, and in regards to individuals.

The suppression or influencing of professional opinion in the Velikovsky case occurred in the following ways:

(A) By word-of-mouth communication before and after the publication of Velikovsky's book. This is an evanescent kind of material, now consisting largely of recollections of scientists and publishers' representatives. (It would consist of items such as: Dr Conant, then President of Harvard, meets the Editor of *Harper's* magazine at the Century Club; he says 'I have only one thing to say about your current issue: "Really!" ')

(B) By letter and 'committee of correspondence'. Item: Before Velikovsky's book is published, Madame Gaposchkin on the basis of *Harper's* article writes a violent review at the request of *The Reporter* magazine and Dr Shapley. This is accompanied by a hortatory message prior to publication.[20]

(C) By seeking recantations. Shapley asked his colleague at Harvard, Dr Robert H. Pfeiffer, to confirm the genuineness of his statements supporting Velikovsky's *Ages in Chaos*: Pfeiffer, Lecturer in Semitic Languages, did so. Atwater was asked by Professor Otto Struve in a menacing letter to reconsider and perhaps clarify his favourable disposition towards Velikovsky. At an A.A.A.S. meeting called especially to deal with problems of publishing ethics growing out of the failure to suppress completely the Velikovsky book, the Macmillan company was permitted to recant and state a safe position. (Boards of review for scientific publishing were suggested and considered by the panel.)

(D) By depriving opposing persons of positions. Their support of Velikovsky's right to be heard and/or of his theories appears to have played a significant part in the forced resignation of Gordon Atwater, Chairman of the Astronomy Department of the American Museum of Natural History and Curator of the Hayden Planetarium, and of James Putnam, a Macmillan editor for 26 years. The converse, promoting the useful allies, is found in Lafleur, of whom *Scientific Monthly*, in heralding a second article a few months later, reported that he had been appointed to a new university and promoted to a departmental chairmanship following his article on Velikovsky.

(E) The techniques of denying and avoiding public discussion, of refusing access to scientific fora and a denial of access to scientific publications – via articles or letters of reply, or even advertising – are amply illustrated elsewhere in these pages.

In addition, the power model of the reception system operates *to restrict* credentials. Velikovsky did not possess orthodox credentials. This was made clear in the review of his work. He was of course, well trained in many fields as, one by one, his readers came around to admitting.

At that time, he had few friends, although among them was Albert Einstein. Shortly after Einstein's death, Professor Bernard Cohen reported that Einstein had spoken in humorous disparagement of Velikovsky. Einstein could not respond, but a number of personal meetings and a good deal of reading by Einstein of Velikovsky's material would refute the surmise. (Cohen himself retracted. *Cf.* the Cohen letter above, p. 15.) We note a handwritten letter in German from Einstein to Velikovsky, 30 days before the former's death, in acknowledgement of a gift of *Ages in Chaos*.

> I look forward with pleasure to reading the historical book that does not bring into danger the toes of my guild. How it stands with the toes of the other faculty, I do not know as yet. I think of the touching prayer: 'Holy St Florian, spare my house, put

fire to others!' I have already carefully read the first volume of the memoirs to 'Worlds in Collision', and have supplied it with a few marginal notes in pencil that can be easily erased. I admire your dramatic talent and also the art and the straightforwardness of Thackeray [Thackrey] who has compelled the roaring astronomical lion to pull in a little his royal tail yet still not showing enough respect for the truth.

Velikovsky made attempts to conciliate the powers, partly in conjunction with his attempts to satisfy the demands of the rationalistic model of the reception system. He appreciated that Shapley and Einstein, along with others, to be sure, were two heavily influential figures on the scientific scene. Einstein was a source of comfort, if not of theoretical support. Shapley was approached in the typical honest manner of 'cranks', that is, in the course of a public forum, without introduction, and then by letter assuming naively the rationalistic operational code that 'to test a theory, you go to a testing specialist who has the required apparatus'.

It may be inquired why Velikovsky chose Shapley and Einstein, and why he engaged in other actions directed at impressing the gatekeepers of science. This behaviour is in the first place 'normal'. It indicates only that he himself was no enemy of authority, but remained throughout a naive and quixotic believer in the symbiosis of the rationalistic and power models. One might pursue farther the psychology of this set of incidents. The strongly controlled but nevertheless necessarily and typically great self-confidence of Velikovsky, which enabled him to be a 'normal' man who could still pursue tremendous hypotheses through many thousands of hours against many adversities, had a side of unconscious intellectual presumption: 'The Lodges speak only to the Cabots.'

The establishment has a final weapon against hostile innovators. It is the *concealed incorporation of their ideas*.

The best-known manifestation of the techniques of secret information is sometimes called the '*silent footnote technique*'. Credit is given in sources, footnotes, and forewords only to those who are members of the establishment in good standing. Also there is a rule of the highly specialized to not cite anyone less highly specialized for fear of being thought too general, too popular. As a clique device, selective footnoting costs an aspirant nothing (except possibly self-respect) and shows that he *belongs* to the group, and he is 'advanced'. It also lets him grace the patronage chiefs and the powerful. It is a vote. A less expensive, less discernible, and more vitriolic tactic is hard to imagine.

To this day, despite a great deal of corroborative evidence and the passage of thirteen years, no scientist has admitted in a work of his own that any glance that he may have given towards the skies, nor any peek into ancient documents, has been provoked by an objective and calm desire to examine Velikovsky's evidence. When relevant findings have occurred, they have not been associated with the name of Velikovsky.

Then, too, using the partially respectable and partly true doctrines of the indeterminacy model, the leaders claim that the innovator plucks his ideas and facts from the air of the times. Examples are the 'ideas are cheap' statement of Philip Abelson, or Harrison Brown's assertions that 'Velikovsky apparently looks upon himself as an original thinker . . .' and 'He quotes some data which we know to be true, some which we know to be dubious and some which we know to be false.' Brown gives not a shred of evidence for this statement. It is baseless, yet a widely circulated canard among scientists is that Velikovsky made so many predictions that some are bound to be true.

Or, using the rationalistic dogma, the establishment propagandists claim that 'there are predictions *and* predictions', meaning that correctness is not the hallmark of good predictions. Science works only on proper, methodical, laboratory work, it is declared. This mysterious science is, of course, only the power and indeterminacy procedures at work. So Velikovsky's catastrophes 'do not upset' scientists: Madame Gaposchkin goes out of her way to express the attitude, 'See how we have accepted the much greater catastrophes recently demonstrated empirically and mathematically by members of the establishment!'

ECONOMIC AND POLITICAL NETWORKS

The tactics used to enhance power within the scientific establishment include bringing in power from the outside. The most obvious external networks activated in the Velikovsky case were the economic and the political.

Here is Dr Velikovsky's description of the fatal interview in May 1950 with the President of Macmillan Company, when the latter requested him to free Macmillan from its obligation to continue publishing *Worlds in Collision*. Mr Brett said:

> Seventy per cent of the business of this company is in textbooks; it is the real backbone of our firm. Therefore we are vulnerable. Professors in certain universities have refused to see our salesmen. We have received a series of letters declaring a boycott against all our textbooks. Please realize how it works. (*Here Mr Brett picked up a pencil and drew some circles.*) Academic circles are not isolated groups; they are united in local organizations, or in professorial associations that are incorporated or represented in larger national organizations. (*And he drew larger circles.*) The American Association for the Advancement of Science in Washington, The American Philosophical Society, and the National Academy of Sciences are groups of national importance where scientists in many fields are represented. In this way the academic pressure may become widespread.

The conversation is pursued and becomes difficult. Velikovsky notes again:

> Mr Brett, though very polite and trying to be pleasant, was definitely committed to his decision to free his house of a book that was arousing wrath among the powerful of the textbook world, and he began again to draw a pattern of circles to show me how the scientific groups are interlocked; how they are centred, and how they can damage a publishing house.

The most readily available economic instrument of the scientific establishment is the 'boycott'. It is well-known but not sufficiently appreciated that the leaders of the scientific field wield a triple influence over publishers. They are authors or sponsors of the leading works in the field. They influence opinion about books; this in turn affects purchasing. And they and their subordinates and followers in other colleges purchase an important part of the books and materials sold in the field and used as texts and required reading. When a publisher's contact men find the doors to the mighty suddenly closed to them, this is more than pressure – it can be a mortal blow.

The establishment moved with speed and vigour to block professional support for Velikovsky's book and to boycott it and its publishers. The following occurs in a letter from Shapley to Macmillan Company *prior to* the publication of the book.

> And frankly, unless you can assure me that you have done things like this frequently in the past without damage, the publication must cut me off from the Macmillan Company.

And on February 20, one month later, and still before the book was printed, in a letter to Ted Thackrey, Editor of *Compass*, Shapley writes:

> In my rather long experience in the field of science, this is the most successful fraud that has been perpetrated on leading American publications . . . I am not quite sure that Macmillan is going through with the publication, because that firm has perhaps the highest reputation in the world for the handling of scientific books.

The book was published after clearing the hurdle of a book of censors instituted by Mr Brett but pressure continued. Macmillan prevailed upon Velikovsky to release it from its contract with him, presenting him with a contract with Doubleday (the book was already on the top of the best-seller list and over 50,000 copies of it had been sold) and making clear that he had no other course to take if his book were to be promoted and marketed. Indeed, the company had already stopped publicizing the book. As every bookman knows, this could be construed as a breach of faith with the author.

Subsequent correspondence indicated the nature of Operation Boycott. D. B. McLaughlin, University of

Michigan astronomer, in a letter of June 16, 1950 to Fulton Oursler, *Reader's Digest*, said in part:

> *Worlds in Collision* has just changed hands, from Macmillan to Doubleday. I am frank to state that this change was the result of pressure that scientists and scholars brought to bear on the Macmillan Company. It is our duty to the public to prevent such fraud insofar as we can.

Paul Herget, Professor of Astronomy at the University of Cincinnati and Director of its observatory, wrote to the columnist Sokolsky, early July 1950:

> I do not believe he [Shapley] was in any sense the leader in this campaign. I was a very vigorous participant myself . . . For your information I enclose copies of some of my correspondence.

After the transfer was made, pressure was brought upon the Doubleday Company.

On June 30, 1950, David C. Grahame, Associate Professor of Chemistry at Amherst, wrote:

> Macmillan Company abandoned it [*Worlds in Collision*] because of the storm of protest it aroused among informed persons, and you, too, may find yourself kept busy answering letters of indignation from scientists the country over. Scientists are now engaged in an active boycott of the Macmillan books, and though scientists are not important buyers of your books, their opinion should be heeded by any publisher who intends to publish a book which purports to be science. I trust that you can be dissuaded.

The Harvard University group was relentless. Professor Fred L. Whipple, who had been Shapley's chief assistant and had relieved him as Director of the Harvard College Observatory, took up the cudgels with Doubleday. On June 30, 1950 he wrote to the Blakiston Company, which was the publisher of his book, *Earth, Moon, and Planets*. Commenting on an article that *Newsweek* magazine had just published on Velikovsky's case (called 'Professors as Suppressors') he says:

> *Newsweek* has unwittingly done the Doubleday Company a considerable amount of harm. They have made public the high success of the spontaneous boycott of the Macmillan Company by scientifically minded people. This in turn amounts to organ-

izing a boycott of the Doubleday Company by the thinking people who buy books. My guess is that Doubleday Company will never publish Volumes 3 and 4[21] . . . In any case, since I believe that the Blakiston Company is owned by the Doubleday Company, which controls its policies as well as the distribution of its books, I am now then a fellow author of the Doubleday Company along with Velikovsky. My natural inclination, were it possible, is to take *Earth, Moon and Planets* off the mraket and find a publisher who is not associated with one who has such a lacuna in its publication ethics.

He would instead, he declared, give the royalties to charity and bring out no new edition. Indeed the entire popularly-written Harvard series on astronomy was soon withdrawn from Blakiston.

Whether a political network became engaged along with the scientific and economic ones is quite unclear. It may even be questioned whether so controversial a subject should be raised. (Perhaps if mere Democrats and Republicans were the participants, one might not hesitate.) And yet, the evidence suggests that an informal left-wing network might well have been in operation. This would help explain the intensity of emotion and activity exhibited by Professor Shapley and various supporters. The political affiliations of Dr Shapley during this period were under scrutiny by official agencies. The 'normal' threats posed by the Velikovsky work might have been intensified by the political attacks Shapley was undergoing. Velikovsky could have been a convenient, fairly helpless target of displaced aggressions.

Yet Shapley was not alone. He was supported by others who were under the same kind of political attack, for example, Kirtley Mather and Edward U. Condon. Were they all displacing aggressions? Was the British evolutionist, J. B. S. Haldane, several thousand miles away, subject to the same collective disorder? In Britain and on the Continent of Europe, *Worlds in Collision* was received differently. Not accepted in many quarters, neither was it vilified. On the other hand, Haldane, an old friend and political ally of Shapley, wrote an exceptional diatribe against Velikovsky, even associating the book with those in America who wished to use Britain as a base for atomic warfare.

If a political network theory were to be assumed, the reasons might be several. The work of Velikovsky could be assumed to defend Jewish nationalism. It could be assumed to defend fundamentalism. It could be considered anti-materialist, anti-determinist, and obscurantist. An attack on it might also give a political apparatus, with its associated branches, some needed exercise, and, what is more, a needed victory at its lowest moment in history. The conflict could moreover serve to bind to the group unsuspecting sympathizers in a common cause of science.

This is conjectural, yet it would be improper to eliminate it entirely from consideration, even at the cost of arousing hostility in readers who, until this page, might have been in full sympathy with our presentation. To illustrate further, there occurred a strange incident that can perhaps be best understood as a network problem.

Shapley was among a group of progressives and more extreme left-wingers who, when the New York newspaper *PM* failed, backed its successor, *Compass*. On February 19, 1950, it reprinted the original *Harper's* article on Velikovsky's book, the very article which, appearing before book publication, caused an immediate hostile outburst from the Harvard group. On February 20, Harlow Shapley, on the stationery of the Harvard College Observatory, wrote to Ted Thackrey, Editor of the *Compass*. 'Dear Ted,' he began, 'Somebody has done you dirt.' The rest of the letter was smoothly persuasive to Thackrey and derogatory to Velikovsky. He referred to *Worlds in Collision* as 'a successful fraud', 'rubbish', and 'astrological hocus-pocus'. Einstein was later to read his letter and call it 'miserable' in a marginal notation.

However, Thackrey, far from cringing, sent back a stinging retort. He stated well the rationalistic ideal, and accused Shapley of trying to suppress Velikovsky's work. Another exchange followed. The *Compass* was not long for this world, however. Thackrey's views on issues such as the Korean War threw the communists and fellow-travellers into deadly opposition to him. Eventually, key backers withdrew their financial support, and *Compass* folded.

But the main struggle over *Worlds in Collision* was not waged in the associated arenas of business and politics. It occurred within the ramparts of science. Furthermore, it was a fairly clear engagement of the one with the many. The hierarchs were not riven by dissent. There has been no revolt. The natural resort of the denied and dispossessed in a power system, factionalism, was not exercised. No faction within science attempted in the name of rationalism to substitute its interest, theories and facts for the prevailing ones.

A different kind of power behaviour within the dynamics of the model is visible. Dr Velikovsky has been more of the hermit scientist than of the hierarch, cabalist, or rebel. The model of this behaviour has the gates of scientific recognition being forced by the single-minded dedicated scholar and a small group of disciples. They create a disturbance that cannot be ignored. The whole picture is one of a power struggle where the odds against innovation are great but the addiction of the innovator to truth is supreme.

In the end, it is the outcome of the power struggle that determines whether the truth is admitted, not the rationalistic tests. Just as a soldier or a bureaucrat will exclaim in amazement over the gargantuan capacity of the collective organism to ingest irrationality and inefficiency, the scientist with any degree of historical perspective must often be shocked at the frequency with which power determines what the laws of human and natural behaviour 'are' and how a corpus of science survives.

THE DOGMATIC MODEL

A final model, the dogmatic, requires exposition. Professor Stecchini has given ample reason to believe that the resistance to the astronomical theories of Velikovsky was motivated by sheer ideology, a dislike of challenge to the orderly universe. Much evidence can be brought forward from other fields of knowledge – archaeology, biblical studies, paleontology, geology, physics and biology – to the same effect: the theories of Velikovsky operating against the prevailing dogma are repulsed vigorously. Every weapon is brought into play against the new ideas – authoritative denunciation, arguments *ad hominem*, tricks of logic and evidence, suppression, denial of rewards, and stony silence.

By the rules of the dogmatic model, what happens is explained solely and adequately by the fact that all believers in the state of present knowledge unite to resist the innovator. New material and men are accepted in the proportion to which they conform with prevailing theories and norms.

Several tests of the dogmatic model may be proposed.

(1) Is there a universal agreement against a work on grounds other than rationalistic? If so, a dogmatic model may fit the case. The spontaneity and generality of denunciation of Velikovsky's work is compelling. The power apparatus is simply not strong enough to explain it. The rationalistic model certainly does not. Nor does the indeterminacy model. Yet the concept of a collective obsession spread among a great many persons on all scientific levels and in all scientific fields would fit the dogmatic mould.

(2) Does the power elite reject new and correct ideas even though the effects of the ideas may be expected to enhance their power? If the answer is an unambiguous 'yes', then the dogmatic model fits. The Velikovsky case is here ambiguous, however. Partly this is owing to the lack of agreement over the correctness of his theories. But other factors cloud the issue too. In 1950 the throne of astronomy, the queen of sciences, was shaky. It could have been bolstered by consideration of the Velikovskian theories. The weakness of classical studies was evident. They could have been rejuvenated. Biology was not

in such a poor condition, but it too could have been aided by vigorous re-examination of evolutionary theory. Geology was vigorous, physics too. They needed no great prestige. All rejected the ideas. Thus power (prestige) was not a determinant, it would seem.

However, power outside is not the same as power inside the disciplines. Time after time in history, power elites succumb because they are more intent on gaining or holding internal power than in maintaining or extending the scope and intensity of their power vis-à-vis the outer spheres. Cavalry generals have been known to risk their country's safety in order to protect the power of their outmoded arm within the military establishments. An authority in the classics might readily sacrifice the chances of his discipline to retain his personal position within it.

We do note a perceptiveness of the larger power issues among fundamentalists and other belief-groups that held a fringe position with respect to modern science. They could see a movement back into science from which they had long been displaced by evolutionary and anti-scriptural doctrines in science.

(3) Do conflicting power factions within the power elite take the same attitude towards plausible innovation? If so, then the dogmatic model is indicated. In the Velikovsky case, whatever general scientific leadership could be said to exist was either antagonistic or silent towards him. If factions existed, then dogmatism can be assumed. The answer is in doubt. The factions may not have existed or perhaps they did not perceive their 'objective interests' (indeterminacy) or perhaps they were in fact dogmatically opposed.

Going into the autonomous fields of science, the situation is somewhat clearer. In no scientific field, of the half-dozen involved, did a faction seize upon the issues. In astronomy, for instance, Struve, who might have opposed Shapley, took a dogmatic position in opposition to Velikovsky. The West Coast empires of astronomy were less unanimous in opposing him. Again, the query: indeterminacy? A cancelling effect between dogmatism and factionalism?

(4) Is there in fact a high correlation between opposition and novelty, where truth is a constant? If so, then the dogmatic model fits. The Velikovsky case alone cannot serve for this test. The measure of truth of the numerous theories is not yet agreed to. The opposition has treated the books wholesale; hence, opinions of one proposition are intertwined with opinions of another.

(5) Where there is awareness and interest in a work among several disciplines that are autonomous power groups, and where the rationalistic code is not applied, is agreement in the appraisal of the work conditioned by the degree to which its theories and approach are novel to the individual fields? If so, then dogmatism, rather than other behaviours, is manifest.

Here again, a sure answer is impossible in the Velikovsky case. Several fields were interested, but each suffered radical assaults. The only group that might have received the findings of Velikovsky without shock would be psychoanalitically oriented anthropologists of folklore. But there are few of these, and they seem scarcely to have been alerted (again the indeterminacy model).

(6) Are statements purporting to be empirically proven propositions of science bluntly made and repeatedly hammered home? If so, the dogmatic model would apply. Time after time, the same simple assertions were made against Velikovsky. This is a well-known rhetorical and propagandistic device, and would fit the power model as such, but it is likely that the assertions were sincerely meant as facts. Examples:

> The earth cannot stop suddenly without disintegrating. (Literally true but the affirmative was never asserted by Velikovsky.)
> The sea levels did not change in historical times. (Incorrect)
> Temples and dwellings from before 1500 B.C. are still standing. (Incorrect)
> Excavations in Ur show no signs of flooding. (Incorrect)
> Eclipses are checked to 3000 B.C. (Incorrect)

Clear records of Venus as a planet with orderly movements exist from before 1500 B.C.[22] (Incorrect)
Velikovsky is not scientific.

(7) Is the language of the reviewers and commentators heavily dogmatic and authoritative rather than rationalistic? If so, then the dogmatic model is operative. In fact, this is the most obvious aspect of the Velikovsky case. In the *New Haven Connecticut Register* of June 25, 1950, there appeared a collective review of *Worlds in Collision* by four Yale professors who were shortly to republish the same review in the *American Journal of Science*. I attempted a crude analysis of the contents of the four successive reviews. *Putting aside the question of the validity* of empirical statements made by the authors, I attempted to discover the proportions of various kinds of formal statements that appeared in the reviews. Using the sentences as the unit of measure, I fitted each statement into one of five categories by its form: a descriptive statement purporting to carry information about the contents of the work; an empirical statement presenting a factual proposition about the scientific material; a logico-empirical statement containing a proposition of factual or conceptual relations; a dogmatic-authorative statement affirming a belief or a consensus of experts; and miscellaneous statements dealing with the personal motives of the author and publisher.

I emerged from this little exercise with 27 statements purportedly descriptive of the work, 4 purportedly empirical statements, 12 purportedly logico-empirical statements, 27 dogmatic–authorative statements and 8 statements dealing with the character of the author and publisher. A separate summing-up of the evaluative loading of each statement resulted in a total of 2 favourable sentences, 31 neutral sentences and 46 negative statements about the work. In the Velikovsky case, then, rationalistic criticism was heavily subordinated to dogmatic–authoritative criticism of a negative character. This kind of material, if pursued through the Velikovsky case and also through many other scientific case studies, might lead to a complete overhaul of the machinery of scientific evaluation. At the very least, it would position the review function on a low level in the order of merit for the rationalistic appraisal of science.

The language of the academic reviewers is unequivocally harsh, strident and hostile. The question arises, however, whether this might not also be an indication of the power system at work. The language of power and the language of dogmatism are often similar: established power is conservative.

Furthermore, we note that the popular reviewers, numbering into the hundreds, are more disposed to rationalistic argument with the Velikovsky ideas than the scientists. This might indicate power, not dogma, to be the issue. The conclusion may be that motives of dogmatism and power are both in evidence. An unnecessary excess of abuse reveals that *Worlds in Collision* struck at dogmatic and moralistic defences as well as at existing power structures.

REFORM OF THE SYSTEM

The documentation of the Velikovsky case cannot be completed here. Much remains to be said. It is enough, however, to the immediate tasks, if it is shown that the Power Model, the Dogmatic Model, and the Indeterminacy Model describe and explain far more of the behaviours observed in the Velikovsky case than the Rationalistic Model.

In the early stages of the Velikovsky case, numerous 'wrong' cues were given. Lacking a conscious, regular system for the reception of new materials, the scientific establishment was governed by intrusive psychological forces organized irrelevantly by ideological and power networks. The frequent, remarkable misreadings of plain textual material are merely one of various indications of a perceptual system operating psychopathologically.

An original spate of publicity was the red flag to the bull. It warned the authorities that an outsider was seeking entrance with strange credentials. In some scholars and scientists, a high level of political anxiety (this was the period of McCarthyism) could join with intellectual anxieties produced by 'strange' and 'discredited' forms of data and proof to form a highly combustible mixture.

The rationalistic system was suppressed and the power system and dogmatic systems were activated. Once events had taken this course, little could be done to evade the conclusion. All involved were fully committed. There was no higher court of scientific appeal, or other checking or remedial agencies. The adjustment thereafter had to occur through unmobilized elements – young, sceptical students (from time to time Velikovsky mentions the young as his justifiers) or dissident scientists or outside intellectuals. Interestingly, the engineering profession is one of the best represented among Veilkovsky's adherents.

The problem that many thought had been solved ages ago – that of recognition of new contributions – turns out to be ominously present. Actually little was solved by the great historical cases of Copernicus, Bruno, Galileo and Pasteur, for the problem has always been conceived as one of improving rationality rather than as one of the applied sociology of science and institutions. It is in every respect like the central problems of political and governmental organization; there, however, a long history of scientific attention focuses on the need for more than personal goodwill and sweet reason to preserve and promote desired behaviours.

Also like the political order, the scientific order consists of a set of sub-universes each with its own goals, routines, organization, and, hence, particular problems. Generalizations about science as a whole and subsequent policies must be based on averages and parameters, and *a priori* could provide less than the total need for policies governing the individual disciplines. That is, a few policies may work for all fields, but each field needs its own; and all such policies should be based upon extensive behavioural research.

Few scientists can be immediately useful in the policy process of science. Most are uneducated to the tasks. They do not understand the nature of ideology. They seem not to know their own psychology or their patterns of social behaviour. They do not know how their organization works or what its policies are. In the end, how can scientists be trusted to fashion solutions to a wide range of social problems to which their special 'hardware' competence must contribute? The answer is that they cannot. Unless and until there is the equivalent of a Copernican revolution (or a Velikovskian revolution) in the form of a sociological revolution in science, natural scientists as a group will constitute a dead weight in public and professional policy, or worse, a potential force of evil.

The beginning of such a revolution must be in scientific self-knowledge. At present, scientists appear to study everything but themselves. An institute for research in scientific procedure is needed to initiate and conduct a wide variety of research projects on the behaviour of scientists. This institute should be amply supported by numerous individuals and groups and should be beholden to none. In its own structure it should predicate the goals that brought it into being. Its activities might be based on the recommendations for reform that are put forward in the passages that follow.

ON THE EDUCATION OF SCIENTISTS

The education of scientists must be broadened to include a knowledge of the aims and methods of the humanistic and behavioural disciplines.

The average scientist needs to know more of the history of science, but especially of an analytic sociological history of science. Unfortunately, the history of science is largely old-fashioned chronological recitation and rationalistic technical analysis.

The sociology of knowledge, epistemology, and pragmatic logic should be regular instruments of all of the sciences and philosophy.

The education of scientists should include ethical training. The cynicism normally provoked by analysis of the type undertaken in the present article can have a destructive effect upon creative and sustained work unless there appear to be social and professional forces working towards rationalistic ideals. The rationalistic model of science itself needs reformulation and reinforcement. Despite its failures in the Velikovsky case, it remains the most acceptable of the model reception systems of science presently conceivable.

The more frequent employment of psychiatric techniques to give specialists insight into their motives and behaviour would help to prevent destructiveness, exclusiveness, and other unconsciously provoked behaviours.

Efforts at unified interpretations of science should be promoted. Presently, the rewards for scholars who work on bridges across the sciences are unattended chairs in philosophy. The largest expenditures, fame, and professional prestige go to the masters of disciplinary secrets.

ON REPORTING ABOUT SCIENTIFIC BEHAVIOUR

Periodic surveys, assessments and agendas of scientific work in every discipline are needed. A clear and frank set of observations about what is and is not going on in science can help prevent a slump into the chaos of indeterminacy and into the evasive and irrelevant actions of the power-hungry. For science and all of its parts, regular reports should be prepared on the costs of maintenance, and on any imbalances between scientific and other social costs and among the various sub-sciences.

The sociology of science should focus upon the new communication systems that are rapidly developing, including linguistics, information storage and retrieval, mechanical translation, and rapid large-scale publication. The invention and control of these systems will soon force decisions that will critically affect power relations within science and society. The existing organizational structures of the sciences are inadequate to deal with such issues.

Most scientific journals are organized along lines of power; scientific controversies are often conducted like political campaigns. The journals lack serious intellectual goals; and they command few resources and skills for the massive tasks of providing free and easy communication. Their reviewing procedures need reform. Professional reviewers' associations might be set up within each scientific association; their members would engage to improve the science of scientific reviews and to use explicit agreed-upon procedures in reporting on new works. Their reviews would carry their associational 'trademark'.

ON THE CONTROLS OF SCIENCE

The associations of science are still among the primitive and puerile mechanisms of modern life. The annual convention of the American Association for the Advancement of Science has perhaps as much to do with the advancement of science as a state fair with the advancement of agriculture, but not more. Yet it is not atypical of the associative activities of science.

At present, and perhaps indefinitely, awareness of the non-rationality of scientific behaviour should favour old fashioned means of promoting scientific freedom. For instance, the semi-independent scientific establishments that have resulted from nationalistic separateness may be preferable to an international establishment with semi-coercive powers.

On the same grounds, a pluralism of support of scientific endeavour is desirable. A multiplicity of foundations, associations, well-equipped universities and other supportive agencies may appear costly, but brings about a larger efficiency through increased initiative and varied development. In this connection, the role of non-governmental companies engaged in research and development, and of independent publishing firms, should not be understated.

It would be well to inquire whether existing institutions have any inherent capacity for trying and sanctioning unprofessional practices among professionals. Two types of problems occur: those of ethics and those of non-rationality. Most contemporary scientists, and the public, perhaps believe that scientific freedom is achieved when outside lay authorities are forbidden to rule on questions of functional ethics and scientific truth. Inquisitions are scorned. Legislative investigations are hateful. The considerable powers of lawyers and medical practitioners for self-government are regarded as inappropriate to scientific affairs.

Is there then no recourse for the scientist who has been damaged by the means detailed in these papers? Perhaps Harvard University has within its authority the right to inquire into the scientific behaviour of its faculty. Its officers might make a determination 'on the merits' that one or more members of the faculty were so irrelevant and destructive in the scientific work as to violate plain standards of scientific competence. They might as a result take remedial action, as, for example, to require apologies, re-tests, re-examinations, discussion in open forums, suspension, reprimand, resignation, or dismissal. Lacking any of these forms of action, can a University be said to be responsible to its own and to the greater community for the quality of the particular activities it performs in the name of the community and of knowledge?

Scientific associations might conduct the same kind of inquiries. Their sanctions might be lighter; their responsibilities, however, are no less heavy. They could extend their authority to questions of apology, hearings, open forums, open journal pages, and suspension or withdrawal of membership.

The machinery and practices so envisioned might be self-defeating. The unorthodox voice is likely to end as the defendant, not the plaintiff, in most proceedings. The rank and file are likely to follow their leaders more than the dissident. Research is needed, therefore, into the conditions under which a hearing procedure and its consequences can be structured independently of the organization as a whole, very much as an independent court system operates in civil law.

The question arises also whether the larger society should ever take a hand in professional affairs. The investment of the public in the Velikovsky case is not inconsiderable. The scope and importance of the knowledge involved are great. Beyond them lies the public concern in how scientific scientists are. And the education being conveyed to the young is of public interest. Nor is it immaterial that a part of the nation's resources is being spent each year to solve technological problems, some of which are connected with national survival. If the public concern is present, what public machinery is to be brought into play – congressional investigations, a national science board to hear and investigate complaints, a congress of scientific associations with a judicial branch?

Such questions warrant intensive study followed by new policies. It is this writer's belief that independent hearing and reporting mechanisms should be invented for use by associations and by joint scientific-public-governmental organs. Legislative and executive machinery should be avoided as far as possible, but quasi-judicial machinery encouraged. Scientists have on the whole tender sensitivities. A mild exposure and embarrassment usually have great corrective value for them.

These then are the conclusions reached. They are as far from the original incidents engendering the case of Dr Velikovsky as were his astronomical, geological, and historical conclusions from his early thought that Freud misjudged Akhnaton.

Immanuel Velikovsky propounded a synthetic theory of the highest order. He reordered classical chronology. He derived important truths from ancient sources that science had abandoned. Profound experiences of man's ancestors are revealed anew. He therefore has given us new understanding of man's nature.

He has shown that the present order of the solar system is quite new and that unaccounted forces help govern it. He has struck at a great part of the Darwinian explanation of evolution. He has upset several major theories of geology and offered substitutes therefore. He found space a vacuum and has made of it a plenum.

A great many of his truths are to be found scattered in the historical and contemporary byways of science. As bits of information and fragmented theories, they meant little or nothing to the many scholars and scientists who may have glanced at them and turned away. With rare imagination and consummate skill, he fashioned them into theories of great scope, compactness, and integration. While his ideas are not at all beyond criticism, as a cosmogonist he appears in the company of Plato, Aquinas, Bruno, Descartes, Newton and Kant. What would therefore be only the duty of the critics of science – to defend ordinary or even mistaken scholars – becomes, by accident, an occasion to defend a great savant of the age.

REFERENCES

1. A person may be *favored* 'unjustly' by the reception system. Thus, many irrelevant elements may enter into rewarding undeservedly a scientist for his behaviors. Whatever principles may be established to correct 'unjust unacceptance' should also be observedly operative in cases of 'unjust acceptance'. It also may occur that 'unjust acceptance' is correlated with 'unjust unacceptance'.

2. Proto-thought is a level of assumptive prejudiced thought midway between unconscious 'thought' and self-controlled thinking. It is prominent in ideological and stereotyped thinking.

3. Cecilia Payne-Gaposchkin, 'Worlds in Collision', *Proceedings of the American Philosophical Society*, Vol. 96 (October 15, 1952), pp. 519, 523.

4. Laurence J. Lafleur, 'Cranks and Scientists', *The Scientific Monthly*, Vol. LXXIII (November, 1951), p. 285.

5. In a review of *Earth in Upheaval*, *Scientific American*, Vol. 194 (March, 1956), p. 127.

6. Harrison Brown, 'Venus and the Scriptures', *The Saturday Review*, Vol. XXXIII (April 22, 1950), pp. 18, 19.

7. In a recent article in *Science*, M. King Hubbert has shown

how an erroneous formula existed in various books over a half century without detection.

... the equation cited was for twenty-five years the most widely used equation in the petroleum industry . . . it was ruefully discovered that the equation in question was neither physically correct nor a valid statement of a result established a century earlier by a Frenchman named Henry Darcy. (*Science*, March 8, 1963, p. 8856.)

8. Edwin G. Boring, 'The Validation of Scientific Belief', *Proceedings*, *op. cit.*, pp. 535–39.

9. 'Orthodoxy and Scientific Progress', *Proceedings*, *op. cit.*, p. 505.

10. *American Behavioral Scientist*, Vol. VI, December, 1962.

11. *Harvard Crimson* (September 25, 1950), p. M 2, and *infra*, p. 59.

12. Cf. James V. Conant, in *Science and Common Sense* (1951), Preface and p. 278, and in New York *Herald Tribune*, February 16, 1951.

13. *Proceedings*, *op. cit.*, p. 525.

14. *Nature*, May 14, 1960; January 7, 1961; March 25, 1961.

15. *Science*, Vol. 138, October 12, 1962.

16. T. S. Kuhn, *The Structure of Scientific Revolutions* (Chicago, 1962), p. 164.

17. *Science and Method* (London, Nelson, n.d.), p. 54.

18. Cf. A. de Grazia, *Science and Values of administration* (Indianapolis, Bobbs Merrill, reprint series, 1962), on science as administration; T. S. Kuhn, *Structure of Scientific Revolutions*, p. 10 seq.

19. A fair estimate of Dr Velikovsky's wage rate considering his total royalties from writing and his total research time on his books, including *Worlds in Collision*, would be $1.35 an hour. He held no university or foundation appointment at any time. The typical Harvard professor could be said to be paid the equivalent of royalties on sales of 30,000 books *every year*.

20. It was in the transition from the mimeographed to the printed version that a clear ethical test was presented and failed by Dr Gaposchkin. We quote here the passage from the mimeographed text and that of the printed text:

The mimeographed version: 'If the biblical story which Mr Velikovsky seeks to establish is to be accepted at its face value, the rotation of the earth must have been stopped within six hours. All bodies not attached to the surface of the earth (including the atmosphere and the ocean) would then have continued their motion, and consequently have flown off with a speed of 900 miles an hour at the latitude of Egypt.'

The printed version (later): 'Let us assume, however, that Dr Velikovsky is right – that the earth did stop rotating. In that case, all bodies not attached to the surface of the earth (including the atmosphere and the ocean) would have continued the motion, and would have flown off with a speed of nine hundred miles an hour at the latitude of Egypt.'

Nota Bene. If the earth, as she says first, decelerated within six hours, the inertial push on objects on the earth's surface would be 500 times smaller than their weight. A man of 160 lbs would experience a forward push of 5 ounces. Dr Gaposchkin now had a clear choice: Someone had called the quantitative error to her attention. She might choose to recalculate the inertia of the slower stop, or, misquoting Velikovsky, imply that he reported an instant stop. She chose the latter. She took out the reference to the six hours and all other qualifications Velikovsky had introduced and kept the 900 m.p.h. reference.

21. An incorrect prediction. Doubleday Company has published, in addition to *Worlds in Collision*, *Ages in Chaos*, *Earth in Upheaval*, and *Oedipus and Ahknaton*. A fifth volume, forming a sequel to *Ages in Chaos*, is in page proofs.

22. We note such phenomena as the following triple play among reviewers: Dr Edmondson of Link Observatory obviously copies in a review from Kaempffert of the New York *Times* who had copied in his review from Gaposchkin's preview that (1) the Venus tablets from before 1500 B.C. describe regular motions of this planet 'exactly as we see it', and that (2) Velikovsky suppressed both this fact and the very existence of the tablets. Both statements are untrue. The tablets describe very erratic motions of Venus, and Velikovsky presented the Venus tablets in his book to support his concept.

ADDITIONAL EXAMPLES OF CORRECT PROGNOSIS

by Immanuel Velikovsky

In 1950 – as it is still largely today – it was generally accepted that the theory of uniformity must be true and that no process which is unobservable in our time could have occurred in the past. It was also believed that celestial bodies, the Earth included, travel serenely on their orbits in the void of space for countless eons. In *Worlds in Collision* (1950), however, I offered these theses: '(1) there were physical upheavals of a global character in historical time; (2) these catastrophes were caused by extraterrestrial agents; and (3) these agents can be identified' (from the Preface). These claims were termed a 'most amazing example of a shattering of accepted concepts on record' (Payne-Gaposchkin).

The consequences of the theory affected almost all natural sciences and many social disciplines. Especially objectionable was the assertion that events of such magnitude took place also in historical times.

Worlds in Collision describes two (last) series of cataclysmic events that occurred 34 and 27 centuries ago. Not only the Earth, but also Venus, Mars, and the Moon were involved in near encounters, when the Morning Star, then on a stretched elliptical orbit following its eruption from the giant planet Jupiter, caused turmoil among the members of the solar system before settling on its present orbit.

The description was derived from literary references in the writings of ancient peoples of the world. The archaeological, geological, and paleontological evidence for the theory was collected and presented separately in *Earth in Upheaval* (1955).

In order to explain how certain phenomena could have taken place – how, for instance, Venus, a newcomer, could obtain a circular orbit, or the Earth turn over on its axis – the theory envisaged a charged state of the sun, planets, and comets, and extended magnetic fields permeating the solar system. This appeared even more objectionable since celestial mechanics had been solidly erected on the notion of gravitation, inertia and pressure of light as the only forces acting in the void, the celestial bodies being electrically and magnetically sterile in their inter-relations. *Worlds in Collision*, in its Preface, was acknowledged as heresy in fields where the names Newton and Darwin are supreme.

The only quantitative attempt to disprove one of my main theses was made by D. Menzel of Harvard College Observatory (1952).[1] He showed ('if Velikovsky wants quantitative discussion, let us give him one'), on certain assumptions, that were I right the sun would need to hold a potential of 10^{19} volts; but, he calculated that the sun, if positive, could hold only 1800 volts, and, if negative, it follows from the equation, no more than a single volt.

In 1960–61, V. A. Bailey calculated that to account for the data obtained in space probes (Pioneer V) the sun must possess a net negative charge with the potential of the order of 10^{19} volts.[2]

In 1953, Menzel wrote: 'Indeed, the total number of electrons that could escape the sun would be able to run a one cell flashlight for less than one minute.'[3] My affirmation of electromagnetic interactions in the solar system became less objectionable with the discovery of the solar wind and of magnetic fields permeating the solar system.

My thesis that changes in the duration of the day had been caused in the past by electromagnetic interactions was rejected in 1950–51.[4] In February 1960, A. Danjon, Director, Paris Observatory, reported to l'Académie des Sciences that following a strong solar flare the length of the day suddenly increased by 0.85 millisecond. Thereafter the day began to decrease by 3.7 microseconds every 24 hours.[5] He ascribed the fluctuation in the length of the day to an electromagnetic cause connected with the flare. His announcement 'created a sensation among the delegates to the General Assembly of the International Union of Geodesy and Geophysics' that year in Helsinki.[5]

V. Bargmann of Princeton University and L. Motz of Columbia University claimed for me the priority of predicting radio-noises from Jupiter, the existence of a magnetosphere around the earth, and the high ground temperature of Venus.[6] They stress also that these discoveries later came as great surprises, though I have insisted in my published works, in my lectures, and in my letters that these physical conditions are directly deducible from my theory.

These claims were not made casually or in a veiled form. Some of my arguments for Jupiter sending out radio-noises can be learned from my correspondence with A. Einstein. I could add that if the solar system as a whole is close to neutrality, and the planets possess charges of opposite sign to that of the sun, Jupiter must have the largest charge among the planets. Rotating quickly the charged planet creates an intense magnetosphere.

In the last chapter of *W. in C.* ('The Thermal Balance of Venus') I insisted that 'Venus is hot' and 'gives off heat' as a consequence of its recent origin and stormy history before settling on its orbit. In 1954, R. Barker suggested that a layer of ice on the night side of Venus is responsible for the ashen light.[7] It is more probably a visible sign of incandescence. When in 1961 the temperature of Venus was found to be ca. 600°K, it was admitted that neither radioactivity nor greenhouse effect suffices to explain why Venus is so hot.

Several of the sensors of Mariner II were beyond their capacity to report temperatures before the nearest point to Venus was reached, 'because temperatures beyond their designed scale were encountered', as reported by C. W. Snyder to the meeting of the American Geophysical Union, December 28, 1962.[8] On December 15, 1962, a day after Mariner II passed the point of closest approach, the 'temperature had inexplicably started to drop'.[9]

It is interesting also to know why the temperature of the upper cloud layer of Venus measured in the 1920's by Pettit and Nicholson (−33°C for the dark side, −38°C for the bright side)[10] was found in the 1950's by Stinton and Strong to be a few degrees lower (ca. −40°C for both sides).[11] Could it be that Venus cools off at this rate? It would point, too, to its youth as a celestial body.

In 1950 the critics of *W. in C.* emphatically objected to the notion that Venus is a young planet or that it erupted from Jupiter.

R. A. Lyttleton (1959–60) showed why the terrestrial planets, Venus included, must have originated from the giant planets, notably Jupiter, by disruption.[12] W. H. McCrea (1960) calculated that no planet could have originated by aggregation inside the Jovian orbit.[13]

R. M. Goldstein and R. L. Carpenter reported to the meeting of the American Geophysical Union at Palo Alto, the last week of December 1962, that radar probes from Goldstone Tracking Station between October 1 and December 17, 1962, confirmed earlier indications that Venus rotates very slowly and retrogradely. According to the press, this led to the following surmises: 'Maybe Venus was created apart from other planets, perhaps as a second solar explosion, or perhaps in a collision of planets.'[14] To this, compare *W. in C.*, p. 373: 'The collision between major planets . . . brought about the birth of comets. These comets moved across the orbits of other planets and collided with them. At least one of the comets in historical times became a planet – Venus, and this at the cost of great destruction on Mars and on the earth.'

In the section 'The Gases of Venus' in *W. in C.* (1950), I concluded that Venus must be rich in hydrocarbons. This theory was termed 'surprising' (H. Shapley, 1946) when, a few years in advance of the publication of my book, I requested that Harvard College Observatory make a spectral search for hydrocarbons in Venus's atmosphere.[15] In 1955, Fred Hoyle proposed, on theoretical grounds, that Venus is covered by oceans of oil and that its atmosphere is clouded by hydrocarbon droplets.[16] I, however, wrote: '. . . as long as Venus is too hot for the liquefaction of petroleum, the hydrocarbons will circulate in gaseous form'. (*W. in C.*, p. 369).

The extraterrestrial origin claimed in my book for at least part of the petroleum deposits, notably those of the Mexican Gulf area, was scorned (C. R. Longwell, 1950),[17] and it was asserted that petroleum is never found in Recent sediments (J. B. Patton, 1950)[18] however, soon thereafter, P. V. Smith (1952)[19] reported the 'surprising' fact that the oil of the Gulf of Mexico is found in Recent sediment and must have been deposited during the last 9,200 plus or minus 1,000 years.

Hydrocarbons were subsequently found on meteorites, a fact termed by H. H. Nininger (1959)[20] also 'surprising': 'These resemble in many ways some of the waxes and petroleum products that are found on the earth.' Several months ago, A. T. Wilson (1962)[21] postulated an extraterrestrial origin of the entire terrestrial deposit of oil. In *W. in C.* (p. 55), presence of hydrocarbons on meteorites was anticipated. The experiment in which high molecular weight hydrocarbons were compounded from ammonia and methane with electrical discharges (Wilson, 1960)[22] supports the view that the planet Jupiter (rich in ammonia and methane) was the source of the hydrocarbons on Venus, on meteorites, and in some of the earth's deposits (*W. in C.*, 'The Gases of Venus').

My contention that Mars's atmosphere must be rich in argon and neon and possibly nitrogen was made early in my work (lecture titled 'Neon and Argon in the Atmosphere of Mars', copyrighted in 1945; test requests addressed in 1946 to Harvard College and Mount Wilson observatories) and repeated in *W. in C.* ('The Atmosphere of Mars'). A few years later, Harrison Brown, on theoretical grounds and independently, arrived at the same conclusion concerning argon: 'In the case of Mars, it might well be that argon is the major atmospheric constituent.'[23] But he thought that rare gases 'are essentially non-existent' on meteorites. In recent years neon and argon have been repeatedly discovered on meteorites (H. Stauffer, 1961),[24] as anticipated in *W. in C.* (pp. 281ff, 367).

Concerning the Moon, I asserted that its surface had been subjected to stress, heating (liquefaction) and bubbling activity in historical times. 'During these catastrophes the moon's surface flowed with lava and bubbled into great circular formations, which rapidly cooled off . . . In these cosmic collisions or near contacts the surface of the moon was also marked with clefts and rifts' (*W. in C.*, 'The Moon and Its Craters'). H. Percy Wilkins (1955) described numerous domes on the Moon and wrote: 'The numerous domes might be regarded as examples of bubbles which did not burst.'[25]

Signs of tensional stresses have been detected on the Moon (Warren and Fielder, 1962);[26] volcanic activity has been unexpectedly discovered by Kozyrev (1958).[27] Sharp outlines of lunar formations could not have persisted for millions of years in view of the thermal splintering due to great changes in temperature, over 300 degrees, in the day–night sequel and during the eclipses. H. Jeffreys (1959)[28] drew attention to this evidence for the youth of the surface features, but made it dependent on the presence of water in the rocks. Since there seems to be volcanic activity on the Moon, water is most probably present in the rocks.

Assertions that the Earth's axis could not have changed its geographical or astronomical position constituted one of the main arguments against *Worlds in Collision.*[29] They gave place to the theory of wandering poles. Th. Gold (1955ff)[33] shows the error in the view of G. Darwin and Lord Kelvin on the subject, and stresses the comparative ease with which the globe could – and did – change its axis, even with no external force applied.

Confirmed is also the conclusion that advanced human culture would be found in the today uninhabited area 'on the Kolyma or Lena rivers flowing into the Arctic Ocean' in northeastern Siberia (*W. in C.*, p. 329) in the region where herds of mammoths roamed. Already in 1951, A. P. Okladnikov,[31] making known the results of his research in northern Siberia, wrote: 'about two to three millennia before our era, neolithic races ... spread to the very coast of the Arctic Ocean in the north and the Kolyma in the east'. Twenty-five hundred years ago copper was worked in the taiga of Yakutsk.

Under the heading 'The Reversed Polarity of the Earth' (*W. in C.*, pp. 114ff.) is written: 'In recent geological times the magnetic poles of the globe were reversed.' The phenomenon that could cause it was described, and the question was asked 'whether the position of the magnetic poles has anything to do with the direction of rotation of the globe'. Complete and repeated *sudden* reversals of the magnetic poles were postulated by S. K. Runcorn (1955)[32] and P. M. Blackett (1956).[33] Runcorn wrote: 'There seems no doubt that the earth's field is tied up in some way with the rotation of the planet. And this leads to a remarkable finding about the earth's rotation itself ... The planet has rolled about, changing the location of its geographical poles.' Complete reversals would change the rising and setting points, west becoming east, as described in many ancient sources collated in *W. in C.* The pioneers in paleomagnetic studies, G. Folgheraiter and P. L. Mercanton,[34] found a reversal of the earth's magnetic field in the Central Mediterranean area in the 8th century before the present era, recorded in the magnetic dip of the Etruscan and Attic vases; their position in the kiln is learned from the flow of glaze. This find is in harmony with the events described on pp. 207–359 of *W. in C.*

Radiocarbon analysis, besides disclosing that some petroleum is of recent origin and deposit, verified also the claim (*W. in C.*, 'The Ice Age and the Antiquity of Man') that the last glacial period ended less than 10,000 years ago. One of the first and most important results of the new method was the reduction of the time of the last glaciation. 'The *advance* of the ice occurred about 11,000 years ago . . . Previously this maximum advance had been assumed to date from about 25,000 years ago,' reported W. F. Libby and Frederick Johnson in 1952.[35] Later this figure was still more reduced; furthermore, it refers to the advance, not the end of the retreat of the ice cover.

Possibly the most clear-cut case of vindication concerns the antiquity I assigned to the Mesoamerican civilizations (Mayas, Toltecs, Olmecs). G. Kubler of Yale University wrote (1950):[36]

'The Mesoamerican cosmology to which Velikovsky repeatedly appeals for proof did not originate and could not originate until about the beginning of our era.'

Kubler showed a discrepancy of over 1,000 years and asserted that events I ascribed to the 8th–4th centuries before the present era could not have taken place until rather late in the Christian era. But on December 30, 1956, the National Geographical Society, on its own behalf and that of the Smithsonian Institution, announced:

> Atomic science has proved the ancient civilization of Mexico to be some 1,000 years older than had been believed. The findings basic to Middle American archaeology, artifacts dug up in La Venta, Mexico, have been proved to come from a period 800 to 400 years before the Christian era. Previously, they had been assigned to 400 or 500 A.D., more than 1,000 years later. Cultural parallels between La Venta and other Mexican archaeological excavations enable scientists to date one in the terms of the others. Thus the new knowledge affects the dating of many finds. Dr Matthew W. Sterling, Chief of the Bureau of American Ethnology at the Smithsonian Institution, declared the new dating the most important archaeological discovery in recent history.

P. Drucker and his co-workers have elaborated on the subject in *Science* (1957) and in the report of the excavation (1959).[37]

H. E. Suess, because of an accumulation of certain discrepancies in the radiocarbon dates, assumes that natural events caused a radical change in the intensity of the magnetosphere and in the influx of cosmic rays sometime in the second millennium before the present era. Several other researchers came to the same conclusion.[38] This is also in harmony with the story related in my book.

Oceanographic research brought several confirming data. H. Pettersson of Goteborg found so much nickel in clay of the oceanic bed that he inferred that at some time in the past there had been a prodigious fall of meteorites.[39] In *W. in C.*, the descent of enormous trains of meteorites and meteoric dust and ash (pp. 51ff) on land and sea is narrated, with reliance on ancient sources. In 1958, J. L. Worzel found a layer of white ash, 5 to 30 cm thick, very close to the bottom, evenly spread over an enormous area of the ocean bed in the Pacific, and he thought of a 'fiery end of bodies of cosmic origin'.[40] M. Ewing cites evidence that the same ash layer of 'remarkable uniformity of thickness' found by Worzel in the Pacific underlies all oceans and assumes 'a cometary collision'.[41] It could hardly be without some recorded consequences of global extent,' Ewing concluded. To this a line from *W. in C.* ('The Darkness') can be quoted: 'The earth entered deeper into the tail of the onrushing comet' with its 'sweeping gases, dust, and cinders' and 'the dust sweeping in from interplanetary space'.

In 1950 a past collision of the earth with a comet was denied, and comets were also regarded as very tenuous and light masses incapable of causing much damage.[42] R. Wildt claimed that the largest comet would have a mass equal to one millionth of that of Venus.[42] But N. T. Bobrovnikoff (1951),[43] Director of Perkins Observatory, took a different view. Several comets seen in the 19th century moved in very similar orbits and 'in all probability, are the result of decomposition of one single body'. He estimated that: 'If put together' these comets 'would make something like the mass of the moon.'

Before Ewing, a cometary collision was postulated in 1957 by H. Urey to explain the tektites and their distribution.[44] G. Baker insists that Australian tektites (australites) have lain in place no longer than 5,000 years.[45]

3,500 years ago the oceans suddenly evaporated and the water level dropped about twenty feet, a fact first noted by R. Daly and later confirmed by Kuenen.[46] Rubin and Suess found that 3,000 years ago glaciers in the Rockies suddenly increased in size.[47] Scandinavian and German authors date *Klimastürze* at 1500 and 700 B.C. – the very periods of great perturbations described in *W. in C.*[48]

In the ocean floor B. Heezen discovered (1960)[49] a ridge split by a deep canyon, or 'crack in the crust that runs nearly twice around the earth'. He wrote: 'The discovery at this late date of the midocean ridge and rift has raised fundamental questions about basic geological processes and the history of the earth and has even had reverberations in cosmology'.

Prof. Ma (Formosa) claims that there was a sudden and total shift in the crust only 26 and 32 centuries ago, as evidenced by the shift of marine sediments (1955).[50] It was argued that in global catastrophes of such dimensions no stalactites would have remained unbroken, but within one year after the atomic explosion, stalactites grew in the Gnome cavern, New Mexico: 'All nature's processes have been speeded up a billionfold.'[51]

Claude F. A. Schaeffer of College de France, in his *Stratigraphie comparée*,[52] on which he worked not knowing of my simultaneous efforts, came to the conclusion that the Ancient East, as documented by every excavated place from Troy to the Caucasus, Persia, and Palestine–Syria, underwent immense natural paroxysms, unknown in modern annals of seismology; cultures were terminated, empires collapsed, trade ceased, populations were decimated, the earth upheaved, the sea erupted, ash buried cities, climate changed. Five times between the third and the first millennia before the present era the cataclysms were repeated, closing the Early and the Middle Bronze Ages in their wake. The number of catastrophes and their dates relative to historical periods coincide in Schaeffer's estimate and in my own. From source material of a different nature – archaeological – he found that the greatest catastrophe terminated the Middle Kingdom in Egypt (Middle Bronze). Thus we are in agreement to a day. The catastrophe that ended the Middle Kingdom in Egypt is the starting point of *Worlds in Collision* (and of *Ages of Chaos*, my reconstruction of ancient chronology).

The recent finds in astronomy, especially in radio-astronomy (sun, Venus, Jupiter), have given confirmation from above; oceanography, radiocarbon, paleomagnetism, and archaeology have carried their shares from below.

REFERENCES

1. D. Menzel, *Proc. Amer. Philos. Soc.* (October, 1952).
2. V. A. Bailey, *Nature*, May 14, 1960; January 7, 1961; March 25, 1961.
3. Menzel, *Flying Saucers* (Harvard University Press), 1953, p. 236.
4. J. Q. Stuart, Princeton University Observatory, in *Harper's*, June, 1951.
5. A. Danjon, *Comptes rendues des séances de l'Academie des Sciences*, 250 #8 (February 22, 1960); 250 #15 (April 11, 1960).

5a. New York *Times*, July 30, 1960.

6. *Science*, December 21, 1962.
7. R. Barker, *J.B.A.A.*, *64*, 60 (1954).
8. New York *Times*, December 29, 1962 (West coast ed.).
9. U.P.I. dispatch from Washington, D.C., in Philadelphia *Inquirer*, December 16, 1962.
10. E. Pettit in Hynek (ed.) *Astrophysics*, McGraw-Hill, 1951, revised by Pettit and Nicholson, *Publ. Astr. Soc. of the Pacif. 67* (1955), p. 293.
11. Sinton and Strong, *Science*, 123, 676 (1956).
12. R. A. Lyttleton, *Monthly Notices*, Royal Astr. Soc., 121 #6 (1960); *Man's View of the Universe*, 1961, p. 36.
13. H. H. McCrea, *Proceedings*, Royal Society, Series A, Vol. 256 (May 31, 1960).
14. *The National Observer*, December 31, 1962.
15. H. Shapley to H. M. Kallen, May 27, 1946.
16. F. Hoyle, *Frontiers of Astronomy*, 1955, pp. 68–72.
17. C. R. Longwell, *Am. J. of Science*, August, 1950.
18. J. B. Patton quoted by F. E. Edmondson, *Courier-Journal*, Louisville, Ky., April 23, 1950.
19. P. V. Smith, *Science*, October 24, 1952.

20. H. H. Nininger, *Out of the Sky* (Dover Publ.), 1959, pp. 89–90.
21. A. T. Wilson, *Nature*, October 6, 1962.
22. *Ibid.*, December 17, 1960.
23. H. Brown in *The Atmospheres of the Earth and Planets*, ed. Kuiper, 1949, p. 268.
24. H. Stauffer, *J. Geoph. Res.*, 66 #5 (May, 1961).
25. H. P. Wilkins, *The Moon*, 1955, p. 42.
26. B. Warren and G. Fielder, *Nature*, February 24, 1962.
27. N. A. Kozyrev, November 3, 1958. Cf. Z. Kopal, *The Moon* (1960), p. 96.
28. H. Jeffreys, *The Earth*, 4th ed. (1959), p. 377.
29. C. Payne-Gaposchkin, *Popular Astronomy*, June, 1950.
30. Th. Gold, *Nature*, *175*, 526 (March 26, 1955); *Sky and Telescope*, April, 1958.
31. A. P. Okladnikov, in *Po Sledam Drevnikh Kultur*, Moscow, 1951; Russ. Transl. series of the Peabody Museum, *1*, #1 (1959).
32. S. K. Runcorn, *Scientific American*, September, 1955.
33. P. M. Blackett, *Lectures on Rock Magnetism*, Jerusalem, 1956.
34. G. Folgheraiter, *Archives des sciences physiques et naturelles* (Geneva), 1899; *Journal de Physique*, 1899; P. L. Mercanton, *Archives des sciences phys. et nat.*, 1907 (t.xxiii).
35. F. Johnson in W. F. Libby, *Radiocarbon Dating* (University of Chicago Press), 1952.
36. G. Kubler, *Am. J. of Science*, August, 1950.
37. P. Drucker, R. F. Heizer, R. J. Squier, *Science*, July 12, 1957; *Excavations at La Venta* (Smithsonian Institute, 1959).
38. Cf. a series of articles by V. Milojcic, *Germania*, 1957 ff, E. Ralph, *Am. J. of Sc.*, *Radiac. Suppl.*, 1959 (note to samples P-214, P-215, P-216).
39. H. Pettersson, *Scient. American*, August, 1950; *Tellus*, I, 1949.
40. J. L. Worzel, *Proc. Nat. Acad. of Sc.*, Vol. 45 #3 (March 15, 1959).
41. M. Ewing, *Proc. Nat. Acad. of Sc.*, Vol. 45 #3.
42. R. Wildt, *Amer. J. of Science*, August, 1950.
43. N. T. Bobrovnikoff, in *Astrophysics*, ed. Hynek, McGraw-Hill, 1951, pp. 310–311.
44. H. Urey, *Nature*, March 16, 1957.
45. G. Baker, *Nature*, January 30, 1960.
46. P. H. Kuenen, *Marine Geology*, 1950, p. 538.
47. Rubin and Suess, *Science*, April 8, 1955.
48. H. Gams and R. Nordhagen, *Mitteil. der Geograph. Ges. in Munchen*, XVI, H. 2 (1923), pp. 13–348. R. Sernander, 'Klimaverschlechterung, Postglaciale' in *Reallexikon der Vorgeschichte*, VII (1926); O. Paret, *Das Neue Bild der Vorgeschichte* (1948), p. 44.

49. B. Heezen, *Scient. American*, October, 1960.

50. T. Y. H. Ma, *Alterations of Sedimentary Facies on the Ocean Bottom*, 1955.

51. Dispatch by W. Hines of the Washington Star from Carlsbad, N.M., in *The Evening Bulletin*, December 18, 1962.

52. C. F. A. Schaeffer, *Stratigraphie comparée*, Oxford University Press, 1948; Im. Velikovsky, Theses for the Reconstruction of Ancient History (*Scripta Academica Hierosolymitana*), 1945.

APPENDIX I

ON THE RECENT DISCOVERIES CONCERNING JUPITER AND VENUS

In the light of recent discoveries of radio waves from Jupiter and of the high surface temperature of Venus, we think it proper and just to make the following statement.

On October 14, 1953, Immanuel Velikovsky, addressing the Forum of the Graduate College of Princeton University in a lecture entitled '*Worlds in Collision* in the Light of Recent Finds in Archaeology, Geology and Astronomy: Refuted or Verified?,' concluded the lecture as follows: 'The planet Jupiter is cold, yet its gases are in motion. It appears probable to me that it sends out radio noises as do the sun and the stars. I suggest that this be investigated.'

Soon after that date, the text of the lecture was deposited with each of us [it is printed as supplement to Velikovsky's *Earth in Upheaval* (Doubleday, 1955)]. Eight months later, in June 1954, Velikovsky, in a letter, requested Albert Einstein to use his influence to have Jupiter surveyed for radio emission. The letter, with Einstein's marginal notes commenting on this proposal, is before us. Ten more months passed, and on April 5, 1955, B. F. Burke and K. L. Franklin of the Carnegie Institution announced the chance detection of strong radio signals emanating from Jupiter. They recorded the signals for several weeks before they correctly identified the source.

This discovery came as something of a surprise because radio astronomers had never expected a body as cold as Jupiter to emit radio waves.[1]

In 1960 V. Radhakrishnah of India and J. A. Roberts of Australia, working at California Institute of Technology, established the existence of a radiation belt encompassing Jupiter, 'giving 10^{14} times as much radio energy as the Van Allen belts around the earth'.

On December 5, 1956, through the kind services of H. H. Hess, chairman of the department of geology of Princeton University, Velikovsky submitted a memorandum to the U.S. National Committee for the (planned) I.G.Y. in which he suggested the existence of a terrestrial magnetosphere reaching the moon. Receipt of the memorandum was acknowledged by E. O. Hulburt for the Committee. The magnetosphere was discovered in 1958 by Van Allen.

In the last chapter of his *Worlds in Collision* (1950), Velikovsky stated that the surface of Venus must be very hot, even though in 1950 the temperature of the cloud surface of Venus was known to be —25°C on the day and night sides alike.

In 1954 N. A. Kozyrev[2] observed an emission spectrum from the night side of Venus but ascribed it to discharges in the upper layers of its atmosphere. He calculated that the temperature of the surface of Venus must be +30°C; somewhat higher values were found earlier by Adel and Herzberg. As late as 1959, V. A. Firsoff arrived at a figure of +17.5°C for the mean surface temperature of Venus, only a little above the mean annual temperature of the earth (+14.2°C).[3]

However, by 1961 it became known that the surface temperature of Venus is 'almost 600 degrees (K)'.[4] F. D. Drake described this discovery as 'a surprise . . . in a field in which the fewest surprises were expected'. 'We would have expected a temperature only slightly greater than that of the earth . . . Sources of internal heating (radioactivity) will not produce an enhanced surface temperature.' Cornell H. Mayer writes,[5] 'All the observations are consistent with a temperature of almost 600 degrees', and admits that 'the temperature is much higher than anyone would have predicted'.

Although we disagree with Velikovsky's theories, we feel impelled to make this statement to establish Velikovsky's priority of prediction of these two points and to urge, in view of these prognostications, that his other conclusions be objectively re-examined.

V. BARGMANN

Department of Physics, Princeton University, Princeton, New Jersey

LLOYD MOTZ

Department of Astronomy, Columbia University, New York

REFERENCES

1. See also the New York *Times* for October 28, 1962.
2. N. A. Kozyrev, *Izv. Krymsk. Astrofiz. Observ. 12* (1954).
3. *Science News 1959*, 52 (Summer 1959).
4. *Phys. Today 14*, No. 4, 30 (1961).
5. C. H. Mayer, *Sci. Am. 204* (May, 1961).

APPENDIX II

VELIKOVSKY 'DISCREDITED': A TEXTUAL COMPARISON

The various writings of Harvard astronomer Cecilia Payne-Gaposchkin against *Worlds in Collision* (*The Reporter*, March 14, 1950; *Popular Astronomy*, June, 1950; *Proceedings of the American Philosophical Society*, Vol. 96, October, 1952) provided a convenient reservoir of damaging testimony from which her colleagues as well as lesser critics drew freely in formulating their own opinions and in preparing further commentaries on the book.

Reproduced below are passages from Gaposchkin's paper that appeared in the *Proceedings of the American Philosophical Society* and the material in Velikovsky's book that she purportedly discredited. The reader may judge for himself who is guilty of faulty scholarship and purposeful misrepresentation.

THE CRITICISM: I

Gaposchkin:

The thesis of the book is scientific, but the evidence is drawn from an immense mass of biblical evidence and Hebrew tradition, myth and folklore, classical literature and the works of the Church fathers. A critic is faced . . . with the herculean labour of laying a finger on the flaws in an argument that ranges over the greater part of ancient literature. [But] when one examines [Velikovsky's] sources, his argument falls to pieces . . . He has not only chosen his sources; he has even chosen what they shall mean.

Let me give one example. [Gaposchkin quotes from

Worlds in Collision:] 'One of the places of the heavenly combat . . . was on the way from Egypt to Syria. According to Herodotus, the final act of the fight between Zeus and Typhon took place at Lake Serbon on the coastal route from Egypt to Palestine.' *But Herodotus says nothing about the battle, or even about Zeus*, in the passage quoted. [The dots denoting an omission and the italics are Gaposchkin's. She next quotes Herodotus in Greek and translates:] 'Egypt begins at the Serbonian shore, where, they say, Typhon is hidden'.

[Gaposchkin makes it appear that Velikovsky invented the battle and its participants, because Herodotus speaks only of Typhon's place of burial, not of a battle.]

THE TEXTS: I

Velikovsky (*Worlds in Collision, pp. 78–81*):

[The quoted sentence in *Worlds in Collision* follows almost three pages of a description of the battle between Zeus and Typhon, quoted from Apollodorus: 'Zeus pelted Typhon at a distance with thunderbolts . . .'] The Egyptian shore of the Red Sea was called Typhonia (Fn: Strabo, vii, 3, 8). Strabo narrates also that the Arimi (Syrians) were terrified witnesses of the battle of Zeus with Typhon . . . 'who . . . when struck by the bolts of lightning, fled in search of a descent underground'.

[Restituted in full, the passage quoted by Gaposchkin reads as follows:] One of the places of the heavenly combat between elementary forces of nature – as narrated by Apollodorus and Strabo – was on the way from Egypt to Syria. (Fn: Mount Casius, mentioned by Apollodorus, is the name of Mount Lebanon as well as of Mount Sinai. Cf. Pomponius Mela, *De situ orbis*.) According to Herodotus, the final act of the fight between Zeus and Typhon took place at Lake Serbon on the coastal route from Egypt to Palestine. (Fn: Herodotus ii, 5. Also Apollonius Rhodius in the *Argonautica*, Bk. ii, says that Typhon 'smitten by the bolt of Zeus . . . lies whelmed beneath the waters of the Serbonian lake'.) [Actually, the Harvard University edition of Herodotus (Loeb Classical Library) connects the quoted sentence about the place where Typhon is entombed with his defeat by Zeus.]

THE CRITICISM: II

Gaposchkin continues:

A cosmic encounter, we read, was responsible for the destruction of the army of Sennacherib by a 'blast of fire'. But none of the three biblical accounts of the event mentions a *blast*: each one ascribes the defeat of the enemy to an angel. (Fn: II Kings, xx, 35; II Chronicles, xxxvii, 2; Isaiah, xxxvii, 36). We do find a blast in the prophecy made by Isaiah *before* the event: 'Behold, I will send a blast upon him, and he shall hear a rumour, and shall return to his own land'. (Fn: II Kings, xix, 7). But the Hebrew word used here means 'wind or spirit' rather than 'fire'.

[Thus Velikovsky is accused of suppressing the 'angel' as the agent of destruction in the story of Sennacherib's débâcle; of incorrectly interpreting 'blast' in Isaiah, xxxvii, 7; and of inventing 'blast of fire', which words do not appear in the biblical narrative.]

[Next, Gaposchkin implies that Velikovsky suppressed Herodotus's version of Sennacherib's defeat:] Herodotus gives a very different account of the defeat of Sennacherib's army, which does not suggest any catastrophe on a cosmic scale. [The passage in Herodotus is printed in Greek, and a translation follows it (Gaposchkin's dots):] Afterwards . . . Sennacherib, king of the Arabians and Assyrians, marched his vast army into Egypt. . . . As the two armies lay here opposite one another, there came in the night a multitude of field-mice, which devoured all the quivers and bowstrings of the enemy, and ate the thongs by which they managed their shields. Next morning they commenced their flight and great multitudes fell, as they had no arms with which to defend themselves. (Fn: *History*, iii; Rawlinson translation.)

[Gaposchkin concluded:] If all readers had complete classical libraries, and could read them; if every man were his own Assyriologist and habitually studied the Bible in the Hebrew and Septuagint versions, Dr Velikovsky would have had short shrift.

[When Velikovsky submitted to the editors of the *Proceedings of the American Philosophical Society* evidence that he *had not* misquoted the Biblical passages, *had not* ascribed 'blast of fire' to a Biblical text, and *had not* suppressed Herodotus's version, he was refused access to the pages of that journal for a rejoinder. As a result, more than one irresponsible writer was misled into echoing Gaposchkin: 'Thus when Velikovsky quotes Herodotus about a battle between Zeus and Typhon and Isaiah on the destruction of Sennacherib's army by fire, you have only to turn to the books cited to learn that Herodotus . . . and Isaiah said nothing of the sort' – this from an article by L. Sprague de Camp ('Orthodoxy in Science', *Astounding Science Fiction*, May, 1954.)]

[As late as the fall of 1962, the reader information service of the Encyclopedia Britannica, in answer to inquiries about the validity of Velikovsky's theories, mailed out a five-page-long compilation of excerpts from critical reviews of *Worlds in Collision.* More than three pages were filled with Gaposchkin passages in the same vein as, and including, those set forth here for comparison with Velikovsky's text.]

THE TEXT: II

Velikovsky (*Worlds in Collision, pp. 230–231*)*:*

The destruction of the army of Sennacherib is described laconically in the Book of Kings: 'And it came to pass that night, that the angel of the Lord went out, and smote in the camp of the Assyrians a hundred fourscore and five thousand; and when the people arose in the morning, behold, they were all dead corpses. So Sennacherib king of Assyria departed, and went and returned, and dwelt in Nineveh.' It is similarly described in the

Book of Chronicles: '. . . And the Lord sent an angel which cut off all the mighty men of valour . . .'.

What kind of destruction was this? . . . It is explained in the texts of the Book of Kings and Isaiah that it was a 'blast' sent upon the army of Sennacherib. 'I will send a blast upon him . . . and [he] shall return to his own land', was the prophecy immediately preceding the catastrophe . . .

The Talmud and Midrash sources, which are numerous, all agree on the manner in which the Assyrian host was destroyed: a blast fell from the sky on the camp of Sennacherib. It was not a flame, but a consuming blast: 'Their souls were burnt, though their garments remained intact.' The phenomenon was accompanied by a terrific noise. (Fn: Tractate Shabbat 113b; Snahedrin 94a; Jerome on Isaiah 1:16; L. Ginzberg, *Legends of the Jews*, vi, 363.)

Another version of the destruction of the army of Sennacherib is given by Herodotus. During his visit in Egypt, he heard from the Egyptian priests or guides to the antiquities that the army of Sennacherib, while threatening the borders of Egypt, was destroyed in a single night. According to this story, an image of a deity holding in his palm the figure of a mouse was erected in an Egyptian temple to commemorate the miraculous event. In explanation of the symbolic figure, Herodotus was told that myriads of mice descended upon the Assyrian camp and gnawed away the cords of their bows and other weapons; deprived of their arms, the troops fled in panic.

[Velikovsky also drew attention to the neglected fact that both versions – in the Scriptures and in Herodotus – include a story of a disturbance (reversal) of the sun's movement in immediate sequence with the above narratives.]

[In a chapter dealing with the folklore of the American Indians, Velikovsky relates a tale preserved by the Mnemoni tribe of the Algonquin nation. The sun had been caught in a noose and restrained from proceeding on its path:] '. . . The Mouse came up and gnawed at the string . . . the Sun breathed again and the darkness disappeared. If the Mouse had not succeeded, the Sun would have died.' (S. Thompson, *Tales of the North American Indians*, 1929). . . . The image of the mouse must have had some relation to the cosmic drama. . . . Apparently the atmosphere of the celestial body that appeared in the darkness and was illuminated took on the elongated form of a mouse . . . This explains why the blast that destroyed the army of Sennacherib was commemorated by the emblem of a mouse . . . Thus we see how a folk story of the primitives can solve an unsettled problem between Isaiah and Herodotus.

INDEX

INDEX

THE ARABS

THOMAS KIERNAN

THE ARABS is an authoritative firsthand portrait of the character and aspirations of this powerful and mysterious people. Chapters outlining the development of the Arab people and of their Islamic religion alternate with vivid passages of reportage and conversation from the author's own Middle East journals.

Journalist Thomas Kiernan – also the biographer of the P.L.O. leader Yasir Arafat – travelled extensively throughout the Middle East in order to ensure that his study was presented without any of the usual distortions of cant and propaganda. In the course of his research he interviewed scores of prominent spokesmen for the Arab cause, and is thus able to explore a striking ambition held by the leaders of the oil-rich Arab states: to gain control of the economies of the industrialized Western nations.

Current world events have generated a widespread desire to understand this enigmatic people and their culture: THE ARABS provides invaluable material in that search for understanding.

0 349 12090 WORLD AFFAIRS £1.95

Also by Thomas Kiernan in Abacus:

YASIR ARAFAT

Also available in Abacus Books

AGES IN CHAOS

IMMANUEL VELIKOVSKY

Taking for his starting point the simultaneous physical catastrophes described in the Book of Exodus and in Egyptian documents, Dr. Velikovsky reconstructs the political and cultural histories of the nations of the ancient world. His reconstruction poses the question – are six hundred years missing in Israel's history, or have six hundred ghost years crept into Egyptian history? Documents are collated for each generation over twelve hundred years and the intriguing march over centuries presents itself as an exciting and fact-filled hunt after the error which caused the histories of the ancient world to become 'ages in chaos' with happenings which never took place, kings who never reigned, and battles that were never fought.

0 349 13582 7 COSMOLOGY £1.50